HARVARD HISTORICAL MONOGRAPHS, LXV
Published under the direction of the Department of History
from the income of the Robert Louis Stroock Fund

Communal Finances in Times of Peace and in Times of War *(Le finanze del Comune in tempo di pace e in tempo di guerra),* painting by Benvenuto di Giovanni, 1467. In Archivio di Stato, Museo delle tavole dipinte, Siena.

FLORENTINE PUBLIC FINANCES

IN THE EARLY RENAISSANCE,

1400–1433

ANTHONY MOLHO

Harvard University Press, Cambridge, Massachusetts, 1971

To the memory of my father

*e che in verità e secondo la
opinione di tutti gli uomini
e' sia stato di qualità che
noi abbiamo da gloriarci assai
di essere suti figliuoli di uno
tale padre.*

PREFACE

This is a monograph on Florentine fiscal history from the turn of the fifteenth century until the early 1430's. In itself this is a rather narrow and highly specialized topic, to which historians have necessarily referred in a rather general and imprecise manner. While studying the political history of Florence during the period generally known as the early Renaissance, I was struck by the paucity of available information on the Commune's finances. It occurred to me, therefore, that a reconstruction of this one dimension of Florentine history might be a desirable, perhaps even valuable, endeavor. The sources are abundant, although some important documents that I ought to have used, and did not, are the records of the Monte, uninventoried and therefore inaccessible to students of Florentine history. In the end, however, the unavailability of the Monte archive did not prove to be an insurmountable obstacle. If the documents of that collection contain the kinds of important and revealing information it has often been rumored they do, no doubt my task of computing communal incomes and expenditures would have been rendered much simpler and shorter. Even so, relying on cameral and legislative records, I believe that I have been able to reconstruct a reasonably accurate and complete picture of the fiscal predicament in which the governors of Florence found themselves during the first third of the Quattrocento.

While I believe that the statistical evidence used in the body of the monograph is reasonably accurate, mistakes and slips are bound to have entered my calculations, all the more because I often tried to consolidate figures that the sources give singly and also because I converted all currencies, silver and gold, into gold florins, a process that, while making it easier for the reader to compare incomes and expenditures for different years, inevitably invites errors. I have sought to minimize these mistakes by using a calculating machine.

While I am confident that the margin of error in the figures that I use to substantiate my argument is not large, I suspect that some of my conclusions, which I offer in tentative and suggestive form in the last chapter, will require considerable revision as our knowledge of early Quattrocento Florentine politics improves. If, on the other hand, my suggestions regarding the relation between fiscal structures and political power are correct, a host of other problems will have to be dealt with, problems whose nature I seek to outline in the conclusion. The consolation of any student of Florentine history must always be that he can turn to the splendid riches of the *Archivio di Stato* and that these unusually complete and informative series of documents, if properly approached, will yield to him their secrets.

During my student days and since, Marvin Becker, a wise and enlightened teacher, has offered me much help and encouragement. I shall always be grateful to him for his friendship and counsel.

Most of the work for this study was completed during the academic year 1968–1969 when, with the aid of generous financial assistance offered by the National Endowment for the Humanities and the American Commission for Cultural Exchanges with Italy (Fulbright Commission), I was able to spend a continuous fifteen months in Florence, carrying out my research *in situ*. Pleasant study accommodations and stimulating conversation at the lunch table were made available to me by the Harvard University Center for Italian Renaissance Studies in Florence at the Villa I Tatti.

It has been my good fortune to enjoy the friendship of Jules Kirshner, R. Burr Litchfield, John Najemy, Carlo Pincin, Richard Trexler, and Ronald Witt, each of whom came to the rescue when help was needed. Guido Pampaloni, before and during his tenure as director of the *Archivio di Stato,* extended a generous hand of hospitality, answered paleographic questions, and offered expert guidance through the riches of the Florentine Archives. Finally, I should like to thank Raymond and Florence Edler de Roover for their extraordinarily generous and useful advice. Their vast learning is matched only by their graciousness to young scholars.

I am dedicating this book to the memory of my father. This is a mere gesture on my part, for I shall never be able to express the affection and gratitude I had for him. Nothing would have pleased me more than the chance to have presented this book to him personally.

CONTENTS

TABLES

Credimus quod cum ad posteriora secula deferetur stupori pro simile visum iri, populum unum tantam tributorum molem substinere potuisse. In tantis igitur difficultatibus, tantisque oneribus rei publice nostre cum singuli cives, longitudine et magnitudine belli, intolerandis expensarum profluviis, integra patrimonia consumerent, clero tamen ita pepercimus, ut nullum ab his subsidium usque ad hanc diem petere voluerimus.

Leonardo Bruni to Pope Eugenius IV, 10.XI.1431

Archivio di Stato di Firenze, Fondo della Repubblica, Missive, Ia Cancelleria, filza XXXIII, f. 53v

ABBREVIATIONS

Unless otherwise indicated, all documents cited in the notes are found in the *Archivio di Stato* of Florence (*ASF*).

To avoid any possible confusion, all dates between January 1 and March 25 have been given both in regular and Florentine styles.

MONETARY EQUIVALENCES

The Florentine monetary system can be reduced to the following set of equations:

Gold Currencies

1 florin = 20 soldi [sous] a oro = 240 denari [deniers] a oro
1 florin = 29 soldi affiorino = 348 denari affiorino
£ 1 affiorino = 20 soldi affiorino = 240 denari affiorino
20 florins = £ 29 affiorino.

Silver Currency

£ 1 di piccioli = 20 soldi (sous) di piccioli = 240 denair [deniers] di piccioli.

Source: Raymond de Roover, *The Rise and Decline of the Medici Bank, 1397–1494* (Cambridge, Mass., Harvard University Press, 1963), p. 33.

1

INTRODUCTION

"From 1413 to 1423, that is, for a total of ten years, we had a tranquil and unchallenged peace, the Commune had few military expenses, and only a few taxes were imposed, so that the land became very wealthy, and it had an abundance of money in it." [1] This was the view of Giovanni di Paolo Rucellai, a Florentine patrician of the Quattrocento, as he expressed it in a resume of Florentine history that he inserted in his private diary in 1456. To him, from the perspective of forty years' distance, the second decade of the fifteenth century seemed more tranquil and uneventful than it might actually have been. His own mature years, after all, were passed in the second and third quarters of the century, a time of endless wars, extraordinarily burdensome taxation, and a precariously balanced political situation. One need not wonder, therefore, that this period — the interlude between the death of King Ladislaus of Naples in 1414 (not in 1413, as Rucellai seems to suggest) and the outbreak of war against Filippo Maria Visconti, Duke of Milan, in the summer of 1423 — stood out so poignantly in his memory as quiet and prosperous compared to his own turbulent times. And if Rucellai's contrast between the 1410's and the 1450's, when he composed his diaries, was somewhat exaggerated, it is nevertheless true that the earlier decade must be considered one of the most prosperous in the history of Florence from 1375, when the war against the Papacy erupted, until the

1. *Giovanni di Pagolo Rucellai ed il suo Zibaldone, I. Il Zibaldone Quaresimale*, ed. Alessandro Perosa (London: Warburg Institute, 1960), p. 46: "Dal 1413 al 1423, che ssono anni 10, avemo una pacie molto tranquilla e sanza sospetto, et il comune aveva pocha spesa di giente d'arme, et non si ponevano graveze o poche, per modo che lla terra ne venne molto pechuniosa e riccha."

closing of the fifteenth century — prosperous both in the sense that economic conditions were favorable to the city's entrepreneurs and that the burden of taxation imposed by the city on its citizens was light and easily supportable.

In 1414, not only had Providence been kind to the Florentines by bringing about the death of their archenemy, the King of Naples, but their own peace party within the city had won a considerable victory, thus checking, though temporarily, the expansionist desires nurtured by some Florentine politicians.[2] Thus Florence was able to consolidate its position in Tuscany and to take stock of its enormously enlarged domain, which now included all large Tuscan cities with the exception of Lucca and Siena. Significantly, no major addition to the Florentine domain was made between 1411, when Cortona was bought from King Ladislaus of Naples, and 1421, when the Florentines purchased the port of Livorno from the Genoese. The efforts of nearly three decades in acquiring large areas of the Tuscan province and in resisting the aggression of Milan and Naples had required the disbursement of large sums, and the Florentines, as if reacting to the excessive spending and military involvements of the previous decades, now proceeded to curtail expenditures and to limit their ambitions for territorial expansion.

Support for Rucellai's view that the tax burden in the 1410's was not oppressive can be found in the Florentine cameral records. Though it is true that the nature of the statistical evidence relating to the fiscal history of the Commune is often fragmentary, figures culled from the existing documents can

2. For the events of those years, consult François-Tomy Perrens, *Histoire de Florence depuis sa fondation jusqu'à la domination des Medicis* (Paris, 1883), VI, ch. 5, and Gino Capponi, *Storia della repubblica di Firenze* (Firenze, 1876), II, ch. 5.

be quite interesting.[3] Unfortunately, for the decade 1414–1423 fairly adequate statistical evidence for the income and expenditures of the Commune has survived only for four years: 1414, a war year, 1416, 1419, and 1420, all three years of peace and relative tranquility. In 1414 the cost of hiring the large mercenary armies with which to combat Ladislaus's ambitions in central Italy had amounted to 548,211 florins, a sum more than double that representing the communal income from the four major gabelles: the gate, salt, contract, and wine gabelles, which together fetched the city only 189,052 florins.[4] This enormous deficit had necessitated the imposition of numerous forced loans (*prestanze*) on the citizens of the Republic.[5] The sum collected during that year, 403,751 florins, represented one of the highest figures for prestanze collected since the over-

3. Charles de la Roncière in his "Indirect Taxes or 'Gabelles' at Florence in the Fourteenth Century," in *Florentine Studies,* ed. Nicolai Rubinstein (London: Faber and Faber, 1968), p. 163, n. 1, suggests that for the first three quarters of the fourteenth century the records of the Camera del Comune (covering the years until 1378) are incomplete and that statistical information found in these records give an incomplete picture of fiscal trends during that period. Though this may be so for the years until 1384, there is little question but that the source from which most of the statistical evidence has been taken for this monograph, the *PC,* offers complete information on all the income and expenditures of the Commune for certain years. On this question, consult Appendix A.

4. In 1414 the *gabella delle porte* fetched a net income of 105,559 florins (*PC,* XXV, ff. 97r–99v); the *gabella del sale,* 58,294 florins (ff. 111r–112r); the *gabella dei contratti,* 10,762 florins (ff. 123r–125r); and the *gabella del vino al minuto,* 14,437 florins (ff. 134r–135r). The expenditures of the *condotta* (the fund for military expenses) for that year, 548,211 florins (to be precise, 475,956 florins and 189,019 lire) are found on folios 20r–43r of that same *filza.* All gabelle incomes refer to net incomes: the gross minus the administrative expenses, which I have deducted from the gross.

5. Regarding the whole practice of forced loans, the reader is referred to chapter 4 and to the bibliographic notes cited there.

throw of the "minor guilds" in 1382.[6] In each of the three peace years, 1416, 1419, and 1420, military expenditures were considerably reduced, standing respectively at 117,434, 118,878, and 93,850 florins, while the annual communal income from the four major gabelles stood at over 200,000 florins. Thus the need for the imposition of prestanze was substantially reduced, and the communal income from that source was scaled down to a total of some 100,000 florins for all three years.[7]

Reduced military involvement and lighter taxation, of course, released for more renumerative business investment substantial amounts of Florentine capital that had previously been channeled into the state's coffers. General business conditions seem to have improved considerably after 1415, and with the one interruption caused by a serious plague in 1417, Florentine commerce and industry experienced one of their most prosperous and buoyant periods of expansion. During these years considerable efforts were made to strengthen the silk industry by introducing the craft of the *battiloro*, the preparation of metal silk threads for silk brocades, and the fortunes of the Florentine banking firms seem to have been quite good.[8] The

6. *PC*, XXV, ff. 220r–227v. The exact sum was 388,834 florins and 59,666 lire. A comparison of this figure with the prestanze collected during other war years indicates the magnitude of the sum collected in 1414. For 1390: 478,430 florins (*PC*, VI, f. 263r); in 1391: 673,936 florins (*PC*, VII, f. 263r); in 1392: 320,458 florins (*PC*, VIII, f. 262r); in 1401: 262,887 florins (*PC*, XVI, f. 207v); in 1402: 300,529 florins (*PC*, XVII, f. 226r); finally, in 1409, the year when war broke out with Ladislaus Durazzo of Naples: 360,356 florins (*PC*, XXIII, ff. 220r–225r).

7. For income from these gabelles, consult Table 2, ch. 3; for expenditures, Table 3, ch. 3; for forced loans, Table 4, ch. 4. Specific folio references are given in Appendix B.

8. Perosa (ed.), *Rucellai: Zibaldone*, p. 62: "E il colmo della riccheza fu da l'anno 1418 a l'anno 1423. Erano in quel tenpo in merchato nuovo e per le vie circhustanti 72 banchi di tavolello e tappeto. Sono d'oppenione

stability of that decade is also reflected in the basic strength of the Florentine silver currency, able for the first time in many years to maintain its value vis-à-vis the gold florin; thus there was a temporary halt in the spiral of currency inflation that, since the middle of the fourteenth century, had brought about the drastic debasement of the Florentine silver currency. The average value of the florin in 1414 was 80 sous, $11\frac{1}{2}$ deniers, while in 1423, at the very outbreak of the war against Milan, it stood at 80 sous, $5\frac{1}{3}$ deniers, having fluctuated within this range during the entire decade.[9] The prosperity and stability of the Florentine economy enabled the Florentines in 1421 to pay a handsome price to the Doge of Genoa, Tommaso di Campo-fregoso, for the purchase of the port of Livorno.[10] The acquisition of this important city, having satisfied the Florentine ambition of becoming a major Italian maritime power, was the occasion for the creation of the communal fleet, which, it was now hoped, would enable the Florentines to compete against Genoa and Venice in the lucrative Levantine commerce.[11]

---

che solo di danari contanti e merchatantia e'cittadini avessono il valore di due milioni di fiorini." On this general theme, see my article "The Florentine *Tassa dei Traffichi* of 1451," *Studies in the Renaissance*, XXVII (1970), pp. 73–118. It is during this period also that the Medici became the Pope's bankers. On this subject, see George T. Holmes, "How the Medici Became the Pope's Bankers," in Rubinstein (ed.), *Florentine Studies*, pp. 357–380.

9. Appendix D gives the monthly exchange rates between silver and gold from January 1388/89 through 1432. The source for this is *ASF, Miscellanea repubblicana*, XXXIII, inserts 1–4.

10. On the purchase of Livorno, *LF*, LII, ff. 91r–93r, and *PR*, CXI, ff. 31r–35r (May 24 and 28, 1421). For the way in which the Florentines paid for Livorno see chapter 5, note 72 later in this book.

11. On the general subject of Florentine maritime involvement after their acquisition of Livorno, see Michael E. Mallett, *The Florentine Galleys in the Fifteenth Century* (Oxford: Oxford University Press, 1967). The details of the first Florentine embassy to a Mohammedan power in the

In the turbulent Italian world of the early Quattrocento a decade of relatively quiet prosperity must have seemed like an anomalous (though pleasant) state of affairs. Already by 1420 it had become evident that the territorial ambitions of Giangaleazzo Visconti's second-born son, Filippo Maria Visconti, Duke of Milan, were bound to upset the diplomatic and political balance of the peninsula. The Florentines, whose principal diplomatic goal from the middle of the fourteenth century had been the maintenance of their predominance in Tuscany, sought to negotiate with the Milanese an agreement whereby each of the two powerful states would be assigned a well-defined sphere of influence and each would avoid interference in the sphere of the other.[12] The Milanese, originally feigning an interest in the proposal, nevertheless proceeded to take over Genoa and made some threatening moves toward important centers of the Romagna. War between them and the Florentines finally broke out when the Viscontian armies appeared in Forlì, a city located some fifty miles from Florence, well beyond the limits of the Milanese sphere of influence. The history of the military reverses suffered by the Florentine forces in the 1420's and early 1430's is well known, since contemporary chroniclers and modern historians have recounted it many times. What is pertinent to the theme of this monograph is that from the outbreak of war in the late summer of 1423 until the conclusion of the first peace of Ferrara, signed on April 18,

---

Levant are given by one of the ambassadors, Felice Brancacci, in his *Diario*, ed. Dante Castellacci, *ASI*, ser. 4, VIII (1881), 157–188.

12. The two best recent accounts from which one can follow the details of the war and also obtain extensive bibliographic references are C. C. Bayley, *War and Society in Renaissances Florence* (Toronto: University of Toronto Press, 1961), pp. 82–151, and *Storia di Milano, VI. Il ducato Visconteo e la repubblica Ambrosiana (1392–1450)* (Milan: Fondazione Treccani degli Alfieri, 1955), pp. 153–291.

1428, the Florentine forces suffered a series of devastating and humiliating defeats. Despite their concerted, and on occasion frantic, efforts to secure the alliance of the Pope, Martin V, and of the Venetians, until late in 1425 the Tuscans found themselves fighting the Milanese alone, and their mercenaries suffered continuous and serious defeats: at Zagonara (July 1424), in the Val di Lamone (March–April 1425), at Anghiari and Faggiola (October 1425). In the summer of 1425 the Milanese forces reached the Tuscan *contado* (territories under Florentine control)[13] and made several sorties up to the city walls. Only the Venetian intervention and the brilliant military successes of their chief mercenary, Francesco Carmagnola, saved the day for the Florentines, leading to the conclusion of the peace of Ferrara.

No sooner had the war against the Visconti been brought to an end than Volterra, one of Florence's most important subject cities, revolted, because it objected to the Florentine insistence that the *catasto*[14] be imposed on the inhabitants of that city. Once again, within weeks of the negotiations of the peace with Milan, Florence was forced to raise large armies in order to discipline her recalcitrant subjects. Though the operation against the Volterrans was completed fairly rapidly, by the fall of 1429 Florence found itself embroiled in the most disastrous war it was ever to undertake: the attempt to annex Lucca to its *imperium*. No other war since the first war against Lucca, fought more than a century before, produced such enormous political and economic dislocations in the very matrix of Florentine society. Continually balked in their hopes of a rapid capitulation by their proud and once powerful neighbor, the Florentines brought to the field some of the largest armies ever assem-

13. See chapter 3, footnote 5, for a discussion of the term *contado*.
14. For a discussion of this form of taxation, see pages 79–87.

bled in Italy and engaged one of the outstanding engineers of the epoch, Filippo Brunelleschi, to devise a plan for flooding the besieged city; in the process, however, they only offered the Milanese and Sienese an excuse to enter the war on the side of the Lucchese. Once again, Venetian initiative enabled the Florentines to extricate themselves from the disastrous expedition against Lucca, their pride badly damaged and their expansionist designs completely frustrated. For a second time representatives of the major Italian powers gathered in Ferrara, where the second peace named after that city was signed in May 1433.

2

COMMUNAL EXPENDITURES: MERCENARIES AND THE PUBLIC DEBT

The wars fought by Florence from the summer of 1423 to the spring of 1433 were unlike any in its history. Only one other decade in the past of the city (the 1390's) had presented to its inhabitants dangers and challenges remotely similar to those of the 1420's. But in the earlier period military engagements were not nearly as constant and exacting as they were to prove later. In the 1390's, while Florence was seeking to preserve its independence in the face of Milanese aggression, war was not fought during every year of the decade. Brief, but crucial, periods of peace, from 1392 to 1395 and from 1398 to 1400, enabled the Florentines and the Milanese to recoup their forces, reorder their finances, and prepare for the next round of fighting. Table 1 shows that military expenditures during these periods of peace were substantially reduced, as were the forced loans imposed on the citizenry.[1]

1. Thus the total military expenditure for that twelve-year period was approximately 5 million florins—4,939,346 florins, to be exact. Often in the past, historians have used the figures offered by Gregorio Dati in his well-known *Istoria di Firenze*. But Dati's calculations can be shown to be wrong, a fact which seems to compromise the reliability of his account, at least insofar as specific events and facts are concerned. Dati, for example, states that the war against Giangaleazzo Visconti cost Florence 7.5 million florins (Dati, *Istoria di Firenze*, ed. Luigi Pratesi [Norcia: Tipografia Tonti, 1904], p. 136). In this same passage he states that the Florentine expenditures from 1375 to 1378, during the war against the Papacy, amounted to 2.5 million florins. This figure also is very exaggerated. An-

Table 1. Military expenditures and forced loans, 1390–1402 (values expressed in florins rounded off to nearest complete figure. Silver currencies converted to gold at current exchange rates, for which consult Appendix D).

Year[a]	Condotta[b]	Prestanze[c]	References in PC[d]
1390	647,062	478,430	VI, 54r–100r; 150r–161r. 263r
1391	810,201	673,936	VII, 45r. 263r
1392	700,909	320,458	VIII, 43r. 262r
1393	140,191	47,778	IX, 43r. 255v
1394	162,213	60,152	X, 48r. 219v
1395	284,104	84,724	XI, 52r. 223v
1396	256,823	119,947	XII, 54r. 222r
1397	587,325	303,100	XIII, 56r. 247r
1399	228,605	118,942	XIV, 48r; 59r. 222v
1400	229,448	121,250	XV, 36r; 62r. 226v
1401	278,441	262,887	XVI, 48r. 207v
1402	614,024	300,529	XVII, 51r. 226r

[a] The volume referring to 1398 is missing.

[b] The sums of the condotta have been taken from the *uscita della condotta* and refer to actual expenditures.

[c] The amounts for the prestanze refer to actual sums collected rather than forced loans assessed on the citizenry.

[d] The first folio references pertain to the condotta, while those following a period refer to the prestanze.

Unfortunately, complete figures representing military outlays for the 1420's and early 1430's have survived for only three

---

other contemporary, who can be shown to have written his account before 1411 while residing in Florence, set the Florentine expenditures during this war at 460,000 florins (Giovanni di Pagolo Morelli, *Ricordi,* ed. Vittore Branca [Florence: Le Monnier, 1956], p. 318): "Ispesesi in questa guerra 460,000 di fiorini." The official registers of the *archivio delle prestanze* seem to justify Morelli's estimate. During the course of the war twenty-two prestanze were assessed, for a total of 580,000 florins. How much of that sum was actually collected is not quite clear. *ASF,* "Prestanze," *filze* 248–343.

years of that decade: 1424, 1426, and 1427. The expenditures recorded for these three years, as well as partial and indirect evidence found in other sources, indicate with little doubt that Florentine military expenses had reached unprecedented and consistently high levels. The sum of 409,283 florins was spent for the pay of mercenaries' wages in 1424, 550,499 florins in 1426, 446,700 florins in 1427.[2] For other years of that decade there are indications that monthly costs fluctuated between 65,000 and 100,000 florins, sums which to contemporaries must have seemed terribly burdensome, if not entirely extravagant.[3]

The principal cause of these expenditures can undoubtedly be traced to the exorbitant demands on the communal Treasury by the numerous mercenaries in the Florentine hire. The question of the relations between the various Italian states of the early Quattrocento and the bands of condottieri (the *soldati di fortuna*) operating in the peninsula during that period, though crucial to an understanding of Italian history of the late Middle Ages, lies well beyond the scope of this monograph. It is clear, however, that as Giuseppe Canestrini suggested in 1851, during the course of the first decades of the fifteenth century the more successful and powerful Italian condottieri had acquired a very

2. For 1424: *PC,* XXIX, ff. 34r–79v. For 1426: *PC,* ff. 26v–41v; XXXI ff. 24r–31v; 40r–43v; 32r–39r; 239r–242v. In this last sum are included 1,582 florins given by the condotta to the *consoli del mare* (consuls of the sea): *PC,* XXXI, ff. 32r–39r.

3. *LF,* LIII, f. 123r (July 16, 1426), in which Lipozzus Cipriani Mangioni calculates expenses at 80,000 florins per month. Giovanni di Jacopo Morelli calculates that expenditures in 1426 were running at more than 70,000 florins per month (*Ricordi,* in *Delizie degli eruditi toscani,* ed. Fr. Ildelfonso di San Luigi [Florence, 1770–1789], XIX, 73). He states that the total cost of the war in the triennium 1423–1425 was around 2.5 million florins (Pellegrini, p. CXXXVII [from *Consulte e Pratiche,* LI, f. 169v, July 3, 1431]): "Ridolfus de Peruzis: Ad partem pecunie: dolendum est de tanta expensa, que ascendit ad 100 m. f. in mense."

prestigious status in the affairs of the peninsula. No longer viewed as simple soldiers in the pay of sovereign powers, they had achieved a quasi-sovereign status, dealing with Florence, Milan, Venice, the Papacy — all the Italian states — as equals.[4] Several of these soldiers were to acquire bases of operation of their own, becoming lords of minor Italian principalities and consequently further consolidating their position. This phenomenon had a far-reaching influence not only on the history of these often colorful condottieri but also on the history of the peninsula as a whole and the individual states comprising it in the early fifteenth century.[5]

As the study of military history has been almost entirely neglected in the last few generations, there exist but a scant number of works devoted to the relations between the Italian political and military establishments of the late medieval and early Renaissance periods.[6] What little evidence is presented

4. Giuseppe Canestrini, "Documenti della milizia italiana," *ASI*, ser. 1, XV (1851), 72–82.

5. Possibly the most famous example of this phenomenon was the takeover of Milan in 1450 by Francesco Sforza, one of the most formidable Italian condottieri of his day.

6. The only recent writer who has addressed himself to this topic is C. C. Bayley, who in his *War and Society in Renaissance Florence — The De Militia of Leonardo Bruni* (Toronto: University of Toronto Press, 1961) sought to present the political, military, and literary background of Bruni's treatise on the citizen militia. But Bayley made no use at all of any archival evidence, and it is the abundant sources in the *Archivio di Stato* of Florence that should serve as the focal point of any such study. In addition to the records of the *Dieci di balia* (*Missive, responsive, istruzioni agli ambasciatori, giornali di entrata e uscita, debitori e creditori*), much information on military expenditures can be gathered from *Camera del Comune — Scrivano — Uscita di paghe; Camera del Comune — Provveditori — Specchio di Entrata e Uscita per vari titoli — Libri del notaio,* in which series one can actually find the names of many mercenaries and of the soldiers serving under them; and *Camera del Comune — Provveditori e Ufficiali del Banco — Spese per le condotte e paghe dei soldati. Filze* 21–30 of the

in this monograph is meant only to suggest the altered status of the mercenaries and the economic consequences borne by the Florentine Commune as a result of this change. One of the principal, and most immediately felt, of these consequences was the increased cost of mercenary service. Starting in 1425, chiefly because of the very serious defeats their forces had suffered, the Florentine statesmen were forced to woo a great number of military leaders, offering them terms that would render service to Florence economically more advantageous than service to Milan. Because of the existing state of knowledge a precise comparison of the number of Florentine soldiers in the city's employ at other times of war is not really possible.[7] Two independent sources of the first half of the fifteenth century set the number of soldiers in the employ of Florence at some six thousand horse and six thousand foot soldiers in 1427.[8]

latter series includes the deliberations of the *ufficiali del banco,* whose importance is discussed in chapter 6 of this monograph. In addition to these most obvious archival references, much other information can be gathered on the activities of the mercenaries from the deliberations and acts of almost every other governmental agency. An example of the type of study that I am referring to is Fritz Redlich, *De praeda militari* (Wiesbaden: F. Steiner, 1956).

7. Gregorio Dati, in his *Istoria di Firenze* puts the numbers of Florentine soldiers at the time of the siege of Arezzo at more than 60,000 men. Clearly, however, these figures should also be accepted with a grain of salt. Pratesi (ed.), *Dati, Istoria di Firenze,* p. 33: ". . . e, come l'ordine fu dato d'accordo, furono il terzo dì intorno alla città d'Arezzo ad assedio 20 mila uomini da cavallo e 40 mila appiè." But a little later, p. 43: "Quella gente d'appiè che tu dicesti poco innanzi che allo acquisto d'Arezzo furono bene 62 migliaia. . . ." As should become clear later, these figures are also too large and do not correspond at all to the actual situation that Dati was describing.

8. Biblioteca Nazionale Centrale di Firenze, *Conventi Soppressi,* C.4.895. *Cronica di Piero Pietribuoni,* f. 119r: "Gente d'arme de'fiorentini per la legha," 6,000 horse and 6,000 foot soldiers. In that same year, continues Pietribuoni, the Milanese forces were composed of 8,550 horse and 8,000

By 1431 their numbers had increased considerably, standing at about eleven thousand horse and eight thousand foot soldiers.[9] Not included in these figures are the several thousand crossbowmen (*balestrieri*) often recruited from among the inhabitants of the contado, whose principal duty was the defense of the countryside. In 1425 it was decided to bring their number to five thousand, while the responsibility for their recruitment and payment was delegated to the subject communes and territories.[10] Finally, in addition to all these, there were the several hundred soldiers — for the most part local recruits — stationed in garrisons near the principal strategic locations of the Florentine domain. Precisely how many soldiers were included in this category is not quite clear. In 1430 there were fully two hundred and eighty such guards stationed in the garrisons of Pisa and Volterra alone.[11]

---

foot soldiers, while the Venetian forces consisted of 8,830 horse and 8,000 foot soldiers. On the general reliability of this source, see Armando Sapori, *Studi di storia economica* (Florence: Sansoni, 1967), III, 6, 19. Marin Sanudo the elder offers the same estimate. *Marini Sanudi Leonardi Filii Patricii Veneti De Origine Urbis Venetae et Vita Omnium Ducum*, in *Rerum Italicarum Scriptores*, ed. Ludovico Muratori (Milan, 1733), XXII, 961: "La Signoria di Firenze con tutte le sue entrate del 1414 avrebbe messo cavalli 1,000. Al presente per le guerre in casa sua può mettere cavalli 4,000. Fuori cavalli 2,000."

9. Pellegrini, p. CXXXVII (from *Consulte e Pratiche*, LI, f. 169v, July 3, 1431): "D. Guglielminus de Tanaglia: De his examinetur per praticam, nam expensa est intolerabilis, reperiendo secum 11,000 equitibus et 8,000 famulis."

10. Reference to this decision is found in *PR*, CXIX, f. 158r, July 16, 1428. The legislative enactment of 1428 was brought about by the persistent complaints of the subject communes, who stated that the stipulated salary of twenty sous per month for each balestriero was costing a total sum of 36,000 lire per year. The government of Florence allowed these subject communities to reduce the stipend of the balestrieri to ten sous per month.

11. The names of these guards are found in *Dieci di balia — Debitori e creditori*, VI, ff. 61v–90r.

For a city the size of Florence to have to put in the field an army of such considerable size was a substantial burden to its citizens. In times of peace, according to the calculations of an early fifteenth-century Venetian observer, Florence could afford to keep an army of some one thousand horsemen.[12] By 1430 it was carrying an army many times that size.

It was not only the number of mercenaries on hire, however, which strained the Florentine budget but also the high wages and fees that the condottieri were able to demand by the third decade of the fifteenth century. In 1260 a *lancia* (a platoon comprising a knight, a shield-bearer, and a squire) commanded the price of six florins per month.[13] By the 1390's the average price paid to a lancia had increased to twelve or fourteen florins per month, although a commander like John Hawkwood could exact as much as eighteen florins per month for the lancie in his service.[14] By the middle of the 1420's the scale of salaries paid to the lancie in Florentine service was not nearly as uniform as it had been in the past. Small bands of soldiers, who could exert only an insignificant amount of pressure on the Florentine government, continued to receive fees comparable to those of the late fourteenth century. The standard price of a

12. Sanudo (see n. 8).
13. D. Waley, "The Army of the Florentine Republic from the Twelfth to the Fourteenth Century," in *Florentine Studies*, ed. Nicolai Rubinstein (London: Faber and Faber, 1968), p. 78.
14. *Camera del Comune — Provveditori — Specchio di Entrata e Uscita per vari titoli — Libri del notaio*, II, ff. 20r–40r, where the following salaries are recorded for the horsemen in Giovanni Acuto's retinue: 18 florins per month per lancia; 11 florins, 7 gold sous, per month per *arcieri doppi;* 6 florins, 13 gold sous, per month per *arcieri scempi*. In addition Acuto was promised a personal allowance of 500 florins per month. Typical rates for foot soldiers are found on folio 50r, where it is recorded that balestrieri received 4 florins per month and *fanti a piè,* 9 lire, 10 silver sous, per month.

lancia for these mercenaries remained at twelve to sixteen florins, as did the price of crossbowmen and archers in their retinue.[15] Soldiers serving the great condottieri of the period, however, saw their salaries increase manyfold within the short period of a few years. Monthly fees as high as sixty florins per lancia, although considered exorbitant by the Florentine authorities, were actually promised by the government to the lord of Faenza in January 1430/31,[16] while some mercenaries are on record as having demanded no less than sixty-five florins for each lancia that they provided the Commune.[17] Attempts to reduce the wages of these soldiers invariably offended their seemingly tender sensibilities, and more than once such an offended mercenary simply marched off the field and offered his precious services to his employer's enemy.[18] Moreover, in

15. See, for example, *PR*, CXX, f. 144r, April 27, 1429, and *PCUB*, XXI, f. 91r, August 10, 1425.

16. *PR*, CXXII, f. 138v, January 10, 1430/31.

17. Pellegrini, p. LVIIII (from *Dieci di balia — Responsive*, IX, n. 41), letter from Averardo de'Medici to the *dieci*, dated April 6, 1431: "Vuole f. 65 per lancia, et per 300 fanti la paga di 4 mesi, la condotta per uno anno, et uno anno a piacimento, con predirlo mesi tre avanti. Et oltre a tutta la presta, vuole per soprapiù f. semila pe'più bisognosi, et f. uno più per lancia, che nonn'anno gl'altri; ma questro con forma et modo non vi faccia dampno per gl'altri, et questo rispetto alla carestia."

18. Canestrini ("Documenti," *ASI*, ser. 1, LXXXIX) cites the example of Carmagnola, who passed from the Milanese to the Venetian forces. Pellegrini, pp. LVII–LVIII (from *Mediceo avanti il principato*, III, no. 74), letter from Francesco Tornabuoni in Venice to Averardo de'Medici, dated April 6, 1431: "I fanti se non saranno rifermi e nonn'aranno, et tutti se n'andranno al soldo del Ducha." Also Pellegrini, p. CXVIII (from *Dieci di balia — Responsive*, IX, n. 65), letter from Niccolò Fortebracci, written on May 29, 1431, to Francesco Foscari, Doge of Venice, explaining why he had left the Florentine service: "La cagione delle presenti è per notificare alla V. S. M. la mia partita dalla M. S. di Firenze et la cagione." Additional examples can be found in *DSSp Aut.*, XXII, f. 156v, October 21, 1432, in which the salaries of certain mercenaries were raised because of

times of crop failure and shortage of grain the condottieri always received an additional allowance in the hope that depredation of the Florentine countryside would thus be averted.[19]

Even more dramatic than the increases in the rates at which individual soldiers were being compensated was the augmented cost of "package" contracts negotiated by the more powerful and influential of the city's mercenaries. John Hawkwood, at the height of his popularity and prestige in Florence, received a yearly personal allowance of 7,200 florins.[20] At the outset of the war against Milan the price of celebrated soldiers had increased considerably, and Florence was able to hire Braccio da Montone on a two-year contract at 30,000 florins per year.[21] Soon, however, even these prices seemed modest compared to bills presented by the mercenaries to the Signory. In the first trimester of 1433, that is, immediately prior to the conclusion of the second peace of Ferrara, Florence had paid 50,428 florins to Niccolò da Tolentino and an additional 59,296 florins, 1 lira,

---

"penuriam victualium et temporis asperitatem . . . et volentes eisdem provisionatos complacere." Also, *DSSp Aut.*, XXIV, f. 11r, April 21, 1431, where the same measure was also taken because "eis [the mercenaries] impossibile esset pro tam pauco salario custodie locorum prout requiretur intendere." See also ff. 38v–39r of the same *filza*.

19. Pellegrini, p. XLIX (from *Consulte e Pratiche*, LI, f. 133r, April 1, 1431): "Antonius Ghezi de Casa [dixit] preterea stipendiarii habent parvum stipendium et male possunt vivere; esset bonum pro una firma augere f. 2 pro lancia, cum hoc ut emendarent illa que auferunt subditis; et hoc modo dabitur occasio ut de suo stipendio vivant et non de rapinis subditorum." See also Pellegrini, pp. XCVII–XCVIII (from *Dieci di balia* — *Responsive*, IX, n. 74): Letter from Averardo de'Medici to the *dieci*, dated May 7, 1431: "Del f. più [which had been promised certain mercenaries] per lancia, come vi si dice, s'intende che l'abbia infino a tanto chello st. del grano valessi XXII soldi, o da indi in giù."

20. *Camera del Comune — Provveditori — Specchio di Entrata e Uscita per vari titoli — Libri del notaio*, II, ff. 2r, 20r for year 1392.

21. *PR*, CXII, ff. 88r–v.

18 sous, 8 deniers, to Michele degli Attendoli.[22] The latter had cost Florence the very respectable sum of 115,492 florins, 10,210 lire, 4 sous, for his services during the previous year (1432),[23] while during that same year Florence had paid 50,000 florins to Count Francesco Sforza, known as *il Conticino*, so that he might remove his troops from Tuscany and observe a policy of neutrality toward the city.[24] It is not surprising that the demands of the mercenaries increased proportionately with the number of concessions that Florence was willing to grant them. Contracts promising large sums of money were being negotiated now not only for service in times of war but also in periods of peace, so that essentially the Florentine government was agreeing to the maintenance of large standing armies during the active lives of her condottieri.[25] One of these mercenaries, reported a Florentine who had lived through the dramatic days of the early 1430's, was being offered "a thousand things, and honors as numerous and as great as one could think; but he always refused by asking for things whose immensity would obscure the sun." [26]

---

22. *PCUB*, XXXI, f. 101v (Niccolò da Tolentino), f. 122v (Michele degli Attendoli).

23. *PCUB*, XXIX, ff. 87v–88r.

24. *PCUB*, XXXI, f. 101v. Many contemporaries took note of this transaction. Niccolò Tinucci, in his "Esamina" (published in the appendix of Giovanni Cavalcanti, *Istorie fiorentine*, ed. I. Polidori [Florence, 1838–1839], II, 419), says: "che mai più in questa ghuerra nè nel passato a uno solo si paghò tale somma di danari." Giovanni di Jacopo Morelli (di San Luigi [ed.], *Ricordi*, p. 93) records the payment and then states: "Dissesi, furono gittati via, perchè non si poteva stare."

25. For one example, see the letter by Averardo de'Medici cited in note 17: "Ma quello che mi dà più noia si è che volea, et questi suoi cancellieri gle l'anno messo del capo, d'avere, finito l'anno a tempo di pace, lance 400 di condotta e fanti 200."

26. Tinucci, in his "Esamina" (Polidori [ed.], II, 418) refers to the

An amusing and characteristic incident involving Florence and one of the mercenaries in her hire took place in the late fall of 1432, and it illustrates the difficulties facing the city in her relations with those soldiers who, though supposedly in the service of the Commune, were actually becoming a determining factor in the city's life. It seems that the Florentine city fathers, pleased with the performance of one of their great captains, Michele degli Attendoli, presented to him, as a token of their appreciation, a golden helmet costing the respectable sum of 2,000 florins. No sooner had news of this event spread in the domain than Niccolò da Tolentino, another of Florence's mercenaries, claimed an equal measure of recognition, so that the Commune was forced to present him a helmet similar to that given Michele degli Attendoli.[27] Four thousand florins in a budget of some three quarters of a million was no doubt a small sum. But only a decade and a half before, in 1419, it had represented 4 percent of the annual expenditures for military affairs, and even in the 1420's many thoughtful Florentines would have felt that such a sum paid to please fickle and insatiable mercenaries was an extravagant waste of money.

Although the above description of Florentine military expenditures may be impressionistic and incomplete, it should make clear the serious financial challenge faced by the Commune's fathers. The crucial question of the 1420's was how Florence's large mercenary armies could be financed, in view of the fact that the Commune had certain other financial ob-

---

negotiations between Florence and Michele degli Attendoli, who kept refusing to sign the contract: "essendogli proferte mille chose, e tanti onori e grandi quanto potessono essere; et egli si tirò sempre indietro con chiedere chose da scurare il sole."

27. The incident is reported by Giovanni di Jacopo Morelli (di San Luigi [ed.], *Ricordi*, p. 106).

ligations as well, the most important being the disbursement of the carrying charges for the public debt (*Monte*).

A detailed discussion of the Florentine public debt must be postponed until a later chapter. But it is important to point out now that at the same time that the Communal government was required to maintain an expensive military establishment it also had to allocate as much as two thirds of the regular communal income to the administrators of the public debt. From a total of some 450,000 florins of net indebtedness in 1347, when it was first funded, the public debt had more than doubled by 1380, standing at about 1 million florins. By the mid-1420's this net indebtedness, that is, the sum that the Commune had actually borrowed and that it was obligated to repay to its creditors in order to amortize the debt, stood at about 2.5 million florins, and before the second peace of Ferrara was to be concluded, possibly 1 million more florins were added to this debt.[28] By the 1420's the carrying charges for the funded public debt amounted to well over 150,000 florins per year, often bordering on the limit of 200,000 florins.[29]

Thus, in years of war, the Florentine citizens in charge of the city's fiscal well-being had to plan on expenditures close to 1 million florins per year. Between 500,000 and 750,000 florins

28. A detailed analysis of the Monte and its budget is found in chapter 4, particularly in footnote 4. It seems ironic that on May 31, 1430, a legislative enactment ordered that the registers kept by the Monte officials be organized and inventoried (*PR*, CXXI, f. 18r), and yet, of all the major archival collections housed in the Florentine *Archivio di Stato* today, the only one unavailable for consultation because of the lack of a reliable inventory is the *Archivio del Monte*. The few registers from this collection to which I refer in the notes of this monograph I was able to consult thanks to the generosity of Guido Pampaloni, who very kindly turned over to me the preliminary notes of a new inventory of these documents, which he is preparing.

29. Consult Table 3, ch. 4.

were ordinarily spent for military obligations (the sum sometimes exceeding 1 million florins), and some 150,000 to 200,-000 florins had to be allocated for the carrying charges of the funded public debt. In addition, of course, the government had to pay its normal administrative expenses, which included the salaries of an expanding bureaucracy, maintenance of prisons, government buildings, roads, and the like. Finally, no government could expect to maintain the trust of its citizens if it did not make some effort to amortize the public debt. Although in periods of war, like the 1420's, the sums allocated to this obligation were curtailed considerably, between 10,000 and 30,000 florins continued to be allocated for this purpose. Thus, the overall expenditures of the city can be calculated conservatively as having been 600,000 to 700,000 florins per year, or, more realistically, in times of war probably more than 1 million florins.

3

COMMUNAL INCOME: TAXES ON THE CONTADO AND THE GABELLES

The large cost of keeping up its military establishment and paying the creditors of the public debt made it necessary for the Commune to have available large sums of cash. Essentially, the Commune had three sources of income: direct taxes imposed on the contado and the subject cities that it controlled; indirect taxes, or gabelles, assessed on the consumption of certain products and on the importation of goods into Florentine territory; and last, forced loans imposed on the city's inhabitants and occasionally on clerics and on the citizens of subject territories. Of the three alternatives, undoubtedly the first two were always considered preferable to the last. By the late 1300's one of the principal financial problems confronting merchants and entrepreneurs, not only of Florence but of the entire European world, was the availability of liquid cash. Thus the obligation to pay any portion of their wealth to the state for purposes that did not directly benefit them was often viewed as an unbearable imposition on the taxpayer. The reluctance of the Florentines to lend their not very abundant capital resources to the state was increased after 1380, when an important law set the interest to be paid to communal creditors at a maximum of 5 percent per year, a rate of return substantially below that which could be obtained in the commercial or banking enterprises of those times.[1] Communal sentiment on this issue was

1. Niccolò Rodolico, *La democrazia fiorentina nel suo tramonto (1375–*

aired during a discussion of a proposal to impose a forced loan on the citizens. One of the councillors, Filippo di Andrea Salviati, on behalf of the residents in the Quarter of Santa Croce, spoke forthrightly, saying: "It displeases them that even for the slightest expenses the Commune has recourse to its citizens' purses. . . . If at all possible, the Commune should rely on its own income and not on the citizens' purses." He then suggested that the gabelles should be reformed and made to produce a higher revenue for the city.[2] Yet, such was the situation during the 1420's that neither the contado nor the gabelles could yield enough income to meet the city's expenses. The reasons for this deficit, which forced the city to rely all the more heavily on the pocketbooks of affluent Florentine citizens, will be suggested in the following sections.

TAXES ON THE CONTADO

Since the publication of Enrico Fiumi's series of excellent monographs on the Florentine economy of the Dugento and Trecento, it is much more difficult to sustain the thesis, dear to the hearts of Marxist historians in the late nineteenth and early twentieth centuries, that Florence methodically exploited its contado during the halcyon years of Italian economic expan-

---

1378) (Bologna: Zanichelli, 1905), pp. 279–280. The entire text of this law was published by Rodolico in the appendix of that book. Some comments on earnings that could be made in banking operations during the 1410's and 1420's are found in chapter 6 of this monograph.

2. *LF*, LI, f. 233r, November 11, 1418: "Filippus Andree Salviati, pro quarterio Sancte Crucis dixit: dolent quod pro minima expensa recurratur ad bursas civium . . . et si fiet poterit comune de suo gubernari et non de bursis civium." See also the comment of Franciscus Blaxi Leoni, who spoke on behalf of the captains of the *Parte Guelfa* on folio 236r of same *filza* (November 20, 1418).

sion. The taxes imposed on the subject territories were not such as to cause economic ruin, nor can one ascertain that any substantial clash existed between urban and rural economic interests that would lead the Florentine entrepreneurs to exploit methodically the inhabitants of their Tuscan domain.[3] Fiumi's research, however, has been concerned primarily with the thirteenth and fourteenth centuries, scarcely taking into account developments following the plague of 1348 and the dislocation suffered by the Florentine economy because of it. There are sufficient indications, in fact, to lead an historian to the conclusion that the basically symbiotic and harmonious relation between Florence and her subject lands, which Fiumi so convincingly delineated, was gradually transformed into a harsh and oppressive rule that tended to erode the economic prosperity of the Tuscan countryside.[4]

It is impossible to make absolutely valid demographic and economic comparisons between conditions prevalent in the Florentine contado at the beginning and at the end of the fourteenth century. Some selected statistics, however, can serve to illustrate the point that economic conditions had become dras-

3. The principal statement of Fiumi's thesis appeared in three remarkable articles in the *ASI*: Enrico Fiumi, "Fioritura e decadenza dell'economia fiorentina," *ASI*, CXV (1957), 385–439; CXVI (1958), 443–510; CXVII (1959), 427–506. Of these, the first is the most important for understanding the economy of the contado. See also his *Storia economica e sociale di San Gimignano* (Florence: Olschki, 1961) and his "L'imposta diretta nei comuni medioevali della Toscana," in *Studi in onore di Armando Sapori* (Milan: Istituto editoriale cisalpino, 1956), I, 327–353.

4. Marvin Becker's recent publications have suggested this development. See his *Florence in Transition* (Baltimore: Johns Hopkins University Press, 1966–1968) and his two articles devoted entirely to fiscal matters: "Economic Change and the Emerging Florentine Territorial State," *Studies in the Renaissance*, XIII (1966), 7–39; and "Problemi della finanza pubblica fiorentina della seconda metà del Trecento e dei primi del Quattrocento," *ASI*, CXXIII (1965), 433–466.

tically altered by the end of the Trecento and that a period of economic regression had come to the Tuscan countryside. According to Fiumi's calculations, the population of the contado[5] during the 1330's was approximately one hundred and fifty thousand to two hundred thousand inhabitants, probably much closer to the latter figure.[6] The first authoritative census of the Florentine contado was undertaken at the time of the imposition of the catasto, in 1428, when it was calculated that about 123,796 people were living under Florentine domination.[7] An-

5. The term *contado* remains one of the most ambiguous in the context of Italian historiography of the twelfth to sixteenth centuries. For the purposes of this monograph *contado* will refer to all Tuscan territories not considered part of the city proper. This definition is quite wrong from the legal point of view, but until further study is completed on the precise meaning of the terms *civitas, contado,* and *districtus,* and the status that each term conferred on the inhabitants of the geographic area it describes, it will be difficult to discuss in a meaningful way the relations between the mother city and its citizens and subjects. William Bowsky and Julius Kirshner make a beginning in discussing these issues in their contributions to *Renaissance Essays in Honor of Hans Baron,* ed. Anthony Molho and John Tedeschi (Florence: Sansoni, 1971).

6. Enrico Fiumi, "Sui rapporti economici tra città e contado nell'età comunale," *ASI,* CXIV (1956), 30.

7. Giuseppe Canestrini, *La scienza e l'arte di stato, Part I. L'imposta sulla ricchezza mobile e immobile* (Florence, 1862), p. 152. Also, Pietribuoni in his *Cronica* (Biblioteca Nazionale Centrale di Firenze, *Conventi Soppressi,* C.4.895. *Cronica di Piero Pietribuoni,* f. 128v): "Estimo posto fino per gli uficiali del chatasto a chontadini del contado di Firenze e di Pisa fuori della città di Firenze e Pisa:

Quartier	Bocche	Teste	Sustanze [in florins]	Catasto [in lire]
Santo Spirito	35,515	10,210	469,300	5,126.1.11
Santa Croce	23,381	6,624	306,322	3,294.9.7
Santa M. Novella	32,842	10,116	486,858	5,360.4.4
San Giovanni	32,058	9,084	419,020	4,600.8.8
TOTAL	123,796	36,034	1,681,500	18,382.0.6"

other governmental survey, undertaken in 1429 by the officials charged with the distribution of salt, concluded that approximately one hundred and twenty thousand people were living in the contado and districtus of Florence.[8] Thus, despite the considerable enlargement between 1330 and 1430 of the territory that was considered part of the contado, there had been an absolute population decrease of about one third. A law enacted in 1414, which outlined the procedures for the imposition of the basic tax (*estimo*) on the contado, specifically states that from the time of the last imposition of the estimo in 1404, the number of households had decreased from 40,711 to 36,333 and that, even more significantly, the total value of all patrimonies held by the inhabitants of the contado had declined from 3,300,358 florins to 2,362,522 florins.[9] By the time of the im-

8. *PR, CXX*, ff. 261v–264r, August 2, 1429, a decree that establishes the minimum requirements for the consumption of salt. On folio 262r it is stated that 120,000 *bocche* inhabited the contado and that they had to consume a total of 24,200 *staia* per year. This same provision established that salt consumption was to be tied to one's catasto assessment. It was calculated that the Commune would collect about 130,600 lire from this gabelle and that this sum was about 35,000 lire less than the salt gabelle had been required to fetch during the last time of its reorganization (*PR, CIII* ff. 14v–15r, April 27, 1414). To make up the difference it was now decreed that a new tax of twenty sous would be assessed on each inhabitant of the contado. The income of this tax, 18,000 lire per year, would still be a full 17,000 lire short from covering the deficit of 35,000 lire, so that it was decided to require the poorer inhabitants of the contado to purchase additional quantities of salt at slightly reduced prices (4 lire, 8 sous, per *staio* instead of 5 lire, 8 sous, per *staio*). It becomes clear from this provision that the deficit of 35,000 lire in the income of the salt gabelle amounts to a decrease in the population of some 18 percent in fourteen years' time.

9. *PR, CIII*, ff. 14v–15r, April 27, 1414. If high assessments continued to be levied on the contadini, "esset dare causam comitatinis delinquere comitatum cum elapsis temporibus ob solutionibus incomportabiles et onerosas." On the estimo of 1404: *PR, XCII*, ff. 274r–v, February 18, 1403/04. On the method of distributing the estimo, see Fiumi, "Sui rapporti economici . . . ," *passim*.

position of the catasto the value of taxable patrimonies had been further reduced to less than one half of what it had been in 1404, standing now at 1,681,500 florins, although one is not quite certain whether this last figure refers to the value of the collective patrimonies before or after legitimately authorized deductions had been made.[10]

The depopulation of the Florentine countryside was indeed a serious problem during the late Trecento and early Quattrocento, and the legislative decrees of that epoch show that contemporaries were keenly aware of its existence. Series of legislative enactments and executive decrees were issued during those years to encourage workers from other parts of Italy to resettle *familiariter* in the Florentine contado. These workers were promised tax exemptions for periods ranging from ten to twenty years, or, if they were originally inhabitants of a territory in the jurisdiction of Florence who had fled to avoid imprisonment for not paying debts to individuals or tax arrears to the state, they were promised an amnesty and were offered an opportunity to repay their debts over a long period, usually up to ten years.[11] The frequency with which these measures appear in the communal registers is a good indication that the problem of an acute labor shortage was not overcome by the passage of these bills and that it continued to present a serious obstacle to the development of a viable fiscal policy toward the contado.

There was also the problem posed by the transfer of large portions of the patrimonies once controlled by the inhabitants of the contado into the hands of Florentine citizens. This prac-

10. See note 7.
11. Examples of this legislation can be found in *PR*, CV, ff. 215v–216r, November 23, 1415; CX, ff. 100v–101r, November 30, 1420; CXII, ff. 143r–144r, October 22, 1422; CXIV, ff. 63v–64r, December 5, 1424; CXVII, f. 45v, June 6, 1427; CXVIII, ff. 472v–473r, November 20, 1427; CXXII, ff. 2r–4v, April 2, 1431.

tice (as was first pointed out by Niccolò Rodolico and recently emphasized by Elio Conti in his multivolume study of the agricultural history of the Florentine state) made the fiscal relations between city and country even more unsatisfactory by shrinking the tax base on which the estimo could be imposed, for property held by Florentine citizens was struck from the tax rolls of the contado and transferred to those of the city.[12]

In view of these two phenomena—the decreasing population and the shrinking tax base of the contado—what can be said of the taxes imposed on the contado? Enrico Fiumi has calculated that during the 1330's the annual per capita tax assessed on the inhabitants of the contado was approximately ten gold sous, in contrast to the fifty gold sous demanded from each Florentine citizen.[13] According to his estimate, of the annual budget of 300,000 florins that Florence needed to meet all its expenditures, the inhabitants of the city contributed 225,000 florins (75 percent) and those of the country 75,000 florins (25 percent). During this period the rate at which the estimo was assessed was ten silver sous per lira,[14] which meant that at the time of collection of the tax, taxpayers were obliged to pay 50 percent of an assessment that had been based on the evaluation of their patrimonies.

By the late Trecento, despite the smaller population of the

12. On this general phenomenon, see Elio Conti's authoritative, but as yet incomplete, *La formazione della struttura agraria moderna nel contado fiorentino* (Rome: Istituto storico italiano per il Medio Evo, 1965–   ), III, part. 2a, 395–491, and the lengthy review of the two volumes of this book that have already appeared (vols. I, and III, part 2), by Giovanni Cherubini, "Qualche considerazione sulle campagne dell'Italia centrosettentrionale tra l'XI e il XV secolo," *Rivista storica italiana*, LXXIX (1967), 111–157, particularly pages 127–145.
13. Fiumi, "Sui rapporti economici . . . ," p. 30.
14. *Ibid.;* also Becker, *Florence in Transition*, I, 3.

countryside and the reduction of the tax base controlled by those still living there, the absolute value of taxes imposed on the contado actually increased over that of the early 1300's. The total tax of 75,000 florins of the 1330's became nearly 97,000 florins in 1392,[15] was reduced to about 85,000 florins in 1399 and 1400,[16] reached the maximum of 154,000 florins in 1409,[17] fluctuated between 125,000 and 135,000 florins during the peaceful years of the 1410's,[18] and then, immediately after the outbreak of war, was once again reduced to the level

15. Precisely 96,707 florins. All folio references are to *PC*, VIII. *Estimo ordinario* (f. 218r): 18,892 florins; *estimo straordinario* (f. 222r): 10,083 florins; *imposta de'contadini* (ff. 340r–v): 21,558 florins; *tassa di lancie* (f. 378v): 5,937 florins; *imposta straordinaria* (f. 289r): 9,879 florins; *macello* (f. 233r): 6,025 florins; *tassa ordinaria de'comuni* (f. 374r): 9,500 florins; *cognora del contado* (f. 225v): 14,833 florins.

16. A total of 82,587 florins collected in 1399, and 85,613 florins in 1400. The following folio references for 1399 refer to *PC*, XIV; for the year 1400, to *PC*, XV:

Tax	1399	1400
Estimo ordinario	17,360 (166v)	16,351 (166v)
Estimo straordinario	23,464 (203v–207v)	27,112 (201r–205r)[a]
Imposta nuova su distrittuali	2,274 (368r)	11,099 (368v)
Tassa di lancie	11,198 (308v)	5,603 (308r)
Macello	6,042 (186v)	5,440 (187v)
Tassa ordinaria	9,416 (300r)	9,138 (297r)
Cognora	12,833 (176v)	10,870 (177v)
TOTAL	82,587 florins	85,613 florins

[a] In 1400 this tax was registered under the heading of *imposta straordinaria su'contadini*, but it is clear that it was the same as the *estimo straordinario*.

17. The high of 1409 is no doubt a result of the Florentine conquest of Pisa and of the high taxes imposed on that city. Specific folio references and breakdowns of these figures for the years after 1402 will be found in Appendix B.

18. See Appendix B.

of the 1390's.[19] During years of peace the percentages contributed by the taxes of the contado to the budgets of the city remained approximately at the level of the 1330's, at about 25
percent, although in times of war, because of the greatly enlarged military budgets, they were considerably lower. Thus,
one may calculate that despite a shrunken tax base in the contado of the late Trecento and early Quattrocento, the annual
per capita tax on residents of the contado at that time was about
twice what it had been in the 1330's, standing at about twenty
gold sous.[20]

The oppressive fiscal demands made on the Tuscan territories
were self-defeating. The more affluent inhabitants of the contado, wishing to avoid the frequent special taxes imposed on the
subject territories and towns, gradually moved into the city,
leaving only the poorer ones behind to pay taxes. Curiously,
despite the high taxes paid by Florentine citizens, those inhabitants of the contado who could, moved into the city, petitioned
for the right of citizenship, and when obtaining it, became eligible for the tax rates applicable to the citizens.[21] This is a clear
indication that the higher tax rates of the city were accepted as
the unavoidable price of political advantages and economic op-

19. See Appendix B.

20. This figure is calculated on the basis of an average annual tax of 100,-
000 florins in addition to the approximately 40,000 florins per year the
Commune collected from the contado and districtus from the salt gabelle
(on which, see note 8). The total population of the contado and districtus
is set at 140,000.

21. Three examples: *PR*, CXIII, ff. 91r–v, August 23, 1423, records the
case of Laurentius Pauli, *biadaiolus,* who was being taxed both in the contado,
where he had his granary, and in the city, where his family was living. He
requests to be struck from the tax rolls of the contado and to be taxed in the
city "in qua familiam educat, gabellas et alia civitatis onera substinet." Two
other similar cases are recorded in *PR*, CXX, April 22, 1429: ff. 101r–v, for
a Maso di Jacopo, and ff. 110v–111r, for Johannes Cambiuzzi, *lannifex.*

portunities available there and woefully lacking in the contado. To offset the drain of manpower and capital from the country-side the Florentine legislators were obliged to raise the rate of the estimo. While for the greater part of the Trecento it had stood at 10 silver sous per lira, in 1384 it was raised to 12 sous per lira, and in 1386 to 15 sous, 9 deniers. During that same decade special surcharges were added to the estimo, amounting to 20 sous per lira (essentially, then, doubling the original assessment),[22] while in 1403 the regular assessment was augmented by four sous and totaled 24 sous per lira.[23] Soon thereafter the rate was further increased, ultimately reaching 40 sous per lira.[24] This figure represents an increase of the tax rate from the level of 50 percent of an assessment based on one's patrimony (10 sous per lira) to 200 percent of that same assessment (40 sous per lira). In addition, special taxes were often imposed on subject communes, particularly the larger and more affluent cities such as Pistoia, Arezzo, San Gimignano and others.[25]

22. From a deliberation of the priors and colleges dated July 31, 1389 (*DSOrd Aut.*, XXIV, ff. 26r–27r). This same measure refers to the imposition of the following *imposte straordinarie:* in 1380, twenty sous per lira; in 1382, a second of the same rate; in 1386, a third at the rate of twelve sous per lira; and in 1387, a fourth of twenty sous per lira.

23. *DSSp Aut.*, XII, ff. 101v–104r, December 11, 1403.

24. The measure is found in *PR*, CI, ff. 36v–37r, April 19, 1412. The bill was strongly opposed, and before its final approval it was voted down on several occasions. *LF*, XLIX, ff. 143r, 147r, 148r, 151r, 152r, 153r, 154r, and 155r.

25. The most important of these taxes was the *tassa di lancie*, which rendered certain localities in the Florentine domain responsible for the payment of a sum equivalent to the maintenance of a specific number of lances. See, for example, *PC*, XV, f. 302r: "Comune e uomini di Pistoia deono dare al comune di Firenze per lor tassa di lancia per tre anni comminciati a dì primo de Febraio 1396 [97] fiorini ottomila per anno, in tre paghe cioè di Genaio, di Magio e di Setenbre, come tocha per rata, a pena del quarto più se non paghano ne'detti termini, e non si possa prolunghare termine ne llevare

In his study of San Gimignano, Fiumi, while recognizing that by the early years of the fifteenth century the total per capita tax burden shouldered by the inhabitants of that city — after 1353 under the domination of Florence — had more than doubled in a period of some three generations, suggests that this resulted not from a policy of conscious exploitation but rather from the increased needs and obligations undertaken by Florence.[26] There is good reason for accepting this interpretation. The Florentine attitude toward the fiscal policy to be imposed on their Tuscan domain was ambivalent and hardly characterized by a singleness of purpose. While on the one hand desperate for whatever contribution the contado could make toward the high expenditures of that period, the Florentine legislators seem to have been aware of their subjects' predicament. Repeated attempts were made to curb the abuses so often perpetrated by unscrupulous tax collectors;[27] reduce the sum owed the com-

---

pena ne sopracciò fare alchuna chosa ne grazia se non pe'signiori e chollegi almeno per xxviii fave, paghandosi la tassagione della grazia che ricievessono chome d'una riformagione scrivendosi per notaio delle riformagioni e non per altri." The *tassa di lancie* was imposed regularly until 1405, after which time several older taxes of the contado were consolidated and paid in one sum. Payments of these taxes after 1405 are recorded in the *PC* under the heading of *imposte straordinarie*. In addition to the *tassa di lancie* before 1405, several other special levies were imposed on the inhabitants of the domain. See, for example, these two entries in *PC*, XIII: (f. 368v) "Entrata di distrittuali, posti [sic] loro per gli ufficiali sopracciò posti del mese di Dicembre, 1396"; total of 12,841 florins; (f. 372r) "Imposta fatta a'distretuali posta per gli uficiali sopraciò posti d'Ottobre 1397"; total of 9,368 florins.

26. Fiumi, *Storia . . . di San Gimignano*, p. 190.

27. The official deliberations of various governmental agencies abound with references to these kinds of abuses. See, for example, *DSOrd Aut.*, XXV, ff. 42r–v, March 22, 1390/91, when the priors heard the accusations leveled against Franciscus Ristori and Laurentius Pieri, "vocatus Ciarpa exactores ad presens deputati ad offitium exactorie pro regulatoribus . . . [qui] faciunt cotidie plures, varias, et diversas inhonestas et inlicitas exactiones, extorsiones

mune by subject lands (a reduction that was offset, of course, by the increase in the tax rates, which, as noted before, had more than quadrupled in some forty years);[28] extend the deadlines for the payment of past taxes; and control the activities of usurers, Jews and Gentiles, who plied their trade in the contado, by carefully regulating the interest rates that the money-

---

et latrocinia a multis et diversis et maxime pauperibus et inpotentibus hominibus et pauperes civitatis, comitatu et districtu flor. contra formam ordinamentorum dicti comunis et contra omnem bonam consuetudinem." The two were removed from office and were fined 500 lire each. Given the very large number of officials needed to administer and collect the taxes on the contado, it is quite clear that the government would have had a difficult time regulating their behavior and eliminating all abuses. On folios 49v–51r of this same *filza* it is stated that the *gabella portarum* alone was to be staffed by the following officials, each of whom could stay in office for a maximum of six months: seven *magistri;* twenty *veditores et proveditores;* two *officiales supra passageriis;* twenty-eight *casserii;* twenty-six *straderii;* six *casserii* and three *straderii* for Arezzo and its district. This one gabelle thus required the services of ninety-two officials. Additional references to these malpractices are found in *Camera del Comune — Statuto dei regolatori dell'entrate e spese del comune, filza unica,* ff. 13v–14r, February 19, 1405/06: "consideranti che i messi et exactori che vanno fuori dela cictà di Firenze a riscuotere le pecunie et cose debite al comune di Firenze, spesse volte molestano e contadini, distrectuali et subditi del decto comune, e da loro extorcono e tolgono pecunie per se proprii e niente rischuotono pel commune di Firenze," the authority of these *exactores* was curtailed, and they were specifically prohibited from collecting private debts.

28. The estimo of the contado was meant to fetch the city a certain minimum sum each time it was imposed. While in the Trecento this sum had been set at 30,000 lire, by the first years of the Quattrocento it had been reduced to 25,000 lire. See, for example, the legislative enactment of April 27, 1414, when this entire question was discussed and the decision was made that because of the substantial reduction in the value of the goods possessed by the inhabitants of the contado, the estimo would now be set at 23,562 lire, a reduction of 6,437 lire from the anticipated sum. This is the same provision already cited, in which there is a reference to the reduction in the number of households in the contado from 40,711 in 1405 to 36,333 in 1414 and to the diminution of the patrimonies owned by the contadini from 3,300,358 florins

lenders could charge their customers.[29] Considerable efforts were also made to make the administration of the estimo more efficient, in the hope that the savings resulting from such measures of reorganization could then be translated into a less onerous tax burden on the inhabitants of the contado.[30]

---

in 1405 to 2,362,522 florins in 1414. Interesting in this context is the fate of the estimo ordered in October 1422 (*PR*, CXII, ff. 137v–139v), which set the anticipated income at 20,000 lire.

The preamble of the act says, among other things: "Auditis infinitis fere querelis factis per comitatinos et alios supportantes extimum ordinarium comitatus continentibus inter alia in effectu quod nisi de nova distributione seu refectione distributionis extimi comitatus provideatur quasi omnia comitatinorum bona, status, et substantia ad exterminium et ruinam exponuntur considerata mutatione substantiarum et status multorum variationem tum propter presentis distributionis diuturnitatem tum propter mortalitatis invasionem que interim multis vicibus patriam conquassavit et fregit in tantum quod multa milia personarum sunt extincta, et volentes . . . inclinati querelis prefatis tam pro conservatione subditorum quam rei publice florentie statu et honore de et pro nova distributione providere. . . ." The task of preparing the new estimo, however, was interrupted by another visitation of the plague (*PR*, CXIII, ff. 165r–v, October 23, 1423), and it was decreed that the old one would remain in effect. In April 1425 (*PR*, CXV, ff. 1r–3r) "remota mortalitatis causa esset per dei gratiam removendus effectus," the new estimo was reordered and set at 20,000 lire. But one year later the officials charged with the task of devising the new estimo were still not finished, and they returned to the legislature with a request that the sum be further reduced to 17,000 lire "ob varias asperitates seu alias causas omnes ad eo pauperes et substantia carentes quod impossibile foret integram suprascriptam distribuere summam" (*PR*, CXVI, ff. 1r–2v, March 27, 1426). Finally, in August of the same year, a further reduction of a few hundred lire was authorized by the legislature. The estimo now was set at 16,450 lire. Thus, from 1414 to 1426 the anticipated income of the estimo had been scaled down from 23,562 to 16,450 lire.

29. For two such examples of attempted regulation of usurers, see *PR*, ff. 27v–28r, June 13, 1420, when the maximum interest rate was set at 25 percent per annum (5 deniers per lira per month); see also ff. 212r–v, February 14, 1420/21.

30. In February 1418/19 a *balia* (special plenipotentiary commission) was appointed "a provedere, ricerchare et examinare tutte et catune spese ordi-

Nevertheless, despite these measures, which in the eyes of the contadini must have seemed mere palliatives, the fiscal vise applied by the city on the contado became increasingly tighter. Communes were falling sadly in arrears in the payment of their

---

narie et extordinarie, utili, inutili, superflue, non buone et non necessarie le quali si fanno et supportansi per lli comuni, populi, ville, luoghi e università del contado e distretto di Firenze, et come si fanno et donde procedano." The task of these officials was to eliminate all unnecessary expenses and to allocate all savings to the Monte officials; their deliberations occupy an entire volume: *Balie*, XXI. Many other provisions regarding the proper taxation of the contado are found in *Camera del Comune—Statuto dei regolatori dell'entrate e spese del comune, volume unico.*

The efforts to introduce a greater measure of rationality into the taxation policies for the contado led to the first rudimentary attempts to create the catasto. The first such law, dealing with the city and territory of Pisa, was enacted on February 17, 1415/16, when special officials were appointed to "informare de substantia, facultate, valore, et statu omnium et singolorum hominum et personarum de comitatu olim pisarum et ibidem habitantium et quorumcunque comunium, universitatum seu locorum eiusdem comitatus tam exceptorum seu taxatorum quam non, videlicet ea comunia que olim quocunque tempore inclusa fuissent sub gabella que vulgariter nuncupata fuit la rinterzata et seu inclusa sub gabella que dicitur della farina et aliorum quorumcunque hominium in dictis comunibus vel quoscunquos ex eis habitantium seu bona immobilia possidentium vel habentium qui non faciant onera vel factiones in alio territorio seu loco subposito jurisdictioni comunis florentie, et ipsam substantiam et facultatem arbitrari et extimare prout equabilius fieri poterit" (*PR*, CV, ff. 303v–306r).

The following enactment is even more specific and anticipates in a very concrete manner the imposition of the catasto. It is a petition of the administrators of the estimo to the priors and the legislative assemblies, incorporated, as submitted, in the text of the law regulating the administration of the estimo (*PR*, CXII, ff. 268v–270r, February 23, 1422/23). The passage is quoted from folio 269r: "Che qualunque persona di qualunque stato o conditione si sia compresa a dovere rimanere nella nuova distributione dell'estimo del contado secondo l'effecto della provisione che d'essa nuova distributione dispone facta e obtenuta negli opportuni consigli del popolo et comune di Firenze del mese d'Ottobre prossimo passato sia tenuta dare per scriptura di sua mano o di mano del prete del suo popolo o di mano di publico notaio agli uficiali dell'estimo del contado o a chui pe'detti uficiali sarà diputato

taxes, thus incurring severe financial penalties. Of the 48,000 florins per year that Pisa was supposed to pay Florence in 1407, only 5,500 florins had been collected in a thirteen-month period.[31] There are cases, not unusual during the first quarter of the fifteenth century, of subject territories being twenty years behind in paying their taxes and petitioning the Signory for a reduction of their assessments and of the penalties imposed on them.[32] In early 1433, well after the suppression of their revolt against their masters, the Volterrans submitted a long and detailed petition to the Florentine Signory describing the pitiful state of affairs in their city and of its inhabitants. Of a tax amounting to 2,300 florins per year, they owed 8,555 florins; they were two years behind in the payment of another tax and three years in arrears in the payment of yet a third. In short, they asked for the consolidation and reduction of all their past debts to Florence, so that they might be able to pay the taxes that no doubt would be imposed on them in the future. The Florentine government agreed, though the new indebtedness of the Volterrans still amounted to several thousand florins.[33]

---

ogni suo bene mobile o immobile e ogni suo credito cholla stima apreso a ta'beni e crediti la quale per lui si faccia ragione vole e giusta infra quel tempo e termine che pe'detti uficiali sarà ordinato. . . ." A statement on how the tax was to be computed follows. Almost the same language is found in another provision dealing with the estimo, in *PR*, CXV, ff. 17v–19r, April 21, 1425. I have been unable to ascertain whether the inventories called for by these enactments were actually prepared.

31. *Signori — Missive Ia cancelleria*, XXVIII, ff. 95r–96r, September 19, 1408. This document was published in P. Silva, "Pisa sotto Firenze dal 1406 al 1433," *Studi storici*, XVIII (1909), 182–183.

32. For one such example, the case of the *popolo* San Bartolomeo de Corbinaria, see *PR*, CV, ff. 29v–30r, where it is recorded that on April 26, 1415, it petitioned the Signory to waive taxes due as far back as 1397. The petition specifically states that the village was being depopulated because of the onerous tax burden.

33. The case is found in *PR*, CXXIII, f. 368r, February 18, 1432/33. For

The state of bankruptcy into which the inhabitants of the contado and of the subject cities had fallen by the early years of the fifteenth century is indicated by the frequent loans that the authorities of subject villages, burgs, and cities had to seek in order to satisfy the Florentine tax authorities. The principal sources of these loans were two: usurers, mostly Jewish, settled in the Florentine territory, and the large banking houses of the mother city.

The presence of Jews and usurers in the Florentine territory, though considered somewhat of an anomaly, was not simply tolerated, but by the end of the fourteenth century openly encouraged, by large segments of the rural and provincial populations. The emigration of the more affluent inhabitants of the contado to the city, and the consequent removal of available sources of capital from the Florentine subject territories, often forced the inhabitants of those areas to rely on the liquid cash that local usurers could lend them. One of the most interesting phenomena of the late Florentine Trecento and early Quattrocento is the interplay of moral precepts and economic imperatives, the latter, because of the exigencies of the moment, overshadowing the former. Time and again, general prohibitions and limitations of usury were enacted by the Florentine authorities in order to protect their subjects from the disastrously

---

an earlier such petition of Volterra, see *Diplomatico, Volterra,* January 2, 1400/01, when the Volterrans stated that they owed the following taxes: 435 florins, 14 sous, for *tassa di lancie* assessed before 1397; 800 florins "pro subsidio etiam defense generalis imposito de mensis Septembris 1399 per rationerios extraordinarios"; 3,000 florins "subsidi lancearum pro tempori trium annorrum 1397–1400." The priors, "considerantes dannis per eos hactenus receptis in guerris proxime preteritis," allowed the Volterrans to pay only 1,308 florins, in two installments. Requests similar to these two fill dozens of folios of the legislative enactments and deliberations of the 1420's and 1430's.

high interest rates charged by the usurers. Yet it was the authorities of these subject communes themselves who requested the Florentine Signory to remove the ban against Jews in their own territories so that their subjects could avail themselves of the capital commanded by the Jewish pawnbrokers. Many such petitions have survived to remind the modern student of the complexity and intricacy of the moral and ethical imperatives operating in late medieval Italy.

In 1399 the authorities of Arezzo petitioned the Florentine priors to approve a pact that they had negotiated with one Gaio, *Judeo,* who would thereafter be allowed to lend freely to the Aretini and in return be granted numerous privileges and concessions in the city.[34] Gaius's pact with the Florentine government provided that he be allowed to exercise his trade in Arezzo for twenty years, after which time both parties were given an option to renew or terminate their agreement.[35] Yet the Florentine government, in a move that reflects the tension between ethics and economics in that age, issued a general ban against all Jews in 1406. Characterizing them as *inimici crucis, domini nostri Yhesu Christi, et omnium christianorum, et exercent usuras contra mandatum ecclesie sancte,* the ban forced Gaio and several other Jewish pawnbrokers out of the Florentine territory. An indication of the crucial role that the Jews played in the Tuscan provincial economy, however, is the fact that the Florentine government, under the pressure from representatives of these subject lands, was forced to abrogate the ban only a

34. *DSSp Aut.,* VIII, ff. 103v–107r, April 28, 1399. A transcript of the entire deliberation can be found in the appendix of the article cited in note 35.

35. For this, and for my subsequent comments on the Jewish moneylenders, see my article "A Note on Jewish Moneylenders in Tuscany in the Late Trecento and Early Quattrocento," in *Renaissance Essays in Honor of Hans Baron,* ed. Anthony Molho and John Tedeschi (Florence: Sansoni, 1971).

few months after its original institution. At least nine localities of the Florentine contado were permitted to invite Jews into their lands from 1406 until 1410, and the surviving records in the Florentine archives seem to indicate that the demands for the services of Jewish moneylenders persisted throughout the entire first half of the fifteenth century.[36] In 1427, after a general ban against the presence of Jews in the Florentine domain, an embassy of Pistoian notables appeared before the Florentine authorities, stating that, unless Jews were allowed to lend money in Pistoia and its contado, the Pistoians would be unable to meet their tax obligations or pay debts they had incurred with private individuals.[37] Similar requests were submitted to the Signory by many other local magistracies, one of which — Cortona — specifically referred to the benefits that would accrue to the poor people (*pauperes persone*) from the admission of Jews into their city.[38] Interest rates charged by usurers are difficult to calculate, although one suspects that they were high. The

36. The ban on the Jews is found in *PR*, XCIV, ff. 232v–233v, January 28, 1405/06; its revocation, in *PR*, XCV, ff. 140r–v, August 6, 1406. Licenses granted to Jewish money lenders from 1406 to 1410 are listed in *Capitoli— Appendice*, XXVIII, ff. 1r–32v.

37. *PR*, CXVII, f. 86v, June 6, 1427: "quod debitis temporibus non valent publicis nec etiam privatis necessitatibus et debitis respondere ex quo necessario compelluntur gravissimis penis subici, ac etiam persepe carceribus opprimi, qua omnia evitarent si in civitate predicta esset aliquis qui ad pignus mutuaret et eorum indigentiis cum pignore subveniret." For another strong condemnation of usurers, Gentile and Jewish, working in the contado, see *PR*, CV, ff. 206v–215r, November 23, 1415.

38. For Cortona: *Capitoli — Appendice*, XXVII, f. 1r. For Volterra: *PR*, CIX, ff. 251v–252r, February 27, 1419/20; *DSSp Aut.*, XXII, ff. 4v–8r, February 4, 1428/29, where maximum allowable interest was set at 30 percent per annum (6 deniers per lira per month). On 29 March, 1432, the Volterrans petitioned and were granted a renewal of this license (*PR*, CXXIII, ff. 5r–v). For Pisa: *PR*, CXXII, ff. 162r–v, August 23, 1431. For Empoli: *PR*, CXXIII, ff. 234r–v, October 10, 1432.

decrees authorizing Jews to lend in the contado often set a maximum of between 20 and 30 percent per year, which meant that
a commune not repaying its loan within three to four years
would have to disburse interest payments ranging from 60 to
90 percent of the amount originally borrowed.

Finally, the inhabitants of the contado and of the subject territories had recourse to the large Florentine banking houses,
which were willing to advance loans to them at substantial interest rates. The plight of Castiglion Fiorentino, for example,
becomes clear in a petition that its representatives submitted
to the Florentine Signory. Though its annual tax assessment
amounted to 900 florins, it already owed back taxes for 4,200
florins, in addition to 1,550 florins borrowed from Florentine
bankers "to pay to the Treasury of Florence the old taxes." Of
this sum, 800 florins had been borrowed from Antonio Davanzati at the rate of 12 percent per annum, and 750 florins from
the bank of Luigi Guicciardini's sons at an annual interest rate
of 16 percent.[39] Even more graphic was the case of Strozza di
Russo de'Strozzi, who had lent more than 18,000 florins to five
localities of the contado, charging them "at the rate of more
than 12 percent," but who, through the years, because of his
clients' inability to repay the capital, had collected more than
17,000 florins in interest.[40] All subject territories under the juris-

39. *Diplomatico — Castiglion Fiorentino*, July 26, 1411.
40. Information regarding this case was found in *Diplomatico — Monte
Comune*, 13 . . . The date assigned to this parchment by the inventory is
wrong. On the *verso* side of the *pergamena*, precisely in the same hand as the
calligraphy of the text, there is the date of December 10, 1453. The contents
of this *pergamena* include an interesting case. Lawyers for the following subject communes were suing Alexio di Jacopo di Strozza de'Strozzi for the
usurious interests that his grandfather had charged them when he had loaned
them money so that they might meet the tax deadlines set by Florence: Pon-
tormo had borrowed 3,616 florins and had paid "pro merito et usuram" 2,650

diction of Florence used the facilities offered them by the prosperous bankers of the mother city[41] and, as should be obvious, the consequences for the economic well-being of the subject communities and for the fiscal policy of the Florentine state were disastrous. By having to disburse a large part of their scarce cash reserves to Florentine bankers, the territories of the Flor-

florins; Poggibonsi had borrowed 9,000 florins and had paid 6,250 florins in interest; Empoli had borrowed 4,020 florins and had paid 2,250 florins in interest; Cerreto Guidi had borrowed 800 florins and had paid 1,330 florins in interest; and Vinci had borrowed 2,400 florins, paying back interest of 5,000 florins! Now these communes wanted to be repaid for the usurious interest that Strozza de'Strozzi had charged them. Unfortunately, the bottom part of this *pergamena* is missing, and I was unable to find out the disposition of the case.

41. For a case when Pisa had to borrow such sums from Florentine bankers, see Silva, "Pisa sotto Firenze . . . ," pp. 292, 594. In 1420, according to Silva, the Pisan authorities had to borrow 15,400 florins from three Florentine bankers (Giovanni da Castelfiorentino, Jacopo di Piero Baroncelli, and Giovanni Bischeri) at 10 percent per year, in order to pay back taxes: "E il bello è," says Silva, "che di quella somma, presa a prestito dal comune di Pisa, neppure un centesimo a Pisa viene mandato, ma tutto è impiegato a pagare i debiti vecchi e a far le scritte dei nuovi." Often, in the records of the Camera del Comune, mention is made of tax payments being made by subject territories through the use of the facilities offered by the large Florentine banking houses. One is not quite certain, however, if these transactions refer to loans taken by these communes in order to pay their taxes or if they had transmitted these sums to Florence through the facilities of these banks. *PC*, LIII, a *filza* devoted entirely to recording tax payments of subject communes, reveals some things of interest. On the first unnumbered folio Bartolomeo di Verano Peruzzi is listed as one of the two *provveditori* of the Camera del Comune; on folio 42r it appears that several subject communities, Pistoia and Pescia, among them, made their tax payments through the facilities of the Peruzzi bank, though it is not quite clear whether they borrowed the money from the Peruzzi or transmitted their payment through them. In any case, this is an instance when the private and public interests of the Peruzzi converged, thus intensifying the fiscal pressures on the subject communes. Other banking firms are mentioned in this volume: The firm of Piero Vellutti & Socii made payments for Pistoia and San Gimignano (ff. 40r–v, 42r), and Mariottus Bencini, *campsor*, made a payment for Arezzo (f. 67v).

entine domain were exporting from their lands capital that could have been more profitably invested there, thus undermining their economy further and also restricting the tax base on which the Florentine authorities could have imposed tax assessments.[42]

A detailed examination of the political repercussions of Florentine fiscal policy in the contado cannot be undertaken here. Two examples must suffice to illustrate the wide extent and the profundity of the changes that this policy brought about. In the late spring and early summer of 1419, despite the relative stability of nearly half a decade, discussions were held in the councils of the Commune on how to alleviate the crushing economic burden imposed by the mother city on its subjects, while at the same time rendering the administration of the fiscal structure more efficient and equitable. A five-man commission of Florentine councillors was finally appointed to survey the procedures by which taxes were imposed on subject lands and to ascertain the precise amount of tax imposed on each administrative unit (*communi, populi, pivieri*) of the domain.[43] The deliberations of these *ufficiali del contado*, which have by accident survived to our day, indicate the dimensions of the problem. While reiterating the usual, but (as experience had shown)

42. See the comments of the anonymous writer in *Ricordi della presa di Pisa*, ed. Ruggiero Nuti, *Archivio storico pratese*, XIX, nos. 3–4 (1941), 126–127: "Ma la detta guerra e assedio fatto a Pisa e nel suo contado costò due milioni di fiorini; che'ntendo ogni milione mille volte mille. Ma i contadini di Firenze sono quegli che delle loro borse sono fatte quasi tutto questo ispendio; e se i cittadini di Firenze pagavano neuno incarico, gli aveano meritati a tenpo XV per centinaio. E venne si grande la fame del denaio, che quasi col pegno non si trovava neuno ricorso. Onde dice bene vero uno mio amico, che dice: 'Per ingiustizia, per guerra e per fame/In breve si distrugge ongni reame.' "

43. *LF*, LI, ff. 270r, 271r, June 2, 1419.

largely ineffectual, censure of usurers and corrupt communal officials, the five officials rescinded the authority of local assemblies to levy taxes on their subjects. Thereafter, only the Florentine Signory and legislature would be empowered to impose levies on any subject territories, while the legislative and executive bodies of these localities would be forbidden even to consider the matter.[44] Private individuals were forbidden to lend any sums at all to these subject territories without the prior approval of the Florentine *ufficiali del Monte* (the administrators of the funded public debt), and even the initiative of Florentine officials serving in the provinces (*podestà* and *castellani*) was carefully limited and defined in fiscal matters.[45] In essence, therefore, the decisions of the officials for the contado were directed toward the complete and substantial redefinition of the fiscal relations between Florence and her subject lands. The ultimate aim of these decisions was to destroy the fiscal autonomy of cities like Prato, Pistoia, San Gimignano, Arezzo, and others, which for generations before, even after their submission to Florence, had enjoyed a large measure of self-determination in these matters. Whether or not a serious effort was made to create a more organized and clearly articulated fiscal structure, and the extent to which such an effort might have succeeded, are questions that only additional study in the archives of Florence and its subject territories will resolve. The decisions of the officials for the contado in 1419 indicate, how-

44. *Miscellanea repubblicana,* CII, insert 1, entitled "Deliberazioni degli ufficiali del contado, 1419." Rubrics 1–3 deal with the diminution of the fiscal authority enjoyed by the local assemblies. The names of the officials charged with these deliberations were Bartolomeo di Tommaso Corbinelli, Giovanni di Francesco Caccini, Tommaso di Vieri Ardinghelli, Andrea di Giovanni d'Andrea [di Neri Lippi] del Palagio, Giovanni di Salvestro Cierridori.

45. *Ibid.,* rubrics 4 and 7.

ever, that contemporary Florentines were keenly aware of the weak points of their contado and of its limited capacity to produce additional income for the communal budget.

If the Florentines were aware of the difficulties they were creating for their subjects, it is also clear that these subjects realized they were being exploited by their masters. The revolt of the Volterrans in 1429 had at its source their discontent with the fiscal policies of Florence. An abortive rebellion in Arezzo in 1431 was inspired by the issue of taxation, and the fact that this rebellion was staged only a few months after the crushing of the Volterran revolt is eloquent testimony of the profundity of the resentment against the Florentines. The leader of the Aretine conspiracy was forthright in explaining his motivation to one of his collaborators: "I should like that you and others side with me, so that we may all escape such heavy taxes," he said.[46] Nor should they allow the Florentines to perpetrate on them the policies that led to the destruction of the Pisans, "whose goods have been robbed and women defiled." They should try to hold on to "that bit of honor and the few goods that we have been able to preserve." [47]

This brief analysis of the fiscal and general economic conditions of the Florentine contado during the first quarter of the fifteenth century suggests that at the very time when the needs of the Florentine state were greatest, and when all its subjects —citizens or contadini—should have made an increased effort

46. Ubaldo Pasqui, "Una congiura per liberare Arezzo dalla dipendenza dei Fiorentini (1431)," *ASI*, ser. 5, LV (1890), 16: "Io vorrei che tu et altri fosse meco, et che noi uscissimo di tante graveze."

47. *Ibid.*: "Notificandovi come io fortemente temo che a voi non intervenga come è intervenuto a'Pisani o peggio, chè sapete come essi sono condotti: la loro robba andata a sachomanno e le loro donne svergognate. E perciò vi aviso che voi siate savi, et provedete per modo sia salvamento dello honore vostro, e delle donne vostre, et simile di quello poco di robba c'è rimasa."

to support the government's diplomatic and military objectives, the Florentine contado, underpopulated and despoiled of much of its wealth, was in no position to increase its fiscal contributions to the central government. From the 1390's it had become evident to thoughtful observers that the inhabitants of the Florentine contado were laboring under a debilitating burden and that efforts should have been made to ameliorate their situation.[48] Not much was done, and after 1424, when military disasters followed one another in alarmingly rapid succession and the military budget increased in equally alarming proportions, the contadini were barely able even to maintain their contributions to the Florentine budget at the levels of the previous decade. While in the 1330's the Florentine contado had been able to contribute fully 25 percent of the city's budget, by the early 1430's its share had diminished to between 10 and 15 percent.

THE GABELLES

The second principal source of income to the Florentine government was indirect taxation on the consumption and importation of goods via the gabelles. In use since the middle of the thirteenth century, these taxes were assessed on common foodstuffs like grain, bread, meat, wine, fruit, and the like. They

48. Already before 1411 Giovanni di Pagolo Morelli had noted in his *Ricordi* (ed. V. Branca [Florence: Le Monnier, 1956], p. 102): "pelle quali [taxes] è suto forza a una gran gente il partirsi, per non avere a stentare in pregione." Silva in his "Pisa sotto Firenze . . . ," p. 287, quotes a statement made in 1417 by Niccolò da Uzzano, who said that the imposition of additional taxes on Pisa "est bursas Pisanorum vacuare." In 1416 the *gabella congiorum vini* on the contadini was revoked. *PR,* CVI, ff. 213v–214v, March 26, 1416: "Considerantes oneribus que supportantur per comitatinos extimum ordinarium comitatus florentie per solventes, et expensis gravibus atque non solum paupertate sed fere miseria universaliter cunctorum comitatinorum. . . ."

included the state monopoly of salt, taxes on the transfer of property or of credits of the public debt (*gabella delle permute del Monte*), and a tax imposed on every notarial document executed by any one of the city's many notaries (*gabella dei contratti*). Finally, they included the import and export duties charged on all items entering or leaving the Florentine territory.[49] During the peaceful and very prosperous fourth decade of the fourteenth century the income from the gabelles, combined with that derived from taxes on the contado, was sufficient to meet the city's expenses. Giovanni Villani, in his celebrated description of Florence, offers the readers of his chronicle a list of all the gabelles then imposed on the inhabitants of Florence and suggests that they produced nearly 75 percent of the annual communal budget.[50]

Communal income from surcharges of this sort depended directly on economic conditions prevalent in the city and its domain. The income from certain basic gabelles was directly related to the quantity of foodstuffs consumed, and though the government could dictate to its subjects the amount of salt they had to purchase each year, it could not dictate the turnover rate of business nor even the amount of wine to be consumed. Therefore, during the third quarter of the fourteenth century, as Flor-

49. On the gabelles, see the recent article of Charles de la Roncière, "Indirect Taxes or 'Gabelles' at Florence in the Fourteenth Century" in *Florentine Studies,* ed. Nicolai Rubinstein (London: Faber and Faber, 1968), pp. 140–192. See also the old but still valuable work of Bernardino Barbadoro, *Sulle finanze della repubblica fiorentina* (Florence: Olschki, 1929). On the serious limitations of this work, see Niccola Ottokar, "Problemi di storia del Comune di Firenze," *ASI,* XCIV (1936), 77–86, and Roberto Cessi, "Note sulla storia della finanza fiorentina medievale," *ASI,* LXXXIX (1931), 85–127.

50. Giovanni Villani, *Cronica fiorentina,* XI, 82.

ence undertook an ambitious program of territorial expansion in Tuscany at a time of rather serious economic stagnation, the government felt compelled to increase the rates at which gabelles were collected in order to maintain the communal income from that source at relatively stable levels. Thus, for example, the rate of the gabelle on olive oil was increased from two sous per *orcio* in 1327 to fifteen sous in 1380; that of wine from ten sous per *cogno* in 1320 to fifty sous in 1380; of hogs from six sous per head in 1333 to forty sous in 1380; and the price of salt trebled, from twenty sous per *staio* in 1315 to sixty sous in 1378. Charles de la Roncière, in his recent pioneering study of the gabelles in the first three quarters of the fourteenth century, has concluded that much of the unrest among the lower orders of Florentine society during that period can be traced to the enormous increases in the rates of the gabelles. It is understandable that these increases should weigh much more heavily on the less affluent inhabitants of the city than on the members of the Florentine patriciate.[51] Be that as it may, it is clear that by the last two decades of the fourteenth century the rates of gabelles stood at substantially higher levels than at the beginning of the Trecento.

Although there were more than thirty different gabelles, each taxing separate items or transactions, the four major surcharges were those of the gate (*porte*), salt (*sale e salina*), contract (*contratti*), and wine sold at retail (*vino al minuto*). During the last two decades of the fourteenth century, for which there are complete and reliable statistics, the combination of these four taxes fetched the city a net income of no more than 289,248

51. Charles de la Roncière, "Indirect Taxes or 'Gabelles' . . . ," pp. 190–192. All information on the rates of gabelles for the years before 1380 are from de la Roncière's study.

florins[52] in 1385 and no less than 189,087 florins[53] in 1390. For the greater part of those two decades the figures representing the net income from these gabelles stayed in the range of 210,000 to 230,000 florins. In 1400, however, with the opening of the third stage of hostilities against Giangaleazzo Visconti, the income from the four gabelles fell, now producing a net of only 185,958 florins in 1400 and only slightly more, 188,-885 florins, in 1401.[54] Because the communal expenses during the first triennium of the new century were considerably enlarged by the military campaigns undertaken against the Milanese, the Ten of War (*Dieci di balia*), who were entrusted with the supervision of the city's military engagements, recommended that the rates of gabelles be increased, so that they would produce a higher income. Their recommendation having been accepted by the members of the plenipotentiary commission (*Ottantuno*), which since 1393 had formulated the city's fiscal policies, a special committee was appointed to review the rates of all gabelles. The members of this committee were given full powers to increase the rates of tax on any items they wished with the exception of grain.[55] The product of the deliberations of these officials was a comprehensive list of the rates of gabelles,

52. All references are to *PC*, II: Gates gabelle (f. 436v), 128,170 florins; salt gabelle (f. 437v), 56,434 florins; contracts gabelle (f. 438v), 30,348 florins; wine gabelle (f. 439v), 74, 296 florins; total, 289,248 florins. These sums represent the net income from each gabelle, the administrative expenses of the office having been deducted from the gross.

53. *PC*, VI: Gates gabelle (f. 167r), 69,420 florins; salt gabelle (f. 181r), 41,321 florins; contracts gabelle (f. 195r), 22,633 florins; wine gabelle (f. 207r), 55,713 florins; total, 189,087 florins.

54. For 1400, *PC*, XV: Gates gabelle (f. 104v), 88,114 florins; salt gabelle (f. 119v), 48,605 florins; contracts gabelle (f. 136v), 12,735 florins; wine gabelle (f. 151r), 36,504 florins; total, 185,958 florins. For 1401, *PC*, XVI: Gates gabelle (f. 104 r), 95,637 florins; salt gabelle (f. 120r), 35,710 florins; contracts gabelle (f. 137v), 21,734 florins; wine gabelle (f. 151r), 35,804 florins; total, 188,885 florins.

which remained in force for more than half a century.[56] Nearly twenty-five folios in length, this inventory lists hundreds of items, from foodstuffs to woolen and iron products, spices and animals, with the rate of the gabelle applicable to each. The new rates, which, as we shall see below, were set at the highest limits they had attained in the previous century, were originally meant to apply only for three years. Nevertheless, because of the Commune's chronic financial straits, and also because the wealthier Florentines preferred this to other forms of taxation, the decree of 1402 was renewed at regular intervals, so that basically the rates established in that year continued to be assessed until the middle of the fifteenth century. Most large Florentine commercial establishments, as well as many governmental agencies, maintained copies of this document, and as a result, it has survived in numerous manuscript copies.[57]

55. The decision is found in *DSSp Aut.*, XI, ff. 51r–53r, May 23, 1402. On the *Ottantuno*, see my article "The Florentine Oligarchy and the *Balìe* of the Late Trecento," *Speculum*, XLIII (1968), 29–58.

56. The entire list of products and the tariff assessed on each after 1402 has been published by G. F. Pagnini, *Della decima e di varie altre gravezze imposte dal comune di Firenze*, 4 vols. (Lisbon cited as place of publication; actually Lucca, 1765–1766), IV. Several manuscript copies of this inventory survive in Florentine libraries. Among those I have consulted are *ASF, Miscellanea repubblicana*, XXXIV, insert 9, and Biblioteca Laurenziana, Ashburnham, 1895. On folio 1v of the latter manuscript one reads: "Le dette ghabelle furono ordinate e chorrette per sei huomini eletti che volgharmente si chiamavano e sei della masserizia per tre anni inchominciando in chalendi Settenbre 1402. E di poi l'anno 1411 fu prolunghato il richrescrimento delle dette ghabelle per dieci, e renduto il primo acchatto dispiacente." Then on folio 23r one encounters this entry: "Finito di chopiare lo stratto di ghabelle sopradetto per me Piero di Jachopo di Pagholo questo dì di Giennaio 1449 a ore nove per Niccholò Chanbini e chonpagni di Firenze, a quali Iddio chonceda onore e utile di merchatantia e dogn'altro loro afare in che s'inpacciassino chon salvamento dell'anima e del chorpo, e anchora per me, schrittore Iddio lo faccia per sua piatà e misericordia.'

57. For bills extending the new rates: *DSSp Aut.*, XII, ff. 24v–27r, April

Table 2 compares some of these rates with those that had prevailed in the fourteenth century.

Even for items for which complete gabelle rates for the fourteenth century have not been compiled, one can make certain tentative comparisons. From a late-fourteenth-century inventory of the Florentine gabelles found in the Biblioteca Riccardiana of Florence we learn that in the late fourteenth century English woolen cloth was taxed at the rate of 40 sous per hundredweight; after 1402 the tax was 1 florin, 16 silver sous. (Converting the florin into silver currency at the rate of four lire per florin, we arrive at a new rate charged on English cloth of 96 sous per hundredweight.) Similar increases took effect in the rates of tax on other products. The gabelle for linen increased from 13 sous to 16 sous per hundredweight; for used cloth, from 16 sous to 18 sous, 8 deniers; for iron bars, from 33 sous to 64 sous; for Parmesan cheese, from 13 sous, 4 deniers, to 15 sous, 7 deniers; for saltwater fish, from 35 sous, 7 deniers, to 50 sous per hundredweight; and finally, for baby lambs weighing less than thirty pounds, from 2 sous, 11 deniers, to 4 sous per head.[58]

During the fourteenth century, because of the all too well-known economic and social disasters that had befallen Florence, the rates of gabelles had fluctuated, often wildly. By the end of

19, 1403; *PR*, CIX, f. 219r, December 29, 1419; *PR*, CXVIII, ff. 586r, 587v, March 15, 1427/28. These rates were still applicable in January 1449/50, as is evident from folio 23r of the Ashburnham MS.

58. Biblioteca Riccardiana, Fondo Riccardiano, 2526. On folio 28r (27r according to the modern pagination): "Iscripto per me Antonio di Ventura per Nanny di Ruberto [Strozzi?]." It may well be that this manuscript was used by an official in charge of collecting the gabelles. The codex is divided into three sections, the first listing the import duties assessed on various items, the second listing export duties, and the third suggesting how an assessor can calculate rapidly the levy to be imposed on animals and fowls.

Table 2. Gabelle rates in the fourteenth and early fifteenth centuries.

	Wheat[a]	Oil[b]	Hogs[c]	Wine[d]	Salt[e]
14th-Century Low	10	2	6	10	20
14th-Century High	24	20	70(?)	60	120
Rate in 1380	12	15	40	50	60
Rate after 1402	12	20	40	65	132–168

Sources: Figures representing gabelles for the fourteenth century are from Charles M. de la Roncière, "Indirect Taxes or 'Gabelles' at Florence in the Fourteenth Century," in *Florentine Studies*, ed. Nicolai Rubinstein (London, Faber and Faber, 1968), pp. 140–192. Figures for the rates assessed after 1402 were taken from Biblioteca Laurenziana, Ashburnham, 1895, and from *ASF, Miscellanea repubblicana*, XXXIV, insert 9. The price of salt charged after 1402 comes from Biblioteca Nazionale Centrale di Firenze, Fondo Nazionale, II.I.160, ff. 34v–35r, and *ASF, Miscellanea repubblicana*, CVI, f. 11r.

[a] Deniers per *staio*.

[b] Sous per *orcio*.

[c] Sous per head. The figure representing the highest rate for the gabelle on hogs in the fourteenth century seems suspiciously high, and even Charles de la Roncière, author of an important essay on fourteenth-century gabelles, questioned it.

[d] Sous per *cogno*.

[e] Sous per *staio*. This was the price for salt charged only to the inhabitants of the city. The contadini, before and after 1402, paid about twenty to thirty sous less.

the Trecento they were substantially higher than those of the early 1300's but, more often than not, below those of mid-century. The rates established in 1402, in most cases, reverted to the highest peaks reached in the 1350's and 1360's. At no earlier time in Florentine history were the inhabitants and subjects of the city required to pay such high indirect taxes for so long a time as in the first half of the fifteenth century. Not until the last quarter of the Quattrocento were gabelle rates increased again, a fact which would seem to indicate that the level of the rates established in 1402 was considered the maximum which could then reasonably be charged Florentine subjects.[59]

What was the net increase in the Commune's income resulting from these higher gabelles, and how helpful was it for balancing the Florentine budget? It seems that the higher rates imposed on the importation of goods fetched an additional 10,000 florins per year, while the higher taxes on salt, the increased fees required for the submission of private petitions to the government, and the lowering of the governmental subsidy traditionally granted to the *Opera* of the Florentine Cathedral (from 2½ percent to 1½ percent of the gross income produced by all the city's gabelles) contributed an additional 14,000 florins.[60] This total of 24,000 florins represented an increase of 10 to 15 percent over the yearly income previously produced by the gabelles.

The implementation of the new regulations thus increased total income from the gabelles substantially: to 221,579 florins in 1403 and 205,541 florins in 1404. These augmented revenues were sustained until the outbreak of war against King Ladislaus of Naples in 1409. Starting in that year, however,

59. For rates applicable in December 1485, see Biblioteca Laurenziana, *Fondo Antinori*, XXVI. The date of this manuscript is found on folio 22r.

60. *PR*, CV, ff. 264r–v, December 30, 1415: "Item quod quantitas percipienda de augmento pretii salis, gabelle dominationum, et de denariis tribus pro libra de assignamento pro opera seu fabrica maioris ecclesie florentine qua dicitur ascendere pro anno ad florenos quattuordecim milium auri. . . ." "Item quod . . . quantitas percipienda de augmento gabelle portarum facto pro certos cives appellatos della masseritia que datur pro anno florenos decemmilia auri vel circa. . . ." These figures reappear in subsequent decrees: *PR*, CIX, f. 219r, December 29, 1419; *PR*, CXIII, f. 229v, December 13, 1423; CXVIII, f. 587v, March 15, 1427/28; *Camera del Commune — Filze miscellanee*, I, f. 88r, December 29, 1419. The original governmental decree establishing the communal subsidy to the *Opera del Duomo* at 3 percent of the gross intake of the gabelles is found in *Camera del Comune — Provisioni Canonizate, volume unico*, ff. 21v–22r, August 1, 1318.

the four major gabelles began fetching less than 200,000 florins, and they remained at that depressed level until the conclusion of the war in 1414, when once again they surpassed the 200,-000-florin mark.[61] With the onset of war against Milan in 1423 the income from the Florentine gabelles plummeted, to 159,044 florins in 1424 and 137,210 florins in 1426, and the gabelles were unable to bring in their former high incomes for the entire duration of the war. Table 3 gives information on the net income from the four major gabelles for those years from 1402 to 1433 for which complete information exists.

The sharp decline of the net yield from the gabelles could result only in disastrous consequences for the Florentine fiscal structure. To repeat what was suggested earlier about the results of the contado's inability to increase its contributions to the Commune's budget, one observes that at the very time Florentine financial commitments were most pressing, the two principal sources of regular communal income proved incapable of meeting them. Rates of indirect taxes being as high as they were, it was impossible to raise them further. Even those communal councillors who recognized the necessity of augmenting the city's intake no longer suggested an increase in gabelle rates; now they were content to recommend the reorganization of the gabelle system so that the collection of these taxes could be rendered more efficient and the widespread corruption among tax collectors and assessors could be reduced.[62]

61. See Table 3, and Table 4, chapter 4.
62. See note 2. In *PR,* CXVIII, f. 505r, December 20, 1427, one finds a good example of the type of corruption existing among gabelle officials. A Pippo di Giovanni di Nuto, resident in the *popolo* di San Lorenzo of the city, had been a collector of the contracts gabelle from 1405 to 1420, during which time he had appropriated certain sums belonging to that office. Having been punished with the amputation of both ears and of his nose and by one year's imprisonment, he was now petitioning the Signory for grace.

Table 3. Net income from the four major gabelles, 1402–1433 (values expressed in florins rounded off to nearest complete figure. Silver currencies converted to gold at current exchange rates, for which consult Appendix D).

Year	Gates	Salt	Contracts	Wine at Retail	Total
1402	85,438	57,241	15,998	33,623	192,300
1403	107,992	69,171	12,748	31,668	221,579
1404	122,837	40,175	14,363	28,166	205,541
1405	118,979	50,612	14,166	26,380	210,137
1407[a]	117,981	61,703	13,194	20,818	213,696
1408	123,986	48,848	13,300	27,600	213,734
1409	109,173	37,097	13,006	18,752	178,028
1411[a]	88,523	51,948	11,463	19,589	171,523
1414[a]	105,559	58,294	10,762	14,437	189,052
1416[a]	115,494	51,319	18,473	20,818	206,104
1419[a]	122,093	51,112	17,539	17,935	208,679
1420	118,046	59,669	17,892	20,080	215,687
1424[a]	92,334	49,378	7,248	13,579	159,044
1426[a]	87,648	26,202	9,500	13,860	137,210
1427	95,471	65,785	11,949	12,093	185,298
1429[a]	103,991	41,165	13,533	13,217	171,906
1430	77,975	47,094	7,599	10,720	143,388
1431	71,557	52,565	10,087	9,952	144,161
1432	70,206	50,420	10,482	7,427	138,535
1433	76,285	([b])	9,001	8,210	([b])

Source: See Appendix B.

[a] Information for missing years not available in *PC*.

[b] Data are incomplete.

Some efforts were made to amend the entire gabelle system. In October 1425, because of the high war expenses, the legislature authorized a standing committee of one hundred and forty-five citizens, who were empowered to formulate general economic policy, to curtail expenditures and assess new ga-

belles.[63] The committee, having met to consider viable alternatives, drastically reduced the salaries of many officeholders and
slightly increased certain minor gabelles, principally those levied on leather and iron products.[64] From 1426 through 1433
numerous measures were taken to institute other small, essentially insignificant, gabelles or to raise by a few deniers the
rates of several isolated items. Thus, for example, the collection
of the *gabella delle porte* was made more efficient for items
stored in warehouses situated immediately outside the city
walls;[65] the gabelles for animals that pastured in the Maremma
were regulated more carefully;[66] and the rates of certain high-
way fees charged animals and passengers were slightly increased.[67] Strict regulations were also enacted for the proper
and prompt registration of all contracts, an official being appointed to audit all notaries' registers so that each contract
might be assessed its due tax.[68] Finally, many instructions were
issued to the administrators (*magistri*) of the wine gabelle on
the need to be ever vigilant so that all wine imported into the

63. *PR,* CXV, ff. 178r–179r, October 22, 1425: "Ut occurentibus expensis
atque gravissimis rei publicae florentine possit ut expendit responderi, ideo
introytos comunis augeri seu novos inveniri et ordinari, atque imponi et solvi
et supportari cupientes. . . ."

64. The decisions of the committee are recorded in *Balie,* XXIII: ff. 61v–
62r, for increased gabelles on leather goods; f. 67r, on shoes; ff. 51r–v, the
re-establishment of some small tariffs temporarily reduced in 1419. The preamble of the enactment states that these new tariffs are imposed "per ac-
crescere l'entrate del decto comune e per corroboratione della forteza e ac-
crescimento de'crediti del Monte d'esso comune."

65. *PR,* CXIX, f. 305r, December 20, 1428.

66. *PR,* CXIX, f. 91r, June 21, 1428.

67. *PR,* CXIX, ff. 90v–91r, June 21, 1428: Pedestrian passengers using
either the *strada di Staggia* or the *strada di Casellino* were to pay a *gabella
del passo* of one florin per person. Those entering on horseback (or on mule
or donkey) were to be charged a gabelle of five florins for the animal.

68. *PR,* CXIX, ff. 23v–24r, May 21, 1428.

city, as well as that sold at retail, would not escape the legal surcharge assessed on it.[69] The single basic item that did undergo substantial price modification because of a higher gabelle was salt. The government, in fact, sought to regulate more closely the quantities of salt kept in warehouses so that large oversupplies would not be left in storage,[70] and both prices and minimum consumption requirements were increased for inhabitants of the city and of the contado.[71]

But excessively high gabelles could be detrimental to the Florentine economy, and some of the assessments made after the years 1423 to 1425 were eventually revoked as being coun-

69. *PR*, CXIX, f. 22r, May 21, 1428; CXXI, ff. 18v–19r, May 24, 1430; CXXIII, ff. 100r–v, May 27, 1432; CXXIV, ff. 42r–43r, April 29, 1433.

70. *PR*, CXVIII, ff. 466v–467v, December 7, 1427.

71. *PR*, CXIX, ff. 304v–305r, December 20, 1428; CXXIII, f. 272v, October 30, 1432, and f. 301v, December 10, 1432. These last two provisions increased the transport charges for carrying the salt from the central storage areas to Arezzo: (f. 272v) "respectu penurie alimentorum pro bestiis ac etiam longioris itineris quod debet fieri metu belli"; (f. 301v) "et actedentes . . . non invenire qui sal et salinam velit portare pro vectura et mercede predicta, volentes ne defectu predicto loca comunis defensione careant. . . ." In this context one should also consult the fundamental provision that established the norms for the consumption of salt in the contado (*PR*, CXX, ff. 261v–264r), already discussed in note 8. Needless to say, the subject communes and territories sought to avoid the purchase of larger quantities of salt than they could afford. An interesting case is revealed in *PR*, CXII, ff. 57r–59r, June 10, 1422. The authorities of Pistoia had willingly accepted their entire allotment of salt from the officials of the salt gabelle, and it seems that they had even volunteered to buy quantities in excess of their regular allotment. Upon investigating, however, the Florentine authorities had discovered that the government of Pistoia was reselling large quantities of this salt to the contadini for prices well below those charged by the Florentine government. While the price charged by the officials of the salt gabelle was 5 lire, 8 sous, per *staio*, the Pistoians "contra formam convencionum inter partes vigentium" were selling this salt for only 4 lire per *staio*. They were then punished by an increase in the amount of salt that they had to purchase from Florence and by the imposition of a monetary fine.

terproductive. A special tax imposed in September 1423 on Florentine merchandise traveling in Genoese boats was repealed in April 1429 on the petition of several Florentine merchants.[72] Another tax, on the exportation of wool workers' carding tools and combs, which had been imposed in December 1426, was abrogated in August 1427 on the petition of the masters of the wool guild, who alleged that it discouraged the workers of the guild from selling their tools and buying new ones.[73] Finally, a higher rate imposed in 1426 on the introduction of iron bars was rescinded in 1431, because it was recognized that it impeded the manufacture of arms at a time when Florence was heavily involved in war.[74]

This, then, was the state of taxes on the contado and of the gabelles during the 1420's. Aside from loans advanced by citizens to the state, other sources of income were difficult to locate. The Church, which according to the allegations of some contemporary Florentines controlled as much as one fourth or one fifth of the city's total wealth,[75] could occasionally be forced

72. The imposition of the tax is recorded in *DSOrd Aut.*, XXXV, f. 12v, September 11, 1423; its repeal, in *PR*, CXX, f. 90r, April 21, 1429.

73. The abrogation of the surcharge (mentioning that the tax had been imposed in December 1426) is in *PR*, CXVII, ff. 275v–276r: "Et quod demum ordinamentum quantum capit et intelligit de veteribus est nocivum artificibus ipsius artis, sine aliquo rei publico commodo, seu alicuius publici damni evitatione. . . ." I was unable to locate the original act establishing the imposition of this tariff.

74. *PR*, CXXII, ff. 284r–v, November 28, 1431, and repeated in CXXIII, f. 135v, June 27, 1432.

75. Many references to the advisability of taxing ecclesiastical property appear in the deliberations of the priors during the late 1420's and early 1430's. On August 3, 1431, in the course of a debate dealing with the communal shortage of funds, Manettus Tucci Scambrilli stated: "Bona ecclesiastica sunt 1/4 vel 1/5 pars omnium bonorum, et defenduntur simul cum nostris; ideo nemo obaudiat, et fiat impositio clericis. Sunt aliqui clerici qui cupiunt requiri et libenter concurrerent; vel stringantur ad emendum 150 m.

to contribute toward the expenses of the city. Such efforts could be costly to the Florentines, however, for they tended to alienate the Papacy, a necessary and much valued ally in those difficult days. Thus, for example, a tax of 35,000 florins assessed on the Florentine clergy in 1426 was reduced by 10,000 florins the next year because of papal pressure.[76] The state, however, succeeded in enacting a law that prevented the often fraudulent transfers of land into the hands of tax-exempt ecclesiastical entities by decreeing that any real estate included in the returns (*denuncie*) of private citizens for the catasto of 1427 carry its tax assessment even after becoming the property of tax-exempt institutions.[77]

In this case, as well, the hopes of Florentine statesmen who had imagined that direct assistance, taxes, or loans from the Church would extricate the government from its serious financial predicament were disappointed. The Church had economic problems of its own,[78] and most of its wealth was in the form of

ff. montis ad 50 per centum. Preterea tollantur tasse a Judeis pro 5 annis ut veniant ad prestandum hic; et ferrent multas pecunias; sed prestatores qui sunt hic substinentur ab amicis pro quibus prestant. Velitis ergo vincere et ad hoc disponatis animum, et eveniet" (Pellegrini, p. CLII [from *Consulte e Pratiche*, LI, f. 180v]).

76. *PR*, CXVII, ff. 308r–v, August 18, 1427. Pietribuoni, in his *Cronica*, f. 120v, has the following entry: "Lunedì mattina a dì X di Novembre [1427] se n'andò a Roma Messer Giovanni de'Vitelleschi da Orvieto, ambasciadore del papa, il quale era stato sei mesi a porre l'anposta di 25 m. fiorini a'preti, et fare rivedere ragioni. Et per racconciare l'estimo a'preti i'libri de'cherichati. Lasciò agli Angnioli. Giovedì a dì 22 di Gennaio 1427 tornò il vichario dell' arciveschovo da Roma."

77. *DSSp Aut.*, XXI, ff. 143r–144v, June 28, 1428. Actually, this is a copy prepared in 1495 of the decision taken by the *ufficiali del catasto*, to whom the copyist refers as the *ufficiali del estimo!*

78. David Herlihy, *Medieval and Renaissance Pistoia* (New Haven: Yale University Press, 1967), pp. 242–243.

lands and real estate. The Florentine government, instead, needed cash, and ecclesiastical contributions of this kind could make only the slightest difference to the enormous Florentine budget.

4

FORCED LOANS

The events discussed in the preceding chapters were bound to have important effects on the fiscal policy that would be applied to the mother city of the large Florentine domain. Before these repercussions are analyzed, however, a brief recapitulation is in order.

By the middle of the 1420's Florentine military expenditures had reached unusually high levels. The condottieri in the city's service were exerting relentless pressure for higher pay and contracts with advantageous terms. At that very crucial time the poverty of the Florentine contado, the economic interruptions caused by the war, and the practical impossibility of increasing the rates of the city's indirect taxes combined to produce in the Florentine budgets immense deficits. Table 4 suggests the magnitude of these deficits, which, if the city were to maintain its independence and preserve the integrity of its large domain, it was bound to cover by tapping other sources of income. In addition to the revenues from the four major gabelles and from the contado, which have been accounted for in Table 4, the Commune had at its disposal the income of certain other taxes, which are not shown in the table. But these judicial fines, gabelles imposed on usurers and prostitutes, and the like fetched the city but small sums, which are more than counterbalanced by additional expenditures (the maintenance of fortifications, administrative expenses of the *Palazzo dei Signori*, subsidies to the *Studio* and the like) that are also omitted from the table.[1]

Thus the only other source that could conceivably have satisfied the needs of the Florentine Treasury was the wealth

1. In Appendix C is reproduced a detailed breakdown of one year's regular communal expenditures.

Table 4. Income and expenditures, 1402–1433 (values expressed in florins rounded off to nearest complete figure. Silver currencies converted to gold at current exchange rates, for which consult Appendix D).

Year	INCOME Ga-bellesb	Con-tadod	Total	EXPENDITURES Con-dottae	Montef	Total	DEFICIT
1402	192,300	82,410	274,710	614,024	166,679	780,703	505,993
1403	221,579	78,503	300,082	585,239	201,501	786,740	486,658
1404	205,541	99,495	305,036	293,132	257,095	550,227	245,191
1405	210,137	110,854	320,991	291,337	241,899	533,236	212,245
1407a	213,696	161,083	374,779	357,563	259,801	617,364	242,585
1408	213,734	143,101	356,835	187,037	276,443	463,480	106,645
1409	178,028	154,686	332,714	460,079	248,766	708,845	376,131
1411a	171,523	70,884	242,407	293,749	234,712	474,461	232,054
1414a	189,052	125,505	314,557	548,211	230,635	778,846	464,289
1416a	206,104	133,360	339,464	117,434	280,171	397,605	58,141
1419a	208,679	81,827	292,030	118,878	271,318	390,196	98,166
1420	215,687	89,925	305,612	93,850	234,281	328,131	22,519
1424a	159,044	83,840	242,884	409,283	218,615	627,898	385,014
1426a	137,210	73,900	211,110	550,499	343,273g	893,772	682,662
1427	185,298	96,021	281,319	446,700	370,316g	817,016	535,697
1429a	171,906	92,348	264,254	—c	264,922	—c	—c
1430	143,388	62,876	206,264	—c	212,164	—c	—c
1431	144,161	—c	—c	—c	188,752	—c	—c
1432	138,535	—c	—c	—c	237,499	—c	—c
1433	—c	—c	—c	—c	—c	—c	—c

Sources: PC, XVII–XXXVI. For specific folio references, consult Appendix B.

a Information for intervening years missing from *PC*.

b This represents net income from the four principal gabelles: gates, salt, contracts, and wine.

c Data are incomplete.

d Net income from contado and districtus.

e Not included are the expenditures of the *castella*.

f This figure represents the total expenditures of the Monte officials, even for those years when they were in charge of the office of the *abbondanza*.

g The expenditures of the Monte for the years 1426 and 1427 include the payment of 134,249 florins in 1426 and 89,815 florins in 1427 disbursed by the Monte officials on behalf of the *ufficiali del banco*. These sums were used to defray the carrying charges and amortize the floating (not to be confused with the funded) public debt. Regarding this practice, consult chapter 6.

of the citizens. Before examining the consequences of the financial burden that in the course of the 1420's and early 1430's the inhabitants of Florence were forced to support, we will consider the total sums that Florentine citizens actually paid to the Camera in the course of that period. Table 5 indicates

Table 5. Forced loans (prestanze or catasti), 1402 to 1433 (values expressed in florins rounded off to nearest complete figure. Silver currencies converted to gold at current exchange rates, for which consult Appendix D).

Year	Annual Deficit	Forced Loans
1402	505,993	300,529
1403	486,658	388,139
1404	245,191	257,095
1405	212,245	272,124
1407[a]	242,585	215,111
1408	106,645	116,127
1409	376,131	360,356
1411[a]	232,054	202,336
1414[a]	464,289	403,751
1416[a]	58,141	4,220
1419[a]	98,166	60,822
1420	22,519	35,797
1424[a]	385,014	560,912
1426[a]	682,662	702,730
1427	535,697	544,328
1429	—[b]	193,231
1430	—[b]	628,758
1431	—[b]	690,293
1432	—[b]	527,209
1433	—[b]	—[b]

Sources: Deficits taken from Table 4. Source of the forced loans is *PC*, XVII–XXXVI. For specific folio references consult Appendix B.

[a] Information for intervening years missing from *PC*.

[b] Data are incomplete.

the sums paid by Florentine citizens to the state, either in the form of prestanze or catasti, from 1402 to 1433. It is obvious from this table that there exists a direct correlation between the annual deficit incurred by the state and the sums borrowed from its citizens. Therefore, the amounts advanced to the government by its citizens provide an approximate index of the level of military expenditures for those years in which the information in the sources was incomplete.

This table makes it clear that the sums that the citizens of Florence paid to the Commune from 1424 until 1433 were considerably higher than they had ever been before in the city's history. During the 1390's a total of 2,441,765 florins was collected during the nine years for which records have survived, an average of 271,307 florins per year. In the first decade of the fifteenth century, during which Florence fought the third and conclusive round of war against Giangaleazzo Visconti and undertook the costly campaign of bringing Pisa under its domination, the total sum of prestanze collected over a nine-year period for which records have survived was 2,178,345 florins, or an average of 242,038 florins per year. Finally, from 1424 through 1432, a total of seven years for which we have complete and reliable statistics, no less than 3,847,461 florins were collected, or an annual average of 549,637 florins, more than twice the annual sum assessed during the 1390's.

THE MONTE

What, then, were the instruments available to the Florentine government that enabled it to collect these funds? What, in other words, were the broad outlines of the fiscal policy pursued by the state with regard to its citizens?

Only twice in its long republican history did Florence experiment with the imposition of what we, today, would call direct taxes. Both attempts were made during the first half of the fourteenth century in the two interludes of signorial government, the first under Charles of Calabria, the second under Walter of Brienne, Duke of Athens. Historians and commentators have conjectured that the association of such a tax scheme with the two much despised *signori* dissuaded subsequent Florentine statesmen from reinstituting it.

Thus, during those years when the combined income from the indirect taxes and from the contado was insufficient to balance the Florentine budget, the sole alternative available to the Florentine state was to borrow money from its citizens. This system, which was initiated in the early years of the Trecento, was gradually refined to the point that in the middle years of the 1340's all the communal debts to the citizens of the state were consolidated and the *Monte Comune* (funded public debt) was created.[2] Bearing an annual interest of 5 percent, credits of the Florentine Monte were negotiable at market values that were established by the demand for them and by the capacity of the Florentine state to discharge interest payments promptly.

After the consolidation of the debt most loans advanced by the citizens to the state were incorporated in it, although occasionally, when especially large sums were borrowed for short periods of time, special Monti were created, with provision made for their liquidation. During the 1350's and 1360's, for reasons that are not quite clear yet, certain loans to the state were promised an interest twice or three times as large as that

2. On the formulation and implementation of communal fiscal policy during the first decades of the Trecento, see Bernardino Barbadoro, *Sulle finanze della repubblica fiorentina* (Florence: Olschki, 1929) and Marvin B. Becker, *Florence in Transition* (Baltimore: Johns Hopkins University Press, 1966), I.

established in the 1340's: thus the *Monte d'un due* fetched interest at a rate of 10 percent per annum, while the *Monte d'un
tre* paid 15 percent per annum.[3] As a result, during the third
quarter of the Trecento, investments in the Florentine Monte
became profitable and quite desirable, fetching as they did a
steady and reasonably lucrative rate of return. As the military
expenses of those decades had become relatively large, at least
in contrast to those of the second quarter of the fourteenth century, the public debt of the Commune had increased substantially, standing in 1380 at about 1 million florins, twice the
amount of its funding some thirty-five years before.[4]

3. The tendency of historians (e.g., Becker, *Florence in Transition,* II, pp.
173–174; Gene A. Brucker, *Florentine Politics and Society, 1343–1378*
[Princeton: Princeton University Press, 1962], pp. 93–95) has been to assume that the institution of these two special Monti reflected a selfish policy
of the patricians who then ruled Florence. Without entirely discounting the
possibility that such motivation was also important, one should examine the
financial conditions of that time. It may well be that because of extreme
shortages of bullion the state had to promise its creditors high interest rates
in order to ensure its own liquidity. In other words, financial considerations
involving, among other factors, the mechanism of the market may have been
just as important as the personal interests of the policy-makers.
4. In discussing the history of the public debt of an Italian Commune of
the period, one should attempt to clarify as much as possible one's definition
of the term. One could, in fact, be referring to two substantially different
figures: the sum of money that the government borrowed from its citizens,
and the sum on which it paid interest. Obviously, these two sums represented
very different aspects of the administration of the public debt. While interest was promised and often paid on a very large sum (which we might call
the nominal communal indebtedness), the amount of money actually needed
in order to amortize the debt (real communal indebtedness) was very much
smaller. On the whole, historians have been imprecise in their use of the
term, and some confusion has therefore arisen. The figure that has often
been used as representing the Florentine communal indebtedness is the one
offered in a recent study by Gene Brucker, "Un documento fiorentino sulla
guerra, sulla finanza e sulla amministrazione pubblica (1375)," *ASI,* CXV
(1957), 169, n. 20. Brucker computes the communal indebtedness in 1378,

In 1380, under the "democratic" government that ruled the city until January 1381/82, a law enacted by the more egalitarian-minded governors of the state once again consolidated the various Monti created since 1347, simultaneously provid-

---

at the conclusion of the Florentine war against the Papacy, at 2,361,802 florins. In itself, however, this is a misleading figure. The source on which Brucker based his computations is a seventeenth-century miscellany on Florentine history, compiled in 1670 by Senator Carlo di Tommaso Strozzi. Strozzi, however, makes no reference at all to the source of his information, so that, at best, his figures should be treated very cautiously. (The precise reference of the document is Biblioteca Nazionale di Firenze, II.IV.380, p. 76). Even if the veracity of Strozzi's figures could be ascertained, however, the problem of what precisely they represent remains to be answered. Do they refer to nominal or real communal indebtedness? The law of 1380 (*PR*, LXX, ff. 187r seqq.; published in full in N. Rodolico, *La democrazia fiorentina nel suo tramonto* (1375–1378) [Bologna: Zanichelli, 1905], pp. 458–475) that reformed the Monte clearly suggests that the real communal indebtedness stood at about 1 million florins, for 50,000 florins per annum were now assigned to the payment on interest, which, according to the provision, could not exceed the rate of 5 percent per annum. It would follow that the difference between real and nominal indebtedness was substantially reduced in 1380. Thus it would seem that the seventeenth-century *spoglio* refers to the nominal indebtedness of the Commune in 1378 (i.e., the sum on which interest was disbursed, or the principal on which the carrying charges of the debt were computed). An analysis of Strozzi's figures tends to reinforce this impression. His document lists the following:

158,608 florins of the *Monte Vecchio,* which amounts in real indebtedness to	158,608 fls.
554,484 florins of the *Monte d'un tre*	185,161
720,000 florins of the *Monte d'un due*	360,400
25,000 florins of the *Monte libero*	25,000
900,000 florins of the *Monte libero d'un due*	450,000

The total is 2,361,802 florins in nominal indebtedness, but only 1,179,169 florins in real indebtedness. In addition to being closer to the figure suggested in the legislative enactment of 1380, the latter is a much more realistic figure, for how could the communal debt have risen from some 450,000 florins in 1347 to nearly 2.5 million florins in 1378 when the costliest war fought by

ing for the payment of an interest rate of no more than 5 percent per year on forced loans inscribed in the new funded debt. Thus, during the last two decades of the fourteenth century and thereafter, forced investments in the public debt became a much less attractive prospect than they had been before. With the increased tempo of military involvement, the higher wages commanded by the Italian and foreign mercenaries, and the consequent need for ever more prestanze, the Monte officials failed to disburse interest to the creditors of the state promptly. This caused economic hardship for those who had anticipated early returns on their investments, depressed the market value of Monte credits, and led Florentine citizens to view the payment of prestanze as an onerous and unpleasant, though at times necessary, obligation toward the government of the city. Though Florentine official pronouncements often refer to the egalitarian spirit that determined the Commune's fiscal policy toward its citizens — each supposedly paying according to his capacity in accordance with a general census of private patrimonies — widespread rumors circulated in the city regarding the unfairness of the existing system. The *grossi e possenti,* it was alleged, paid much less than their fair share of taxes, while those least capable of doing so had to underwrite the city's principal expenditures. Difficult though it may be to prove these contentions, there is no question but that forced loans had become by the 1380's and 1390's an unpopular measure

---

Florence during that period had required the assessment of forced loans totaling only 580,000 florins? See chapter 2, note 1. In this context one should also note that the legislative enactment of 1380 sought to control the increase in the real communal indebtedness by refusing to redeem credits of the Monte for a higher price than paid for them. Thus the high profits that in the past had been secured by speculators of the public debt would now be substantially reduced.

with Florentine citizens.[5] In order to assist those unable to pay
their full assessments the Florentine government allowed those
who wished to do so to pay only a portion of their taxes — one
half to one third, depending on the amount of the original as-

Table 6. Prestanze assessments in Gonfalon Drago di San Giovanni,
1381–1406.

Year	Total Households[a]	Payment Ad Rehabendum	No Payment	Reference
1381	791	397	93	567
1384	587	200	107	877
1390	796	253	([b])	1253
1395	708	182	174	1395
1397	837	127	342	1609
1399	1,201	63	743	1756
1402	1,304	51	860	1964
1404	838	98	([b])	2058
1406	601	95	([b])	2280

Source: All references in last column are to volumes of *ASF, Prestanze.*

[a] The total number of households fluctuated not because of great demographic changes but rather because of changed decisions by communal officials
regarding the extent to which poorer families should be taxed.

[b] Data are incomplete.

sessment — but these people had to waive all future claims to
collect interest on their payments or to be eventually reimbursed
for their loans to the government. The extent to which the obligations of the private citizens to the state increased during the
late fourteenth century is demonstrated by Table 6, which,
using as a sample one of the city's sixteen administrative units,

5. For some comments on this question, see my article "The Florentine
Oligarchy and the *Balie* of the Late Trecento," *Speculum,* XLIII (1968),
39–49.

Gonfalon Drago, Quarter of San Giovanni, lists the number of households assessed prestanze from 1381 to 1406, the number of those able to pay their full assessments as prescribed, and the number of those making absolutely no payment at all. Those paying fully before the predetermined deadlines were described as paying *ad rehabendum* and became full creditors of the government; those paying nothing at all were denied all political rights and were liable to all the penalties imposed by the Florentine authorities. The rest paid either *ad perdendum,* paying a portion of their assessments in order to remain politically eligible and to avoid the imposition of fines or other penalities but also losing the right to collect interest or to be eventually reimbursed for their payments; or they sold their assessments to speculators who subsequently assumed all claims against the state for those payments.

It therefore becomes clear that as taxation became more onerous, the number of those paying *ad rehabendum* in the hope that their payments would constitute real business investments tended to diminish, while any attempts to enlarge the tax base by including in the rolls the names of poor families were bound to fail because of the utter inability of these people to pay their taxes.

Prestanze and the whole system of deficit financing as it developed in Florence, however, proved to be burdensome not only to the individual rate payers but also to the very government that had instituted the fiscal system. The greater the communal need for money, the more frequently were prestanze assessed, while in turn the Commune had to allocate increasingly substantial sums for the disbursement of interest to those citizens who had paid *ad rehabendum.* Not only that. Soon after the passage of the law of 1380, which, as was mentioned, provided for the payment of an interest rate of no more than

5 percent per annum, it was discovered that in order to induce citizens to make payments in times of great financial stress much more substantial returns would have to be promised. Thus, special Monti were established that fetched interest rates of 8 and 10 percent per annum. It is true that more revenue accrued to the state because of these additional inducements, but it is also true that the carrying charges of the public debt increased to the point where they represented the greatest portion of the Florentine budget. The 50,000 florins per annum stipulated in the law of 1380 were nearly 79,000 florins in 1388,[6] and 92,386 florins in 1393,[7] and after 1394 they surpassed the 100,000-florin mark, never to become less than that. Not included in these sums are payments for the amortization of the debt or for the carrying charges of the higher interest-bearing Monti, all funded after 1390.[8]

6. The carrying charges for the year were 78,348 florins (*PC*, V, f. 269r, under entry "Monte al danaio per lira"). In addition, during that same year (f. 265r) 27,343 florins were expended for the "diminuzione del Monte."

7. *PC*, IX, f. 281r. In addition, the following sums were also allocated to, and expended by, the officials of the Monte: 30,978 florins for the "diminuzione del Monte per tratte" (f. 285r); 29,995 florins for the "diminuzione del Monte per compere" (f. 284v); 16,884 florins (the scribe's figure of 19,156 florins is wrong, for he made a rather obvious mistake in his addition) "per rendere il 12° accatto" (f. 289v); 17,899 florins (once again the scribe committed an error in addition) for "rendere i prestanzoni" (f. 291v); finally, a total of 23,186 florins was paid during the course of that year to compensate Florentine citizens who, having bought ecclesiastical property during the War of the Eight Saints, had been forced to return it after the war, and who were promised compensation for their losses by the state (ff. 286v–287r).

8. This phenomenon, i.e., the constant and rapid growth of the Monte's budget, is used by Marvin Becker as the focal point of his treatment of Florentine history (*Florence in Transition*, I, II). Much of Becker's interpretation, despite the intemperate criticism leveled against it by Lauro Martines, must be accepted as offering an interesting and potentially useful perspective from which to view the evolution of the Commune. But even then,

During the 1390's and early 1400's total communal indebtedness increased to the point where the city officials were hardly able to cope with it, and they were often forced to postpone the payment of interest. Such a step would be taken only very reluctantly, for it undermined the confidence of the citizens in the capacity of the state to honor its obligations to them, a condition that would further increase the reluctance of many to pay prestanze assessed on them in the future.[9] By 1415 the

---

an important problem still remains unresolved. Assuming that the growth of the Monte could have contributed to the triumph of a certain type of political ethos, what is it that distinguished the evolution of Florence from those of the remaining Italian communes of the Trecento and Quattrocento? Venice, Genoa, even Lucca and Pisa, were also saddled by burgeoning public debts, and yet no historian has viewed those Monti as particularly relevant to the evolution of Genoese or Venetian public morality. How, then, does one account for the differences between the developments on the banks of the Arno and those elsewhere? In this context one should note that a potentially important difference between the Florentine and Venetian public debts lay in the inability of the Florentine officials to quote consistently high prices for Monte credits on the open market. In contrast, credits of the Venetian public debt were quoted at uniformly high levels, sometimes even reaching points above par. (For the Venetian public debt, see Gino Luzzatto's *Il debito pubblico della repubblica di Venezia* [Venice: Istituto editoriale cisalpino, 1963].) But the political or cultural significance of this phenomenon is rather difficult to ascertain.

9. The decisions to postpone the payment of interest on the credits of the public debt are recorded in *LF,* XLIV, ff. 173r–175v; XLV, ff. 64r–v, January 16, 1396/97; XLV, ff. 89r–v, April 16, 1397; XLVI, ff. 40v–41r, September 13, 1398; XLVI, ff. 127r–128r, December 19, 1399; XLVI, ff. 135r–136r, January 30, 1399/1400; and XLVII, ff. 90r–v, May 29, 1402. The institution of this practice was recognized by the few contemporary chroniclers whose writings have survived to our day as being of some importance. The sole such chronicle of the 1390's, which is actually more of a political diary kept by an anonymous Florentine, devotes an entry to it (Biblioteca Nazionale Centrale di Firenze, *Codex Panciatichianus,* CLVIII, f. 171r): "E fe fare questo Giovanni Biliotti una leggie che si possa parlare di disfare il monte, dove prima era pena chapitale a chi ne parlasse. E vinto per gli oportuni consigli si fe ricresciere molte gabelle perchè in comune entrino danari, acciò che il

Commune was paying interest on a total communal indebtedness in the Monte of about 3.1 million florins, or nearly three times the sum of 1380.[10] Existing documentation, which in the face of the very large and complete but entirely disorganized

monte si disfaccia, e chi v'à conperati su danari non debia riavere altro che il proprio capitale. Grande favelare se ne fe per la città per gli uomini che v'ano su i danari loro. E fe levare via il terzo de gli'nteressi alle chiese che dove si rendea cinque per cento si renda meno il terzo, e così a'chontadini, e levate via le tratte de'beni delle chiese venduti per tre anni." Another anonymous chronicler of those years, the author of the pseudo-Minerbetti, also refers to the enactment of this measure (*Cronaca volgare di anonimo fiorentino dall'anno 1385 al 1409*, in *Rerum Italicarum Scriptores* [Città di Castello: Lapi Editore, 1915], XXVII, part 2a, 162): "Furono queste cose fatte contro alla fede data per lo Comune a coloro che doveano avere; e molti cittadini ne ricevettero grandi danni; ma il Comune per la grande nicistà il fece, avvegna che fosse contro alla promessa fatta loro." Domenico Buoninsegni, whose *Istoria Fiorentina* (Florence, 1580) has been used by many subsequent historians as a source for the developments of the 1390's, did nothing more in reporting this event than copy the passage he found in the pseudo-Minerbetti (compare page 722 of his *Istoria* with page 162 of the anonymous chronicle).

10. On December 30, 1415, a provision stated that the annual carrying charges for the public debt amounted to 185,000 florins (*PR*, CV, f. 264r): "Item non obstantis aliis provisis quod ad restitutionem et pro restitutione pagarum retentarum omnium montium pro tempore quattuor annorum proxime preteritorum initiatorum die primo mensis Januarii anni MCCCC-undecimi et finiendorum die ultimo presentis mensis Decembris que dicuntur ascendere quantitatem florenorum centum ottuaginta quinque milium auri. . . ." Since one fourth the annual interest due was retained each year, it follows that the total interest withheld during four years equaled the annual carrying charges of the public debt. For the sake of calculation, one may set the average interest rate paid by the Commune to its creditors at 6 percent per annum. During this time the *Monte Comune* fetched an annual interest of 5 percent; the *Monte de'prestanzoni*, 8 percent; and the *Monte di Pisa*, 10 percent. But since most forced loans were inscribed in the *Monte Comune*, one may venture to set the average interest rate at 6 percent. It would thus follow that the total nominal indebtedness of the Commune (i.e., the capital on which it disbursed interest payments) amounted to about 3.1 million florins.

archive of the Monte must remain fragmentary and rather inconclusive, tends to suggest that during the tranquil and prosperous decade 1414–1423 the face value of the Florentine public debt was reduced by about 175,000 florins.[11]

With the outbreak of war in the summer of 1423 the problems besetting the entire fiscal structure — the prestanze, the communal indebtedness, the difficulty of financing wars and concurrently coping with the carrying charges of the funded public debt — presented themselves most forcefully and dramatically. If the city were to wage war and survive, it would have to rely on the purses of its citizens. In turn, any reasonable pecuniary expectations that the state might have of individual Florentines would depend on three factors: the existence of economic conditions that would allow the inhabitants of the city to pay their assessments; a realization on the part of all concerned that the fiscal structure was relatively equitable and placed no unfair burdens on specific groups or individuals; and the capacity of the Monte officials to satisfy the legitimate claims of those who through the years had invested, albeit under duress, in the Florentine public debt. As the decade wore on, a situation arose that would prove to have extraordinary consequences for the future of the city: the unavailability to the state of large sums of cash on relatively short notice. The fiscal history of Florence during that crucial decade was to revolve around these issues, which, as the crisis deepened and the possibility of resolving it seemed to become more remote, dominated increasingly the minds of communal councillors and legislators.

11. By 1419 the carrying charges of the public debt had been reduced to 183,000 florins (*PR*, CIX, f. 219r, December 29, 1419), while in 1423 they stood at 175,000 florins (*PR*, CXIII, f. 227v, December 13, 1423).

DISTRIBUTION OF FORCED LOANS

Immediately after the onset of the war the first problem confronting the Florentine lawmakers was that of the distribution of taxes among the citizenry. The issue of the *distributio* was by no means new in the 1420's. From the time the system of forced loans had first been instituted, statesmen and laymen had debated the question of the most equitable way of distributing the prestanze so as to reduce as much as possible the number of complaints about them. Should the distribution be carried out on a city-wide basis according to each citizen's capacity to pay, or should the total sum to be collected first be parceled out among the sixteen administrative units of the city (*gonfaloni*) and then subdivided among the inhabitants of each district by the more authoritative and trustworthy citizens of each? Ideally, of course, which of the two arrangements was used should not have made much difference, for an individual's assessment should always have been commensurate with his financial standing. But in a world so full of suspicions, cliques, and family and business factions, where a person's *brigata* always stood behind him to offer its support, and when personal, direct influence among the lawmakers often carried a determining weight in the resolution of most issues, any theoretical debates about an egalitarian Florentine tax structure were bound to be irrelevant. What Florentines suspected most was that some of their more prominent compatriots would escape with an undeservedly light tax assessment because of a friend's or a relative's membership on the tax commission. These suspicions were all too well founded, for there exists sufficient evidence that every member of the Florentine society on whom prestanze were assessed, regardless of social background or financial standing, sought to cultivate the friendship and sympathy of

tax assessors.[12] Thus most Florentine legislation regarding the
distribution of taxes was directed toward creating a system
so complex that it would tend to neutralize any attempted acts
of favoritism.[13]

During times of peace and prosperity, when the total number of prestanze called for relatively modest sums, complaints
against the distribution of taxes were expressed only occasionally and not very forcefully. So, for example, the distribution
of forced loans decided upon in 1411, which remained in effect
for the duration of the war against Naples, was not rescinded

---

12. This is one of the prominent themes in Gene Brucker's recent *Renaissance Florence* (New York: Wiley, 1969), especially chapters 3 and 4.
Typical, and far from uncommon, is the situation described in the following
letter from Lapo Mazzei to his friend Francesco Datini, dated April 4, 1391
(*Lettere di un notaro a un mercante del secolo XIV — Con altre lettere e
documenti per cura di Cesare Guasti* [Florence, 1880], I, 9): "Francesco di
Matteo [Bellandi da Prato], e a bocca e per lettera, m'ha detto della novità
che'l Gonfalone del Lione rosso v'ha fatta: che se il pensiero loro avesse
auto effetto, vi danneggiavano uno migliaio di fiorini o più: non dico sanza
cagione, ma e'non seppono fare, grazia di Dio! Altra via aveano, e non la
vidono. Io ho fatto levare dalla Camera, in carta, la prestanza e l'estimo; e
stamane avea fatta la pitizione per darla: e a caso trovai i vostri dal fondaco,
che voleano consiglio da ser Viviano. Dissi non facessono, e manda'negli;
e die'loro il modo. Eglino ci sono bene solliciti; e io non dormirò: e penso
che come uno uficio che fia sopra ciò disputato, si raunarà, che tra eglino e
io vi faremo spacciare; però ch'avete ragione chiara. E già n'ho parlato
con alcuni amici di quegli uficiali, che sono sedici. Per altra vi dirò più
oltre. A Dio v'accomando. LAPO MAZZEI notaio vostro." Mazzei's letters to
Datini contain many references to instances in which important communal
officials were asked to intercede directly on behalf of the wealthy Pratese.
All prominent Florentines invariably sought the help of communal officials
charged with assessing taxes, and one's power in the city could be measured
to a large extent by the success one met in avoiding payment of one's proper
taxes.

13. I have dealt with some of these issues in my article "The Florentine
Oligarchy and the *Balìe* of the Late Trecento," *Speculum*, XLIII (1968), 29–
58.

until the spring of 1422. In the meantime, from 1414 onwards, as the number of forced loans was substantially reduced, the complaints against the "distribution of 1411" were not taken very seriously and failed to produce any tangible results.[14] During times of great financial stress, however, the focal point of much citizen discontent was the distribution of the prestanze, so that in order to mute these complaints communal officials were forced to order new distributions. During the 1390's, when taxes were higher than they would be again for the next thirty years, no fewer than five different distributions were carried out, each coming under attack immediately after its enactment.[15]

The system devised in 1422 was no more acceptable than those enacted during the last decade of the preceding century. Soon after its institution it was attacked for allegedly being unfair and was replaced by another, ordered in December 1424.[16] The new arrangement, as well, failed to satisfy those objecting to the heavy tax burden, and for the first time, in the

14. The very long and complex provision outlining the mechanics by which the new distribution would be instituted can be found in *PR*, CXI, ff. 331v–334v, March 5, 1421/22. But despite the complexity of the mechanism established by this decree, complaints arose almost immediately, and another mode for distributing the forced loans had to be decided upon (*PR*, CXII, ff. 18v–20r, May 6, 1422): "Et qualiter ut per multos assertum est dicti noves pro gonfalone [appointed in previous March] non ea mentis sinceritate qua decent ad prestantiandum predictas novas partitas in minore quantitate debita se dirigunt ut aliis ipsis partitis in taxa sui gonfalonis, inclusis ipsius gonfalonis conditionem meliorem facere possent. Et volentes dictas partitas aliter et per alios prestantiari debere, et per eos maxime a quibus omnis privata affectio separat esse credatur," they revoke the authority of the officials appointed in March and appoint in their stead a new group.

15. Molho, "The Florentine Oligarchy," *passim,* especially pages 39–49.

16. *PR*, CXIV, ff. 33r–35r, October 12, 1424. The officials appointed to the task were to level the assessments "habendo respectum ad deum et ad salutem patrie et coscientias suas."

mid-1420's, one begins to encounter in the deliberative records of the Commune references to the need for a more systematic, accurate, and judicious method of distributing the communal taxes.[17] But the catasto, which these references foreshadowed, was not put into effect until after a new distribution, this one ordered in January 1425/26. The preamble of this legislative enactment, speaking as it does of the need for greater equality in the assessment of taxes and for ensuing peace among the citizens, is entirely representative of the rhetoric one encounters in the majority of these laws.[18]

17. The earliest reference I have found in which a statesman recommended the imposition of the catasto is dated March 24, 1424/25. In a debate regarding the distribution of forced loans Rinaldo degli Albizzi said (*LF*, LIII, f. 62r): "quod, habita licentia dicendi, loquentur aperte. Et quod differentia et examinatio est longi. Et quod dominatio est commendanda. Pars dicit [Rinaldo was speaking on behalf of the quarter of San Giovanni] provisionem iustam et dant fabam nigram, et altera dicit quod si crederent exgravium esse fiendum egenis quod darent fabas nigras, sed quia timent dicunt quod proponatur quotiens, et alias poterunt melius iudicare. Et de catasto quod fiat." Ridolfo di Bonifazio Peruzzi, speaking on behalf of the quarter of Santa Croce, immediately seconded Rinaldo's statement: "Catastum fiat." Later that fall, when the same issue was once again being discussed (*LF*, LIII, f. 89v, November 23, 1425), Giovanni di Bicci de'Medici, representing the quarter of San Giovanni, spoke out strongly in favor of distributing the forced loans more equitably, without, however, ever mentioning the catasto by name.

18. *PR*, CXV, ff. 274r–278v, January 12, 1425/26. The new distribution, to be executed on the basis of an anticipated yield per forced loan of 50,000 florins, "ut cum maiori equalitate, pace quae civium gravissima onera qua per defensione rei pubblice conveni substineri supportentur." Only a few weeks later, the officials charged with distributing the new forced loans returned to the legislature asking for authorization to decrease the sum from 50,000 to 45,000 florins (*PR*, CXV, ff. 295v–296r, February 27, 1425/26): "Et quod ipsi prout tenentur exequi commissione sibi factam volentes reperiunt impossibile fore tam gravem summam imponere, cum inveniant multos cives ob diversos casibus suam totam fere substantiam consumpsisse, quibus omnibus in vigente ad hac distributione prestanzonis

Whether or not the promises contained in the rhetoric of this enactment were actually fulfilled by this last distribution is not quite known, for the records of the deliberations and actual assessments devised by the communal officials do not seem to have been preserved. What is known is that this law was originally intended to remain in effect for only one year, after which time the older, and seemingly discredited, system was to be reinstated. Interestingly, a number of merchants, feeling that the time limitations imposed on the new distribution compromised its effectiveness and soundness, petitioned the Signory for its indefinite extension. The language of their petition is revealing, for it suggests how vast was the power of the Florentine entrepreneurial class in the city. Praising the new distribution of prestanze for being more equitable than those of the past, the merchants, who unfortunately remain unnamed, then stated that unless assurances were given that it would be enforced indefinitely, many of their confrères would be tempted to send their money abroad, thus creating an even more acute cash shortage in the city. Some, on the other hand, fearing the inordinate burden of taxation, were ready to retire from their businesses, thus withdrawing their profits from the tax base and consequently diminishing the income of the city. Under this kind of direct and none too subtle pressure the government conceded, amending the original bill to the satisfaction of the petitioners.[19]

---

erat imposita summa florenorum otto milium auri, et ad praesens non iudicant possibile fore eisdem imponere mille."

19. *PR.* CXV, f. 297r, February 27, 1425/26: "Et qualiter secundum audita, multi cives putantes necessarium fore prope finem anni distributionem reficere, et sua occultent pro ipsis leviora sufferentes pondera conantur suas substantias et precipue pecuniam numeratam ad alienas partes per viam cambiorum facere transportari, in tantum quod aliquanti sper cognoscitur

In retrospect, it is easy to perceive why even this new distribution failed to placate a large segment of the Florentine population. Taxes being as enormous as they were, complaints were bound to continue for the simple reason that the existing system by which they were imposed offered no great guarantee of fairness.[20] Thus, the original demand for a more scientific and rational system of taxation persisted, and when in 1426 the important issue of aiding certain friendly and trusted Genoese families against the Milanese was being discussed, the tempo of deliberations regarding the adoption of the *catasto* increased noticeably. Aware that the fundamental desire for equality that underlay much Florentine rhetoric remained unfulfilled in the realm of fiscal policy, communal councillors offered forceful suggestions that the catasto be imposed without delay. The existing system of taxation, said Rinaldo degli Albizzi, does not foster *caritas inter cives*. The Venetian example, however, showed that through the catasto, "in the future, that city [Florence] would be governed and ruled better." [21] Whoever opposes

---

pecunia numerata deficere. Et quod tam ex hoc quam etiam quia ipsi cives, et precipue trafficantes stantes dubii de ipsa distributione reficienda se retrahunt ab exercitiis eorundem, ex quibus damna gravia in introytibus publicis proveniunt et maiora parantur, et ipsi rei publice et privatis incommoda satis dura. . . ."

20. Many of the legislative enactments of those months refer to the bitterness and discontent that existed in the city. One example is the provision of January 16, 1426/27 (*PR,* CXVI, f. 241v): ". . . civile odium in pluribus extinguetur, et cives ipsi particulari rancore deponito nec non nove distributionis suspitionis cessante animosius suam mercaturis exercitia reperiunt et suam rem pubblicam salubrius gubernabunt."

21. The discussion on the institution of the catasto has been published in full by Pietro Berti, "Nuovi documenti intorno al Catasto fiorentiono," *Giornale storico degli archivi toscani,* IV (1860), 32–62. Albizzi's statement is on page 43.

the catasto, said Matteo Castellani, "wishes to conceal his patrimony and defraud the Commune." [22] The refrain of most speakers during the debates of 1426 and early 1427 was that, if the city were to meet the challenge posed by the expansionist policies of Filippo Maria Visconti, it must devise a more equitable system of taxation so that assessments would conform to the relative wealth of individual rate payers.[23] In a series of dramatic discussions undertaken during the spring of 1427 it became obvious that even those who hesitated to accept the suggested measure would have to cede to the pressure exerted by the malcontents. Giotto di Bartolomeo Peruzzi, speaking on behalf of the quarter of Santa Croce, emphatically stated on March 7, 1426/27, "The inequalities in the distribution of taxes have been greater than at any time since the city was founded by Charlemagne, and if the present priors succeed in enacting the catasto, they would deserve to be praised by having their names inscribed in golden letters." [24]

Peruzzi's hope that the catasto would be imposed during the

22. *Ibid.,* p. 44: "Matteus Castellani dixit quod qui hoc [the catasto] negat vult substantiam suam occultare, et Comune defraudare et non debita solvere."

23. *Ibid.,* pp. 46–47: "Giovanni Andree Minerbetti dixit quod quando facta fuerit inquisitio omnium cives vias ad solvendum habebant. Et Veneti sic agunt et subditi omnes eorum solvunt." Since the publication of Berti's article, it has been often assumed that the sole advocate of the catasto was Rinaldo degli Albizzi and that Cosimo de'Medici, while originally opposing the measure, was finally forced to support it. But, as Ugo Procacci recently pointed out, this view of the problem may be oversimplifying Cosimo's opinions and position. See Ugo Procacci, "Sulla cronologia delle opere di Masaccio e di Masolino," *Rivista d'arte,* XXVIII (1953), 3–35, especially page 21, note 30, for a "revisionist" discussion of this problem.

24. Berti, "Nuovi documenti . . . ," p. 52: "Giottus Bartolomei Peruzzi pro quarterio Sancti Crucis dixit quod inequalitates maxime sunt et maiores quam unquam fuerint post hedificationem Karoli magni citra; et si Domini catastum perficient licteris aureis describi merentur."

priorate of March/April 1427 was not fulfilled, but, under the inexorable pressure of large segments of the population, the communal legislature finally enacted the measure instituting the catasto on May 22, 1427.[25] Discarding the old system of assessing taxes on the basis of approximate estimates of patrimonies (estimo, or *stima*), the catasto now required all inhabitants of the city, and eventually those of the contado and of subject territories as well, to submit detailed declarations of their entire patrimonies. The law of 1427 provided for a tax of 0.5 percent on the capitalization of each individual's total wealth. Capitalization was to be computed on the basis of a return of 7 percent per year, allowance having been made for the deduction of all debts and charges and of 200 florins for each member of a household. Moreover, one's private home, be it a modest house or a sumptuous *palazzo,* was exempted from taxation.[26] The remaining net capital was subsequently taxed at the rate of 0.5 percent. In addition, there was a head tax of between two gold sous and six gold sous on each male member of a household between the ages of eighteen and sixty.

Undoubtedly, the adoption of the catasto constituted one of the most significant enactments in the history of Florence. The point was not missed by contemporaries and future historians. For the first time in its history, said Matteo Palmieri, the Florentine merchant-humanist of the second quarter of the Quattrocento, Florence asked its citizens to pay taxes according to a

25. The final provision establishing the catasto is found in *PR,* CXVII, ff. 38v–43r. The text of the law has been published in full in Otto Karmin, *La legge del catasto fiorentino del 1427* (Florence, Vallechi, 1906).

26. For a brief summary of the provisions of the law establishing the catasto, see Raymond de Roover, *The Rise and Decline of the Medici Bank, 1397–1494* (Cambridge, Mass.: Harvard University Press, 1963), p. 25, and my article "The Florentine *Tassa dei Traffichi* of 1451," *Studies in the Renaissance,* XXVII (1970).

stima vera di sustanze instead of at the arbitrary discretion of tax assessors.[27] Giovanni Cavalcanti, a shrewd and sometimes acerbic commentator of those times, deals in two different places of his narrative with the reaction of Florentine citizens to the imposition of prestanze and subsequently to the enactment of the catasto. Whenever prestanze were imposed in the city, cries of despair would invariably be heard among the citizenry. "One would say, 'Oh! damned *patria,* why do you nurture such malicious people [the members of the tax commission]? . . . And another one said, 'They count even the mouthfuls of food we eat at home. It is not as if they wish to leave me my necessities, but they deny me even these, so that they will lead me and my family to dishonor and sin.' Thus, throughout the entire city the poor and weak complained about the excessive taxes." [28] But when the catasto finally was enacted,

27. *ASF, Acquisti e doni,* VII, f. 2r: "+ 1427 a dì 10 di Luglio. Richordo in primo chome da sopradetto dì adrieto a Firenze mai più fu chatasto ne mai posono le graveze secondo stima vera di sustanze ma ponevansi in varii modi, alchuna volta ponendo venti huomini a tutta la terra e chiamonsi ventina. Altra volta per ghonfalone, e erano vario numero d'huomini, alchuna volta furono sette, altra volta nove, e da lloro si chiamavono quando settine e quando novine. E i detti huomini aveano a porre secondo loro discretione a chi pareva loro quella prestanza vileano."

28. Giovanni Cavalcanti, *Istorie fiorentine,* ed. Guido di Pino (Milan: Aldo Martello, 1944), p. 15: "Poste e scoperte le gravezze, pianti e rammaricamenti, picchiamenti di palme e di guance per tutta la città si sentiva. L'uno diceva: O maledetta patria, perchè sei tu nutrice di sì malvagi genti? L'altro nominava chi era stato la cagione della sua gravezza, dicendo: E'sa bene che mi è impossibile pagare sì sconcia cosa: se egli appetiva il mio luogo, perchè non me lo chiedeva egli in vendita? e per meno del giusto pregio glielo avrei dato. L'altro diceva: E'mi annoverano i bocconi; e, non che mi voglino lasciare il bisogno, ma mi niegano il necessario, solo per inducere la mia famiglia a disonore e peccato. Ah Dio, perchè indugi tanto a sobbissare questa malvagia gente? L'altro malediceva chi la ripose, e amendò le caverne e le spelonche che la crudeltà di Totila rappresentavano

Cavalcanti reports a dream which he had: Here was *Letizia*, "come amongst this people in order to preserve the wealth of its citizens." Henceforth, happiness would reign in the city, for people would no longer be asked to contribute exorbitant taxes, and no one would be ruined by the burden the city was asking its citizens to shoulder.[29] Finally, Niccolò Machiavelli, in a characteristically pithy statement, suggested that for the first time the Florentines had agreed to be ruled by impartial and unchangeable laws rather than by the arbitrary decisions of human beings.[30] In February 1430/31, when the issue of po-

---

ai nostri antichi. E così per tutta la città li miseri ed impotenti si compiagnevano delle non misurate gravezze."

29. *Ibid.*, pp. 108–110: "L'una era che di vaga donzella aveva sembiante, la quale di vaghi fiori la sua fronte adornava di bella grillanda: il suo dosso d'un vago verde era vestita: in mano portava uno strumento non mai più veduto. Le corde parevano quando una cosa e quando un'altra; ma il più delle volte, mi assembravano agli spillieri che feriscono le viste a chi fiso riguarda nella luce del sole. Questo strumento con tanta dolcezza sonava, che sorda e mutola, a lato a quello, la cetera d'Orfeo saria stata, se non come cosa che da niuno piacere fusse composta: con la testa alta, e con lampeggiante riso, e con favella angelica parlava, e così lo strumento e la voce accordava dicendo: Io sono Letizia, venuta in questo popolo a mantenere le sustanze dei suoi cittadini; perocchè io veggo che a quell'ora sarà consumato il cento che il mille; e così niuno desidererà le possessioni dell'altro. Volesse Dio che al tempo delle grandissime spese fusse questo modo e quest'ordine del Catasto trovato! conciossia cosa che le nobili schiatte sariano ancora in possessione delle loro ricchezze: e così come questi, tutti quelli che il governo non hanno della Repubblica terrebbono le loro ricchezze. Quante fanciulle si maritarono a ricchi, che poi vissero in povertà solo perchè l'un dì quello che avevano, l'altro dì sotto il peso delle gravezze, era loro tolto! Molte altre parole usava in su quello mai più veduto strumento: le quali parole dall'ordine del dire me ne comandò silenzio; avvegna dio che le cose dette sono spesse volte odievoli e senza rimedio; e così ciascuno può piuttosto crescere alle cose non dette che levare delle dette."

30. Niccolò Machiavelli, *Istorie fiorentine*, ed. Plinio Carli (Florence: Sansoni, 1927), I, 201: "Avendola [the tax] pertanto a distribuire la legge e non gli uomini."

litical representation of various classes was being discussed in a council meeting, one of the representatives, magister Galileus Johannis Galilei, offered the following suggestion for establishing social harmony in the city: "Since the catasto, the taxes have been well distributed; the one defect of our city that still remains to be corrected is the unjust distribution of offices." [31]

Thus, with the adoption of this momentous measure, the Florentine statesmen had confronted successfully one of the principal problems that had plagued their city since the middle of the fourteenth century. While it is true, as many historians have subsequently pointed out, that the catasto did not offer an absolute guarantee that all their wealth, particularly liquid investments, would be properly declared by the Florentine entrepreneurs, it nevertheless offered a fiscal structure and the necessary machinery to ensure, if properly respected and enforced, a more equitable distribution of the tax burden.

Before proceeding with the analysis of fiscal policy during the 1420's it is necessary to examine the precise role that the catasto was meant to fulfill. Several historians have been tempted to interpret it as a kind of panacea, which, after its imposition, tended to alter the entire structure of Florentine fiscal policy by eliminating the need for forced loans. Thus, continues this argument, the city had the opportunity of diminishing its total debt and channeling its resources to more essential and constructive expenditures instead of having to allocate large portions of its budget to the carrying charges of the funded public

31. Pellegrini, pp. XXXVI–XXXVII (from *Consulte e pratiche*, LI, f. 124v, February 21, 1430/31): "Magister Galileus Johannis Galilei dixit quod examinentur cause et invenientur radices huius morbi, ut possi adhiberi medela. Causa discordiarum solet esse quia aut honores aut onera non certe distribuuntur inter cives. Onera nunc sunt bene distributa per Catastum; restat ut defectus sit in honoribus distribuendis.''

debt. Essentially, then, these historians have suggested that the catasto involved the imposition of direct taxes. This interpretation, however, is wholly untenable, for the catasto did not seek to eliminate the system of deficit financing sanctioned and employed in Florence since the middle of the Trecento. Its purpose was actually threefold: (1) It sought to eliminate the older system which often made the citizens of a gonfalon collectively responsible for the assessment imposed on that district of the city.[32] Instead it established unequivocally the principle of in-

32. For references to this practice, see *PR*, CXIII, ff. 79v–80v, July 21, 1423; *PR*, CXIV, ff. 4r–v, June 9, 1424; *DSSp Aut.*, XX, ff. 15r–v, August 13, 1423. The notarial register of ser Bartolomeo di ser Piero di ser Ricomano de Coiano de'Migliorati records the minutes of the officials of the gonfalon Lion d'Oro, quarter of San Giovanni, who were entrusted with confiscating goods of tax delinquents so that the gonfalon's tax assessment might be paid to the central authorities (*ASF, Notarile anticosimiano*, M 546, f. 73r): "Cives honorabiles florentini et omnes dicentes et asserentes et affirmantes se esse de dictum vexilliferum leonis ad aurum et in dicto vexillifero prestanziati in simul omnes congregati in dicta ecclesia Sancti Laurentii ad mandatum et requisitionem suprascripti Antonii ser Tommasi, vexilliferum gonfalonerii predicti, pro negotiis dicti gonfalonis utiliter exercendis dicentes et asserentes habere baliam et potestatem et auctoritatem omnia et singula infrascripta faciendum vigorem reformationis et secundum formam statutorum et ordinamentorum comunis Florentie quocunque tempore editorum, considerantes quod summe necessarium et utilem est quod per homines et personas dicti vexilliferi leonis ad aurum eligantur et seu constituantur et ordinentur sindicum cum camerario, notario, scribano pro exigentibus debitis et seu reditis dicti vexilliferi, et quod dictum ipsum vixillum in suis iuribus non ledatur, ymo de bono in melius gubernetur, ideo pro bono, pace et utilitatem dicti vexili et hominium et personarum eiusdem vice et nomine dicti vexili et omni modo, via, jure, forma et causa quilibet magius, melius, validius et efficacius potuerunt, fecerunt, constituerunt, creaverunt et solemniter ordinaverunt dicti vexili et hominium, personarum eiusdem veros, legiptimos sindicos procuratores, actores, factores et certos nuptios spetiales infrascriptos nominatos. . . ." Among the specific powers assigned to these men were those "ad agendum, causandum etcetera; ad patendum et exigendum etcetera; ad faciendum capi et relaxari omnes et singulos debitores dicti vexili et de bonis eorum et cuislibet eorum sequestrari et in solutione peten-

dividual responsibility for the payment of taxes. After 1427 each household was held responsible before the communal authorities for the accurate and full payment of its taxes. (2) It ensured that computation of one's patrimony would be based not solely on real estate and other tangible assets but also on liquid wealth, such as cash and business investments. It is this aspect of the catasto legislation which aroused the ire and opposition of many businessmen, who were quick to point out the uncertainty and precariousness of this type of assets. It is unfair, these entrepreneurs argued, to levy a tax on movable property, "which people possess today and lose tomorrow." Such a tax was an obstacle to the proper operation of business, they claimed, and it also caused the flight of capital.[33] (3) The catasto ensured that the great injustices in the apportionment of taxes that had been a feature of the city's fiscal history in the past were eliminated. While before 1427 it could have been argued that the principal burden of taxation had been borne by the middle strata of Florentine society, because the more affluent escaped with assessments that did not accurately reflect

dum et capiendum." In addition, they had the right "ad acquirendum, et petendum et accipiendum et recepiendum . . . mutuo et in depositum aut in cambium etcetera aut alio quoquo modo ommes et singulas quantitates pecuniarum." On folios 122r–124r, November 15, 1425, is recorded a case in which these officials confiscated the property of a Piero di Vigiano di Novo da Vespignano: "ex nunc dicta bona, tanquam bona dicti Pieri Vigiani servatis incorporaverunt et declaraverunt dicta bona spectare, pertinere ad dictum vexilliferum vigore prestanziarum et residuorum qua debentur per dictum Pierum dicto vexillo."

33. R. de Roover, *The Rise and Decline of the Medici Bank*, p. 25. This point may well explain Cosimo de'Medici's lukewarm support of the catasto. Rinaldo degli Albizzi, who seems to have derived most of his wealth from landed investments, would have favored the imposition of a tax based on liquid and immobile wealth. The Medici, of course, would have preferred the continuation of the older system, which did not include liquid property in the computation of one's assessment.

their real wealth, after the imposition of the catasto it was plain that such injustices and imbalances were meant to be eliminated.

The catasto of 1427, however, did not eliminate the system of forced loans and deficit financing. It simply distributed these loans more equitably and assessed them by taking into account all movable and immovable assets. All the catasti assessed on the urban inhabitants after 1427, as will become clear later in this monograph, were meant to be loans of the citizens to the state. And all, with very few exceptions, were interest-bearing, promising in many instances higher rates than before. It is important to keep this point in mind; otherwise the true magnitude of the crisis that was to befall Florence in the first years of the 1430's will be hard to comprehend.[34]

THE TAX BURDEN

While it may be true that the timid attempts from 1422 to 1427, and subsequently the dramatic and efficacious solution devised in that year, effectively resolved the question of the distribution of taxes, the essential fiscal problem confronting the policymakers of the city continued to present itself, increasing in immediacy and forcefulness as the years progressed. The question that Florentine statesmen must have asked themselves is this: Granting that the tax load is distributed fairly, how can a city of Florence's size, and one commanding the resources that the city did during the opening decades of the Quattrocento,

34. The comments in this section refer to the catasto for the city of Florence. The law of 1427 instituted the catasto not only for Florence but also for the entire Florentine domain in Tuscany. But rural catasti, though often collected simultaneously with catasti imposed on the city, were meant to be substitutes for the old estimo. They were not interest-bearing forced loans, as were catasti imposed on citizens, but they were direct taxes.

raise the necessary cash to finance its diplomatic and military adventures? Gregorio Dati, the author of a *History of Florence from 1385 to 1406,* had described in some detail the military expenses borne by his compatriots during those earlier wars. As an accurate historical source on the events he described, his *Istoria* is of little value, because of the author's obvious tendencies to exaggerate and to undertake extensive polemics against the Milanese.[35] But Dati, himself an active participant of the heated and dramatic debates of the late 1420's, had understood and articulated one of the essential problems plaguing his contemporaries: At a certain point in the *Istoria,* which is set in the form of a dialogue between a Florentine and a group of foreigners, the older and wiser Florentine enumerated the expenses that his city had undertaken in order to combat the mercenaries in the Pope's hire from 1375 to 1378, then to resist the Milanese aggression, and finally to conquer Pisa in 1406. A young man in the audience then asked in wonder, "But where did the Florentines find all this money? I did not think that so much gold existed in the world!" [36]

Where would, in fact, the Florentines find all the gold they needed to pay their mercenaries? Was the treasure of the citizens sufficient to meet the challenge of the decade, and if so, would they be willing to turn it over to the state if taxes were distributed in an equitable and judicious manner? And what effect would the continued allocation of enormous sums to military expendi-

---

35. See chapter 2, note 7. The most recent attempt to date Dati's *Istoria* can be found in Hans Baron, *From Petrarch to Leonardo Bruni — Studies in Humanistic and Political Literature* (Chicago: University of Chicago Press, 1968), pp. 138–150.

36. Pratesi (ed.), *Dati, Istoria di Firenze,* p. 137: "Domandoti: questa mi pare delle maggiori cose che io intendessi mai; che io non arei mai creduto che tanto oro fusse al mondo, e non so inducere lo intelletto a credere come questo esser possa, se tu non me lo chiarisci in qualche modo."

tures have on the economic well-being of the city, its merchants, and its workers? [37]

The concept of an annual anticipated budget decided upon by the communal authorities was entirely unknown in Renaissance Florence. As the need arose, expenses were met on a month-to-month basis. Whenever the communal Treasury was in danger of exhausting its available resources, the members of the Signory, often in consultation with other branches of government, would decide on the number of prestanze that need be assessed in order to cover the city's expenses. Final authority for the enactment of such tax bills usually rested with the communal legislature, although at times special plenipotentiary commissions (*balie*) entrusted with the administration of the communal fisc could also impose such forced loans.[38] Such a commission was in fact active from 1423 to 1425, during which time it imposed on the city no fewer than forty-six prestanze, thirteen prestanzoni (large prestanze usually amounting to twice the size of a normal forced loan), and a residuo (the uncollected balance of prestanze already imposed, taking the form of a new tax) on the fifty-seven loans assessed during that period.[39] These taxes amounted in all to between 1 million

37. Dati answers this question by stating that the almost insurmountable difficulties of the war years forced the Florentine merchants and industrialists to modify antiquated customs and find new ways and outlets, which would not have been discovered in normal times. In addition, although acknowledging the problems that war and military financing presented the city, he suggests that, to a minor extent, war expenditures were beneficial to the city's economy because they brought additional business to the city's entrepreneurs.

38. Molho, "The Florentine Oligarchy," *passim.*

39. The deliberations of this balia are found in *DSSp Aut.,* XX. Folio references for the prestanze imposed during that period follow: 11r–13r, June 8, 1423; 17v–19r, September 7, 1423; 28r–29v, November 3, 1423; 30r–31v, December 11, 1423; 32r–34r, January 28, 1423/24; 35r–37v, March 3, 1423/24; 41r–43r, May 18, 1424; 44v–47r, August 5, 1424; 50r–52r,

and 1.25 million florins, although it is safe to assume that not the entire sum was collected by the communal authorities. We do know, for example, that of twenty-four prestanze that were meant to yield 480,000 florins, the Commune was able to collect only 402,000 florins, or approximately 84 percent of the anticipated yield.[40] Though the records of the balìa entrusted with the administration of the communal fisc during 1426 do not seem to have survived, starting in 1427 we have continuous records of every forced loan imposed on the citizenry. Their number is legion, indeed, and their enumeration would serve no other purpose than to reinforce the impression gained by the figures already presented in Table 5.[41]

September 25, 1424; 57v–59r, October 25, 1424; 65r–67r, December 1, 1424; 67r–69v, January 15, 1424/25; 75r–77v, May 11, 1425; 79v–82r, June 2, 1425; 82r–85r, July 7, 1425; 85v–88v, August 7, 1425; 89v–93r, August 23, 1425. Often each assessment would involve the imposition of more than one forced loan. Folio references to the imposition of residua follow: 15r–v, August 13, 1423 (residuo for five prestanze); 59r–61v, October 27, 1424 (residuo for twenty-three prestanze); 62v–64r, November 22, 1424 (residuo for five prestanze); 70r–73r, March 9, 1424/25 (residuo for twenty-four prestanze).

40. *DSSp Aut.*, XX, f. 74v, April 28, 1425: "Veduto tutti i ma'paganti e fogne [partite] d'ogni gonfalone e sbattuto della tassa, et simile veduto i debitori d'ogni gonfalone e fattone le somme e gittatogli sopra buoni paganti del quinto et ultimo residio di prestanze ventiquattro della novina, troviamo essere i debitori di tutti i gonfaloni, rechato a una somma fiorini settantotto miglia et quindici, et fatto la ragione d'ogni gonfalone troviamo ne toccha come appresso diremo, et così vi rapportiamo questo dì 28 Aprile, 1425."

41. The references to the imposition of forced loans, prestanze or catasti follow: *PR*, CXVI, ff. 236v–238r, January 13, 1426/27; CXVIII, ff. 26v–30r, October 23, 1427; CXVIII, ff. 463r–466r, December 5, 1427; CXVIII, ff. 529v–532r, January 30, 1427/28; CXIX, ff. 136v–138v, July 7, 1428; CXIX, ff. 139v–140v, July 7, 1428; CXIX, ff. 162r–163v, August 4, 1428; CXIX, ff. 164r–165v, August 4, 1428; CXIX, ff. 170r–171v, August 21, 1428; CXIX, f. 269r, November 26, 1428; CXX, ff. 26v–28r, March 7, 1428/29; CXX, ff. 171v–173r, May 30, 1429; CXX, ff. 204r–v, June 13, 1429; CXX, ff. 400v–

Prestanze or catasti could be imposed for fairly modest sums, as was the case on four different occasions in 1428 and 1429, when one half a catasto was assessed in order to pay back wages of many of the city's foreign judges; an additional one fourth of a catasto was assessed to underwrite the expenses of a small expeditionary force sent against Faenza; yet a third half of a catasto was levied in order to pay the salary of Marchionne degli Estensi, lord of Feanza and one of Florence's principal mercenaries; and finally, one twelfth of a catasto was assessed to pay the expenses incurred in a ceremony staged during the arrival of Martin V's nephews in the city.[42] Forced loans, however, could also be assessed for substantial sums, meant to repay large debts incurred in the past and to reinforce the cash reserves of the state. So, for example, on December 12, 1429, seven catasti were imposed; on January 4, 1430/31, an additional four; on July 11, 1431, twelve more; and on Febru-

---

403v, December 12, 1429. *DSSp Aut.*, XXII ff. 49r–51v, December 22, 1429; ff. 57r–59v, January 11, 1429/30; ff. 109r–111v, March 7, 1429/30; f. 121r, May 5, 1430; ff. 143v–145v, August 11, 1430; f. 149v, September 6, 1430. *PR*, CXXI, ff. 1r–2v, April 6, 1430; ff. 6v–8r, May 16, 1430; ff. 36v–38r, June 20, 1430; ff. 43r–46r, June 28, 1430; ff. 70r–v, October 27, 1430; ff. 86r–88v, November 23, 1430; ff. 102r–103v, December 8, 1430; ff. 119v–121r, December 23, 1430; ff. 128r–131r, January 4, 1430/31; ff. 164v–168v, March 5, 1430/31. *DSSp Aut.*, XXIV, ff. 7v–10r, April 16, 1431; ff. 13r–17r, May 5, 1431. *PR*, CXXII, ff. 45v–47r, May 30, 1431; ff. 92v–94r, June 21, 1431; ff. 131v–138r, July 11, 1431; ff. 193v–195r, September 18, 1431. *DSSp Aut.*, XXIV, ff. 45r–48v, September 6, 1431; ff. 56r–59r, November 9, 1431. *PR*, CXXII, ff. 297v–299v, December 21, 1431. *DSSp Aut.*, XXIV, ff. 76r–79r, January 11, 1431/32. *PR*, CXXII, ff. 336r–341r, February 6, 1431/32; CXXIII, ff. 221v–223r, September 20, 1432; CXXIII, ff. 278r–283r, November 15, 1432; CXXIII, ff. 410r–411v, February 27, 1432/33; CXXIV, ff. 117v–120v, July 23, 1433; CXXIV, ff. 180r–v, August 11, 1433; and CXXIV, ff. 256v–257v, March 12, 1433/34.

42. See note 41 under dates August 4, 1428; August 21, 1428; May 30, 1429; and June 13, 1429.

ary 6, 1431/32, no fewer than thirty-six catasti.[43] By the late 1420's and early 1430's the assessment of four or six catasti, often on two or three occasions each year, became a common practice. To appreciate fully the heaviness of the tax burden one has to remember that every catasto amounted to 0.5 percent of an individual's net capitalization, so that the thirty-six catasti of February 1431/32 required the payment of a sum equal to 18 percent of the total amount of all net capital available in the city. From the beginning of 1428 until the end of 1433, in addition to certain special levies, the citizens of Florence were asked to pay 153⅝ catasti. Since each catasto assessed at the rate of 0.5 percent a tax on net capitalization — which, by the structure established in 1427 and by the definitions provided by the Florentine legislators, was much smaller than gross capitalization — it follows that over a period of six years the city undertook to collect in taxes 76 percent of the total net capitalization available in the city, or an average of 12.6 percent per year. If we remember that according to the calculations of the communal officials the average return of investments in the city was about 7 percent per year, we realize that on the average, during the years 1428 to 1433, each Florentine citizen was required to pay taxes amounting to approximately 180 percent of his income! [44]

How do the fiscal demands made by the Florentine state on its citizens during the 1420's and early 1430's compare with the obligations of Florentine taxpayers during a previous generation? The figures offered in the introductory comments to this chapter made it clear that at no time before had the level of forced loans — prestanze or catasti — been so high as dur-

---

43. See note 41 under relevant dates.

44. The total number of catasti has been computed from Matteo Palmieri's diary (*ASF, Acquisti e doni,* VII, ff. 9r, 20r).

ing the decade that separates the eruption of war with Milan in 1423 from the exile of Cosimo de'Medici in 1433. It may be instructive, however, to examine three individual cases, so that the effect of this policy on individual citizens of the Commune may be discerned. In this case we can rely on the private account books of some famous Florentines — Francesco di Marco Datini da Prato, who flourished at the turn of the fifteenth century; Matteo di Marco Palmieri, famed humanist and assiduous recorder of his private fortunes, who came to maturity during the late 1420's; and the family of Giovanni di Bicci, and Cosimo di Giovanni de'Medici.

Francesco Datini, the famous merchant of Prato, has attained his modern fame not necessarily because of his exceptional success in accumulating one of the great private fortunes of his day, but rather principally because by a fortunate set of circumstances most of his private and business papers — account books, bills of exchange, correspondence — have survived to our day. This great repository of documents allows one to study the complex process by which Datini was able to construct his vast business empire, and to analyze the location of his resources during his long business career. His private account books, as one might expect, contain extensive information on the fiscal relation that developed between himself and the Florentine Commune after 1394, when Datini was granted Florentine citizenship.[45] For the purposes of this study we shall con-

---

45. See the two letters sent by Lapo Mazzei to Datini in Mazzei, *Lettere . . .* , I, 55–56 (June 27, 1394): "Stasera alle ore 23 fui chiamato a' Collegi: e uscito ch'io fu'della audienza, senti'nei Dodici nuovi parlare molto bene sopra questa materia. Guido temperò bene il liuto, poi ch'io ebbi parlato. E'l fine è, che gli anno approvato la liberazione dell'estimo, e trattovi d'ogni gravezza di contado, do grande concordia." Also pages 61–62 (July 13, 1394): "No sta bene che voi siate veduto fermo a Prato, in quel tempo che si fa l'estimo, e in quel tempo che siete stato fatto cittadino." On July 15,

sider the forced loans levied by the Commune on Datini during a seven-year period, from 1400 through 1406, years when the tax burden reached its highest level before the late 1420's. These were the years, one will recall, when Florence fought the last and decisive round of war against Giangaleazzo Visconti, re-established its hegemony in Tuscany, and finally took over Pisa after a prolonged and costly siege. Table 7 shows that during these years Datini paid, under the numerous forced loans assessed on all citizens, 15,337 florins. At the same time, in those years he received from the officials of the Monte, for interest on his investments in the public debt and for partial reimbursement of his capital, a sum of 6,455 florins, so that the balance sheet of his various transactions with the state during those years shows a deficit of 8,882 florins, or 1,296 florins per annum.[46] Datini's net worth is rather difficult to calculate, and the two scholars who have addressed themselves to this question have offered two somewhat different figures. Cesare Guasti, the nineteenth-century editor of Lapo Mazzei's letters to Datini, calculated the latter's total patrimony at his death in 1410 at some 70,000 florins,[47] while more recently Federigo Melis has suggested that Datini's fortune exceeded 100,000

Datini made a large payment to the Camera del Comune. This payment, equivalent to fifty-three times his regular prestanza assessment(!) must have been related to Datini's recent acquisition of Florentine citizenship (*Archivio di Stato di Prato, Carte Datini*, 607, f. 1v): "Il Chomune di Firenze de'dare, 15 Luglio [1394], paghorono per me Francesco di Marco e Stoldo di Lorenzo [& Co., this being the name of Datini's subsidiary firm in Florence] a'sindachi del ghonfalone de Llione Rosso per la tassa mi feciono in due volte, si paghò fiorini ottociento, f. 800 d'oro."

46. References to the sums of money that Datini collected during that period as interest for his investments in the Monte are found, in almost all cases, in the folio facing the versos cited in Table 7.

47. Mazzei, *Lettere* . . . , p. CXXXIX.

florins at the time of his death.[48] Assuming a realistic figure to be about 75,000 florins,[49] the annual deficit in Datini's transactions with the Monte would amount to 1.7 percent of his total capitalization, a figure indicating that even during those difficult years the tax burden imposed by the Commune on its citizens was quite manageable.

Matteo Palmieri's situation in the late 1420's, however, was quite different. In addition to composing many literary and historical works during a lifetime devoted to the *studia humanitatis,* Palmieri kept a remarkable account book, in which he faithfully recorded all his transactions with the Camera del Comune and the officials of the Monte: prestanze and catasti that he was assessed and that he eventually paid; interest he received from the officials of the Monte; copies of the catasto declarations, which he filed periodically, and the like. It is from this manuscript, now housed in the Florentine *Archivio di Stato,* that one can learn about Florentine fiscal policy as it affected the lives of individual citizens. The total assessts controlled by the Palmieri family from 1427 until 1433 fluctuated from 4,794 florins in 1427, when the declarations for the first catasto were filed (by Matteo's father Marco, who was still alive), to 5,264 florins in 1430/31, and back to 4,711 florins in 1433, when the third catasto was being prepared. To these assets one should add a few hundred florins for the value of Palmieri's private residence, which, like all private homes, was exempt

48. Federigo Melis, *Aspetti della vita economica medievale* (Siena: Monte dei Paschi di Siena, 1962), I, 331–333.

49. In 1409, shortly before Francesco Datini's death, one of his scribes or accountants calculated that his total worth was 67,802 florins (*Carte Datini,* 600, ff. 80v–82r). This estimate, no doubt, left out such items as the merchant's palace and some of his other holdings. Raising the sum to 75,000 florins would seem to offer a reasonable, though by no means absolutely accurate, estimate of Datini's total worth.

Table 7. Forced loans paid by Francesco Datini, 1400–1406 (values expressed in florins, gold sous, and gold deniers).

Date of Payment	Name of Tax	Interest Rate (percent)	Amount Paid	Reference
Jan. 10, 1399/1400	1a doppia–cinquine	5	103. 9. 6	607, f. 3v
Jan. 21, 1399/1400	3a–cinquine	5	51.13. 9	607, f. 3v
Feb. 20, 1399/1400	3a della massa	5	106.17.11	607, f. 3v
Apr. 29, 1400	4a doppia–cinquine	5	103. 8. 0	607, f. 3v
May 4, 1400	5a doppia+residuo	5	131.10. 1	598, f. 88v
June 22, 1400	3 della massa	5	106.18. 2	607, f. 3v
Oct. 15, 1400	delli assentati	5	155. 2. 4	607, f. 3v
Dec. 1, 1400	6a scempia	5	51.13. 6	607, f. 3v
Jan. 11, 1400/01	7a del piaciente	5	106.17.11	607, f. 3v
Apr. 23, 1401	$\frac{2}{3}$ acchato del sale	5	34.10. 0	607, f. 3v
May 2, 1401	8a–cinquine	5	51.15. 0	607, f. 3v
May 11, 1401	9a–cinquine	5	51.13.10	607, f. 3v
July 9, 1401	10a e 11a delle cinquine	5	102. 0. 4	607, f. 3v
Oct. 13, 1401	15 delle cinquine	5	775.10. 0	607, f. 3v
Apr. 3, 1402	13a delle cinquine	5	106.18. 0	607, f. 3v
May 10, 1402	6 delle ventine	10	540. 0. 0	598, f. 29v
May 26, 1402	residuo cinquine	5	34.18. 3	607, f. 4v
July 8, 1402	4 delle ventine	10	360. 0. 0	598, f. 29v
Aug. 9, 1402	2 delle ventine	10	180. 0. 0	598, f. 29v
Aug. 26, 1402	2 delle novine	10	180. 0. 0	598, f. 29v
Jan. 3, 1402/03	doppia della massa	5	180. 0. 0	607, f. 4v
Feb. 26, 1402/03	1½ delle ventine	10	135. 0. 0	598, f. 69v
Mar. 24, 1402/03	3 bandite allo schonto delle 15	5	270. 0. 0	607, f. 4v
Apr. 30, 1403	3 delle ventine	8	270. 0. 0	598, f. 69v
June 18, 1403	4 delle ventine	8	360. 0. 0	598, f. 69v
June 18, 1403	doppia della massa	5	180. 0. 0	607, f. 4v
July 21, 1403	4 delle ventine	8	360. 0. 0	598, f. 69v
Sept. 7, 1403	4 della massa	5	360. 0. 0	607, f. 4v
Dec. 14, 1403	2 della massa	5	180. 0. 0	598, f. 137v
Dec. 17, 1403	3 della massa	5	270. 0. 0	607, f. 4v
Feb. 20, 1403/04	2 della massa	5	180. 0. 0	607, f. 4v
Mar. 11, 1403/04	2 della massa	5	180. 0. 0	607, f. 4v

Table 7. (*Continued*)

Date of Payment	Name of Tax	Interest Rate (percent)	Amount Paid	Reference
Apr. 16, 1404	2 della massa	5	180. 0. 0	607, f. 4v
May 27, 1404	3 della massa	5	270. 0. 0	607, f. 4v
Aug. 16, 1404	1a doppia–cinquine	5	184. 0. 0	607, f. 4v
Sept. 12, 1404	3 delle cinquine	5	276. 0. 0	607, f. 4v
Nov. 20, 1404	3 delle cinquine	5	276. 0. 0	607, f. 4v
Nov. 13, 1404	1½ delle cinquine	5	138. 0. 0	599, f. 6v
Jan. 8, 1404/05	2 delle cinquine	5	184. 0. 0	607, f. 4v
Feb. 23, 1404/05	2 delle cinquine	5	184. 0. 0	599, f. 6v
May 15, 1405	7a delle cinquine	5	92. 0. 0	599, f. 6v
July 10, 1405	1½ delle cinquine	5	138. 0. 0	599, f. 6v
Oct. 6, 1405	5 delle cinquine	5	460. 0. 0	599, f. 6v
Oct. 6, 1405	8 prestanze	8	736. 0. 0	599, f. 6v
Nov. 20, 1405	4 prestanze	8	368. 0. 0	599, f. 6v
Feb. 10, 1405/06	3 della nuova	5	257. 7. 3	599, f. 6v
Jan. 11, 1405/06	3 della nuova	5	257. 7. 3	599, f. 13v
Jan. 23, 1405/06	residuo	5	253. 7. 8	599, f. 191v
Mar. 13, 1405/06	5 prestanze	8	465. 7. 6	599, f. 197v
Mar. 24, 1405/06	4 prestanze	5	343. 3. 0	599, f. 191v
Apr. 26, 1406	4 prestanze	5	343. 3. 0	599, f. 235v
May 26, 1406	5 prestanze	10	428.18. 9	599, f. 261v
June 16, 1406	5 prestanze	10	428.18. 9	599, f. 261v
July 19, 1406	5 prestanze	10	428.18. 9	599, f. 261v
Aug. 16, 1406	5 prestanze	10	428.18. 9	599, f. 261v
Sept. 16, 1406	3 prestanze	10	257. 7. 3	599, f. 261v
Sept. 1406	—a	8	428.18. 9	599, f. 200v
Oct. 2, 1406	2 prestanze	10	171.11. 6	599, f. 261v
Oct. 19, 1406	5 prestanze	10	428.18. 9	599, f. 261v
Nov. 29, 1406	4 prestanze a schontare nel residuo	5	368. 0. 3	599, f. 300v
Jan. 31, 1406/07	residuo	5	743.15. 0	599, f. 235v

Source: All references in last column are to the *Carte Datini, Archivio di Stato di Prato*.

a Data are incomplete.

from taxation and therefore not declared in the returns (*portate*) filed by the Palmieri. Thus, though we do not have evidence as complete as that available for Datini, we can conclude that Palmieri's total assets during this period were about 5,000 florins.[50] The catasto assessment levied on the Palmieri in 1427 was 17 florins, 15 gold sous, 2 gold deniers; in 1430/31 it was slightly reduced, to 17.3.4; and in 1433, because of a number of debts that Matteo had incurred principally to clothe his newly acquired wife, it was scaled down again by a few sous.[51] Yet, from November 1428 until 1433 *pater et filius* Palmieri had paid no less than 2,634 florins for various catasti levied on the citizenry, while concurrently receiving from the Monte no more than 482 florins for payment of interest and for the capital that they had invested in the state.[52] Thus, during those five years Matteo Palmieri had contributed to the state 2,152 florins in excess of what he had received from it, for an annual loss averaging 430 florins, or an annual taxation at the rate of approximately 8.6 percent of his gross capitalization. This is an annual

50. *ASF, Acquisti e doni*, VII, ff. 2v–7r (for 1427), ff. 12r–19r (for 1430/31), ff. 22r–26v and ff. 27v–29v (for 1433).

51. *Ibid.*, ff. 7r, 19r, 26v.

52. Professor Elio Conti of the University of Florence is about to publish a critical edition of this important source, and for this reason I shall not offer the detailed breakdown of figures for Palmieri as I do for Datini and the Medici. The following synopsis of Palmieri's tax payments should suffice:

Year	Payment in Florins	Reference[a]
Nov. 1428–1430	676	f. 82r
1431	643, 1 lira, 5 silver sous	f. 82r
1432	978, 11 silver sous, 8 deniers	ff. 84r, 88r
1433	337, 1 lira, 5 silver sous, 4 deniers	f. 88r

Source: ASF., Miscellanea Repubblicana, VII.

[a] Payments of interest are recorded on folio 81v.

percentage five times as high as that contributed by Datini! One suspects that during the five-year period a large part of Palmieri's income went to pay his high taxes. There are good indications, in fact, that by the early 1430's Palmieri and many other Florentines of his social standing were beginning to lose confidence in the Commune's ability to honor its obligations to its creditors. When filing his catasto return in 1433, having listed all his Monte credits, Matteo Palmieri added that he was not quite sure if that portion of his declaration was entirely complete, for the Monti "are so numerous and diverse, that it seems to me impossible to keep account of them all." [53]

One final example should suffice to illustrate the difficulties that Florentine citizens, even the most affluent, were encountering during the late 1420's and early 1430's because of the Commune's fiscal policy. Thanks to the meticulous and exhaustive study of the Medici bank recently published by Raymond de Roover, we have a reasonably complete and accurate idea of the total wealth and resources commanded by the Medici family during the first four decades of the fifteenth century. From 1397, when Giovanni di Bicci de'Medici, the real founder of the dynasty, created the Medici banking firm, until 1420 the Medici family collected a total of 113,865 florins in profits, or an annual average of 4,950 florins.[54] During the following fifteen years the Medici bank established itself as the most vigorous and dynamic business concern in Florence, possibly in all Italy. The Medici during that period were successful in acquiring the position of papal bankers, and because of the great advantages that came their way in their privileged status within the Curia they were able to accumulate within a fifteen-year

53. *Ibid.*, f. 25r: "ch'e' sono sì variati che mi pare impossible averne conto."

54. de Roover, *The Rise and Decline of the Medici Bank,* p. 47, Table 8.

period profits higher than those of the preceding twenty three years: 124,255 florins, or an annual average of 8,283, a figure more than one third higher than that of the previous period.[55] One should recall that these figures represented the profits of the most successful business establishment of Florence. Unfortunately, we have no figures representing the tax assessments and tax payments of the Medici during the first two and a half decades of the fifteenth century. From the secret account books of the late 1420's and early 1430's, however, we learn that from 1425 until early 1433 Giovanni di Bicci and Cosimo di Giovanni de'Medici paid a total of 91,441 florins in prestanze and catasti, receiving an interest and partial amortization of their investments in the Monte of only 15,981 florins. Thus, during that period the net cost of the Commune's fiscal policy on the Medici amounted to 75,460 florins, or an annual average of 9,432 florins. This sum exceeded by more than 1,100 florins the annual profits of the Medici family from their very lucrative holding company (see Table 8).[56]

Such heavy financial burdens were bound to produce adverse reactions among the citizens. It has already been noted that in 1423/24 the yield of a prestanza was about 80 percent of its anticipated income. That percentage was gradually reduced as the decade progressed, so that by 1427 an impost was no longer expected to fetch the city more than 50 to 60 percent of its face

55. *Ibid.*, p. 55, Table 11.

56. It should be pointed out that it is rather difficult to state with any degree of certitude whether these sums represent the total tax payments of the Medici during these years. All the tax payments recorded in the *libri segreti* were made through the *tavola* of Florence, and it may well be that Giovanni di Bicci and Cosimo made some payments to the catasto officials directly. Given the nature of the available evidence, it seems almost impossible to ascertain the magnitude of the sums, if indeed there are any, paid by the Medici but not recorded in the secret account books.

Table 8. Payments to Camera and receipts from Monte of Giovanni di Bicci and Cosimo de'Medici, 1425–1433 (values expressed in florins, gold sous, and gold deniers).

Year Ending	Paid	Received	Difference
March 24, 1425/26	15,740.12.16	0. 0. 0	15,740.12.16
March 24, 1426/27	11,160. 6. 4	711.13. 0	10,448.22. 4
March 24, 1427/28	7,123.26. 0	1,540.17.10	5,583. 8. 2
March 24, 1428/29	5,292.14.10	2,227.22. 0	3,064.21.10
March 24, 1429/30	3,410.28. 3	3,111.10. 7	299.17. 8
March 24, 1430/31	14,930.14. 8	2,258. 8. 1	12,672. 6. 7
March 24, 1431/32	18,948.21. 5	3,899.26. 1	15,048.24. 4
March 24, 1432/33	14,834. 8. 5	2,232. 0. 0	12,602. 8. 5
TOTAL	91,441.17. 3	15,981.10. 7	75,456. 6. 8

Source: Mediceo avanti il principato 153, *Libro segreto* II (1420–1435), ff. 33r, 49r, 65r, 74r.

value, and that only after long months had elapsed from the time of its enactment.[57] Unfortunately, for the years following 1428, changed accounting methods of the scribes employed in the Florentine Camera do not allow one to measure the exact yield of each forced loan. It is safe to assume, however, that as the pressure on the Treasury mounted and the consequent demands made on the Florentine citizens increased, the trend outlined above became even more pronounced.

The government, of course, possessed powerful weapons with

57. See, for example, *PC*, XXX, f. 349v, for a reference to a double prestanza that fetched the Treasury only 27,215 florins of its anticipated total of 50,000 florins. Also *PC*, XXXI, f. 267r, where it is mentioned that the twenty-first prestanzone, due in mid-October 1427, had produced a yield of only 28,629 florins of its 45,000 florins by the following March. Many other examples can be found in the *PC* of various years under the heading *ritratto di varie prestanze*.

which to pressure its citizens into paying their assessments in full and within the prescribed deadlines. From the outset of the fiscal crisis in the middle of 1423 until the peace of Ferrara in 1433, it tried, intermittently and often simultaneously, to encourage and intimidate its citizens into meeting their fiscal responsibilities. The most attractive inducement it could offer to the inhabitants of the city was the promise of interest rates sufficiently lucrative to attract their capital. This, of course, was a difficult promise for the state to keep. Its military expenditures were so high that during the 1420's it had been forced to institute a complex system that increased the cash reserves of the state by withholding one fourth the interest due to the creditors of the Monte. Thus investors in the *Monte Commune,* instead of receiving a return of 5 percent per year, found themselves receiving interest at the rate of only 3.75 percent. Similarly, those who had been promised a rate of return of 8 percent per annum for their investments in the *Monte de'prestanzoni* received only 6 percent.[58] Thus the government, at the very moment when it should have offered its prospective creditors more lucrative terms for their investments, found itself in the awkward position of having to follow precisely the opposite course. It therefore had to resort to expedient arrangements. While, for example, withholding one fourth the interest due to investors in the *Monte Comune* (who had been promised a rate of return of 5 percent per year), it created a different Monte, known as the *Monte de'cinque interi,* into which were inscribed the payments of prestanze or catasti if made within fifteen days of the time of their imposition. This Monte, as its name indicates, paid interest of a full 5 percent, without the usual deduc-

---

58. For provisions ordering the withholding of one fourth the interest due Monte creditors, see *PR,* CXIII, f. 226v, December 13, 1423; CXVIII, ff. 583r–589v, March 15, 1427/28; CXXII, ff. 313v–325r, January 21, 1431/32.

tion of the one fourth.[59] Shortly after the adoption of this measure, yet another inducement was offered those capable of paying their assessments within fifteen days, by effectively raising
the promised rate of return from 5 to 6 percent per annum. This
measure was adopted, says the legislative enactment, "so that
the citizens will be aided in paying their extremely onerous levies with greater facility." [60]

59. *PR*, CXIV, ff. 90r–92v, December 12, 1424: "Illi qui solvent infra
primum terminum assignatum vel assignandum pro solutione talis oneris
seu ad solvendum ipsum onus in libris et registris novi montis qui appellari
debeat il monte de'cinque interi . . . et habeant et habere debeant huiusmodi
creditores pro dictis eorum creditis interesse et donum infrascriptum videlicet,
describendi in monte novo qui dicitur de'cinque interi ad rationem florenorum
quinque auri pro anno et pro centinario et ad rationem anni et centinarii
florenorum vere sortis scripte integrum, videlicet sine aliqua retentione quarti
que usque nunc pro creditoribus montis comunis fieri consuevit. Et alii
creditores describendi in libris montis comunis ordinati ante presentem
provisionem, videlicet ad rationem florenorum quinque auri pro centinario
et pro anno et ad rationem anni et centinarii florenorum vere sortis scripte,
sed cum retentione quarti ipsius interessi prout in ordinamentis ipsius montis
comunis pro creditoribus eiusdem clarius est." See also *DSSp Aut.*, XX, ff.
67r–69v, January 15, 1424/25.

60. *PR*, CXV, ff. 263v–267v, December 30, 1425: "Ut cives facilius ad
supportationem gravissimorum onerum inducantur persequentes ad finem
qua praticata et tandem relata fuere per plurimos viros eruditos et expertos
in gubernatione rei publice florentine . . . [deciderunt et ordinaverunt] quod
omnes et singuli qui pro se vel alio solvere animo rehabendi integre veram
sortem quarumcunque seu pro quibuscunque prestantiis, prestanzonibus,
residuis, piacentibus, dispiacentibus vel aliis quibuscunque oneribus seu
gravedinibus etiam secundum quamcunquam distributionem prestantiarum
vel similum onerum et sub quacunque forma tenore appellatione vel effectu
imponendis infra unum annum proximum futurum incipiendum die primo
mensis Januarii proxime futuri, et quilibet ipsorum intelligantur esse et sint
creditores comunis florentie illius quantitatis et summe quam pro vera sorte
et supra animo rehabendi solverint. Et possint et debeant per scribanos
montium dicti comunis scribi et registrari ut creditores et pro creditoribus
eiusdem comunis in libris et registris montium prefati comunis in illis
videlicet in quibus describi debebunt secundum effectum infrascriptum.
Videlicet: quod illi qui solvent infra primum terminum assignandum pro

If promises of higher returns did not produce the desired results, however, the government could impose extraordinarily strict penalties on tax delinquents. To begin with, in every tax bill imposing a forced loan were incorporated a number of clauses that specified the penalties awaiting those not honoring the terms of the law. In addition, supplementary punitive laws were continually enacted, outlining with great precision the infringements of personal liberty that would befall tax delinquents. These included disenfranchisement from the political process by inclusion of their names in the lists of debtors to the Commune (*specchio*), thus disqualifying these persons from holding communal office;[61] confiscation of their goods equal to

---

solutione et ad solvendum tale onus in libris et registris montis qui appellatur vulgariter il monte de'prestanzoni sive magnarum prestantiarum libertatis et una simul cum aliis ad presens creditoribus dicti comunis in dicto monte prestanzonum. Et qui solverint post ipsum primum terminum quandocunque scribi debeant in monte comuni qui vulgariter appellatur il monte comune vecchio. Et quisque ipsorum describatur creditor pro illa seu in illa quantitate seu quantitatibus que pro vera sorte ut supra rehabendi animo solute fuerint, et que per dictum comune restitui debent. Et quod postquam sic descripti fuerint habeantur, censeantur et sint pro veris et ut veri creditores dicti comunis in montibus suprascriptis. Et habeant et habere debeant huiusmodi creditores pro dictis eorum creditis remunerationem, donum, damnum et interesse infrascriptum, videlicet describendi in monte prestanzonum seu magnarum prestantiarum libertatis ad rationem florenorum octo auri pro anno et pro centinario et ad rationem anni et centinarii florenorum vere sortis scripte in libris dicti montis cum retentione quarti ipsius remunerationis donni, danni, et interesse. . . . Et alii creditores . . . habeant et habere debeant ad rationem florenorum quinque auri pro centinario . . . et cum retentione quarti ipsius interesse. . . ." This measure was renewed one year later (*PR*, CXVI, ff. 285v–289v, February 17, 1426/27) for the following reason: "Quia onerum gravissimorum frequentissima impositione durante expedit fessos cives tam longis temporibut diuturna que solutione gravatos meriti et interesse sublevatione iuvare ut si in uno ut necessitas exigit fere ad impossibile sunt coacti, in altero restaurationis remedio faveantur. . . ."

61. The two following contemporary references to the effectiveness of the *specchio* should make it clear that the economic hardships imposed by the

the value of their debts to the Commune; and often their rele-
gation to the ranks of the magnates (the politically disenfran-
chised noble class).[62] Appointment of the dreaded *ufficiali delle
vendite* (officials of the sales) was always considered an ominous sign in Florence, for these officials were authorized to
confiscate and sell the patrimonies of tax delinquents. Given
the nature of the fiscal crisis during the 1420's and the heavy
tax burden imposed on the citizens of Florence, it is not at all
surprising that laws appointing the members of this office were
enacted several times from 1423 to 1433.[63] Even more serious
was the measure enacted on October 15, 1425, which rendered
his relatives responsible for an individual's prompt payment of

state on its citizens often produced serious political repercussions. Pietribuoni
reports that Piero di Michele di Forese Salviati was drawn to the priorate on
28 June, 1429, "e gli fu notifichato ch'egli era in sullo specchio per le gabelle
de'contratti, e andossene la sera a chasa sanza compagnia come s'era usato.
Et con uno fante colla lanterna, se n'andò solo a chasa. Et dipoi s'intese
ischabiato et stracciato" (*Biblioteca Nazionale Centrale di Firenze, Conventi
Soppressi,* C.4.895. *Cronica di Piero Pietribuoni,* ff. 125r–v). Giovanni di
Jacopo Morelli writes: "Io Giovanni Morelli in questi dì fu' tratto Capitano
di Pisa del 33. Ebbi divieto per la gabella del vino" (*Ricordi,* in *Delizie degli
eruditi toscani,* ed. Fr. Ildelfonso di San Luigi [Florence, 1770–1789], XIX,
123).

62. See, for example, *DSSp Aut.,* XX, ff. 77v–78v, May 11, 1425.

63. *PR,* CXIV, ff. 35v–37r, October 12, 1424, states that the priors, the
colleges, the *sei di mercanzia,* the *otto di guardia,* and the captains of the
parte guelfa were to appoint the sales officials. These latter were authorized
to confiscate the goods of citizens owing for the payment of past prestanze;
these goods could be sold at public auctions only if the debt to the Commune
amounted to at least one half the sum to be realized by the sale. The contracts
gabelle was to be assessed on these transfers, while the salary of the sales
officials was set at 5 percent (12 deniers per lira) of the income the Commune would realize from these sales. Similar provisions were also enacted
in *PR,* CXVI, ff. 36r–39r, May 27, 1426; CXVI, ff. 248v–252r, January 22,
1426/27; CXXII, ff. 29v–33r, May 15, 1431; CXXII, ff. 276r–v, November
17, 1431.

taxes. The sales officials were now instructed by the legislation authorizing their appointment to sell the property of a tax delinquent to members of his immediate family (*proximioribus coniunctis in grado sanguinis*). If they were financially unable to buy the confiscated goods, they were to offer the goods "step by step to other relatives in their family. And if these were unable to buy them, they should [try to sell these goods] to those who are located closer, or who are neighbors of these properties that are for sale; if these were not able, then [the goods were to be sold] to any one, even to a person unknown [to the tax delinquent]." [64]

Even more shocking to the sensibilities of stolid Florentine citizens, however, must have been a bill enacted on December 9, 1432, according to which the sales officials were instructed to confiscate not only the real estate of tax delinquents but also their investments in the Monte. This was, indeed, a serious measure, because from the very time of the funding of the Monte in the 1340's, the Florentine government had repeatedly and solemnly promised that Monte credits would not be confiscated for any reason at all, neither for the satisfaction of private or public creditors nor even as a penalty for seditious actions against the Florentine state. But the government, not

64. *PR*, CXV, ff. 170r–173r, October 15, 1425: "Offerire debeant gradatim ad alios coniunctos in parentela. Et si non essent habiles ad proximiores seu propinquiores sive vicinos bonorum vendendorum, et si non essent habiles tunc ad quoscunque etiam extraneos." This measure would seem to indicate that the ties of *parentela* were still very strong in the third decade of the Quattrocento and that some recent attempts to characterize this age as one in which the traditional structure of the family was breaking down may have overstressed isolated and uncharacteristic incidents (see Richard Goldthwaite, *Private Wealth in Renaissance Florence* [Princeton: Princeton University Press, 1969]). Here, for example, is an instance in which all members of a family, including rather remote relatives, are made responsible for an individual's prompt payment of taxes.

entirely content to breach its promises to tax delinquents, also decreed that goods confiscated and sold to the tax delinquents' relatives were to be paid for by the latter's Monte credits.[65] Moreover, a sales tax of 10 percent was soon imposed on such forced sales of tax delinquents' real estate or of Monte credits, so that the purchaser of this property, even if he obtained it involuntarily, was required to pay from his own funds the 10 percent surcharge.[66] Such steps, while obviously undermining the confidence of the Florentines in the good faith of their government, had the great advantage of contributing to the diminution of the public debt and of the carrying charges allocated to it.

Disenfranchisement from the political process and confiscation of patrimony could also be accompanied by actual physical punishment. Two bills enacted on July 3, 1432, provided that the communal judges were bound to prosecute tax delinquents within the deadlines established by the communal authorities, so that thereafter Florentine citizens could stop hoping to avoid punishment by relying on the inevitable delays with which most cases were heard in the city's courts.[67] On that same day it was also decreed that prisoners who were in the malodorous prisons of the city (*stinche*) on account of tax debts could no longer be given special treatment but thereafter must be kept constantly chained and supervised, as was customary with all other criminals.[68]

Too many threats and excessively punitive measures, however, aroused even further the restlessness and discontent prevailing in the city, particularly among the less affluent and most

65. *PR*, CXXIII, ff. 306r–v, December 9, 1432.
66. *PR*, CXXIV, ff. 3r–v, March 26, 1433.
67. *PR*, CXXIII, f. 141r, July 3, 1432.
68. *PR*, CXXIII, ff. 141v–142r, July 3, 1432.

oppressed. The revolt of 1378, when the workers of the woolen industry (*ciompi*) had looted and burned their masters' properties and for a brief time imposed their own régime on the city, had left a deep impression in the minds of Florentine entrepreneurs. The signs in the mid-1420's were ominous and tended to give rise to much worried talk. In late August 1426 the house of Niccolò di Andrea Carducci, one of the twenty citizens entrusted with devising a new system of prestanzoni, was set on fire. The communal legislature, alarmed at the seriousness of the offense, immediately offered a prize for information that would lead to the arrest of the culprit, making clear in the legislative enactment that the connection between the crime and Niccolò Carducci's position was obvious: *quo factum putatur ex eo quia idem Niccolaus fuit unus ex viginti civibus deputatis ad faciendum novam distributionem prestanzonis civitatis florentiae.*[69] A series of public trials in the spring and summer of 1428/29 further accented the discontent so ubiquitous and menacing to the position of those in power. One of the accused, a member of an old and powerful family, the Tornaquinci, was brought to trial for having refused to pay his prestanze and catasti for three continuous years. The indictment against him is explicit: Inspired by a diabolical spirit, having lost all his respect for God and for the state of Florence, Chirico di Piero Tornaquinci was contributing to the erosion of age-old communal liberties and the possible subjugation of the city by a hateful and tyrannical régime by his refusal to pay his taxes for three continuous years.[70] But even those who were not pos-

---

69. *PR*, CXVI, ff. 155v–157r, August 29, 1426: "Fuit immissis ignis et appositus hostium domus habitationis prudentissimi viri Niccolai Andree Carducci . . . et non sine maximo periculo personarum ipsius Niccolai et sue familie."

70. *PR*, CXX, ff. 22v–23r, February 15, 1428/29: "Quia dictus Chiricus

sessed of a diabolical spirit and who did not refuse to make prompt payment of their taxes were disgruntled and annoyed by the financial burden imposed on them. "I advise you," wrote a Florentine to a friend who was in Greece, "that here we have nothing but plague, wars, and extravagant expenses." [71] That same visitor to Greece received another letter from Palla di Nofri Strozzi, one of the most eminent Florentines of his day, advising him that so heavy and potentially damaging was the tax burden that in times such as theirs one's principal preoccupation should be the maintenance of one's own patrimony. [72] As a final illustration of the explosive situation, and the erosion of the citizens' trust in the government that the continued policy of deficit financing produced in the city, one can cite a reference in the diary of a pacific and very respectable Florentine merchant, Giovanni di Jacopo Morelli. While discussing the gradually deteriorating state of Florentine finances in 1426, well

---

spiritu diabolico instigatus deum pre oculis non habendo, nec statum bonum et tranquillum inclite civitatis Florentie, scienter dolose et appensate animo et intentionem prefatam civitatem, populum et libertatem eius tirannide submictendi et submicti faciendi cessavit tamquam rebellis et non zelator inclite libertatis pacifici, tranquilli et boni status civitatis florentie solvere prestantias et onera hactenus iniuncta." See also folio 92v, April 21, 1429, and folios 186r–v, June 10, 1429. Pietribuoni, in his *Cronica,* f. 117r, says: "A tempo de'detti priori si die bando a più cittadini perchè non aveano paghate le prestanse. ne prestanzoni, tra'quali fu Giacopo di Vanozzo de'Bardi, et Chiricho et Nicchòlo di Piero Tornaquinci."

71. Biblioteca Laurenziana, Ashburnham, 1830, II, 409, letter from Nanni degli Strozzi in Florence to Neri di Donato Acciaioli in Athens, dated July 25, 1424: "Io ti adviso di qua non è se non moria, guerra, et spendio grandissimo."

72. *Ibid.,* II, 430, letter from Palla [di Nofri] Strozzi in Florence to Neri [di Donato] Acciaioli in Romania, dated 8 July, 1424: "Questi son tempi da por da parte ogni altra volontà e ingegnarsi provedere a facti suoi per ogni via possibile. Già si può dir siamo circa a quaranta prestanze da poi questi fatti comminciarono." On this same theme, *Ibid.,* I, 4, 5.

before the crisis had reached its most acute state, Morelli exclaims, "Go ahead and make war; encourage war; keep feeding those who incite war. Florence has never lived without wars, nor will she be able to live without them, until four of the major citizens are decapitated each year!" [73]

To allay the discontent and mollify the spirits of its citizens, the Florentine government during the 1420's, much in the same manner as it had done in previous periods of intensive military engagements and of large expenditures, was forced to temper the punishments with which it threatened potential tax delinquents. Repeatedly during the 1420's bills were enacted in which clear reference was made to the difficulties encountered by large segments of the population in paying taxes. The government, states one of these provisions, understanding that "experience shows that debtors of the Commune will be induced to pay more promptly if they are pardoned than if they are punished," proceeded to defer the deadlines for the payment of taxes past due.[74] Other laws are even more explicit and blunt in describing the predicament of Florentine citizens: "Unless the deadline for the payment is extended," recorded a communal scribe in the preface to a tax bill, "citizens will not be able to pay and will become liable to serious penalties. We must, therefore, enact some legislation in order to exempt them from these penalties." [75] As the 1420's progressed, and with the passing of

---

73. Giovanni di Jacopo Morelli (di San Luigi [ed.], *Ricordi*, p. 73): "Fate guerra, inducete guerra, date poppa a chi nutrica la guerra. Mai è stata Firenze senza guerra, ne starà perinsino non taglia la testa ogni anno a 4 de'maggiori."

74. "Quia ut experientia demonstravit gratia semper citius quam pena debitores comunis ad solvendum induxit" (*PR*, CXVIII, f. 448r, November 14, 1427).

75. *PR*, CXVII, ff. 149v–150r, July 18, 1427: "Cum per frequentiam impositionis onerum publicorum plures ad eo impotentes effecti sint ad solven-

each year, the burden on the citizens became even more heavy, series of bills were enacted, extending the deadline for the payment of taxes or offering a general grace to those who had already incurred penalties for their failure to pay taxes imposed in the past. References are made in some of these bills to individuals owing their prestanze for periods of ten, fifteen, or more years, and one wonders what psychological effect must have been produced among the Florentine citizens by the almost constant revision, amendment, and correction of laws that had been designed to increase the revenues of the city and also to inspire respect for the law among the inhabitants of the city.[76]

While always free to hope for the passage of a bill granting general amnesty to all tax delinquents, Florentine citizens could at the same time have recourse to the communal authorities, petitioning (before 1427) that their assessment was unjust and requesting its diminution, or (after 1427, when because of the catasto, complaints of injustice would no longer be sustained) that their cash reserves were simply inadequate to meet the tax assessment, whose magnitude was largely based on investments in land or in the Monte. Hundreds of such petitions were submitted each year to the Signory and subsequently processed to

---

dum quod incideant in penas plurimas atque graves, et nisi in eorum favorem aliquid pro predictis statuatur non est verisimiliter quod a talibus penis exemantur."

76. Many examples exist. Already on August 29, 1422, Luca di Paolo Razanti petitioned for grace for the prestanze that he had owed since 1401. Although his assessment during those years fluctuated between 16 sous and 1 florin, 19 sous, 11 deniers, he owed in all nearly 175 florins. "Et quod prout notum fere omnibus esse putat pupillus remansit . . . opulentam substantiam possidens qua tota in onerum publicorum solutione consumpta est ante que ad annos discretionis pervenit tam indiscrete gravatus fuit." Numerous other such decrees can be found in the legislative records of those years. Some examples: *PR*, CXV, ff. 120r–v; CXVI, ff. 30v–31v; CXXI, ff. 14v–15r; CXXI, ff. 131v–132r.

the legislative chambers. Usually the government reached an agreement with the petitioner, in the greater number of cases consolidating his past debts and possibly reducing the assessment. Twice in the 1420's, however, the government sought to regulate the practice of submitting private petitions that requested a reduction or postponement of prestanze payments. In the fall of 1423 it was decided that no such petition would be entertained unless it was accompanied by an inventory of all the claimant's patrimony. Property omitted from it, with the exception of cash and household goods not subject to taxation, if discovered, would be automatically confiscated by the government and the petition rejected.[77] In 1427 it was also decided that petitions requesting the reduction of prestanze assessments would not be admitted unless the petitioner had already filed his catasto return.[78]

Extension of the deadline for the payment of taxes, and general amnesties of penalties incurred by tax delinquents, could be considered little more than palliatives meant to facilitate the collection of taxes and to avoid the creation of a spirit of revolutionary discontent among the communal citizens. The state, however, also had to demonstrate that the exigencies of the situation had impressed themselves with clarity on the minds of those governing it, and that its operations reflected the new needs and demands of a period of unprecedented crisis. One observes, therefore, a clear movement during the 1420's toward a more rational, efficient, and careful administration of the Florentine fisc.

77. *PR, CXIII,* ff. 147r–v, October 1, 1423.
78. *PR, CXVII,* ff. 121r–v, June 26, 1427.

5

ADMINISTRATIVE AND
ECONOMIC EFFECTS OF
HEAVY TAXATION

ADMINISTRATIVE EFFECTS

As might have been expected, the first repercussions of these efforts toward a greater measure of efficiency in taxation were felt among the ranks of the communal bureaucracy that was entrusted with the administration of state revenues. Complaints against the mismanagement of government funds had always been heard in the communal councils during the Trecento and the early Quattrocento, but they seem to have assumed a particularly intense level after 1423. The inhabitants of the quarter of Santo Spirito, reported their spokesman Giovanni di Tommaso Corbinelli in a council meeting, complained that government funds were continually being misspent. He further demanded the curtailment of the initiative of communal officials in determining how the city's revenues should be spent, and asked "that taxes not be imposed for one reason, and the money be spent for another." [1] Under such strong and explicit pressure a series of measures was enacted that limited the initiative of such officeholders and attempted to guarantee their aptitude for holding those offices. In July 1428 the long-sanctioned tradition of drawing the names of gabelle officials from especially prepared pouches (*borse*) was abandoned in favor of

1. *LF*, LIII, f. 99v, January 21, 1425/26: "Et quod denaria non imponantur pro una causa et pro altera solvatur."

appointing them directly. The extraordinary precautions taken in this measure, which established several steps in the selection of these officials, could indicate that rather than aiming at the appointment of special political favorites to these posts, the principal intention of the communal legislators was to appoint trustworthy and competent men.[2]

Shortly thereafter, in December 1429, an important restriction was imposed on the traditional perquisites and freedoms enjoyed by communal officials. Often during earlier periods a Florentine appointed or elected to a government post would cede his position to a friend or relative, reaching with him mutually satisfactory financial arrangements. After 1429 cashiers (*camarlinghi*) serving in any communal office were prohibited from relinquishing their offices to anyone but their closest relatives. Thus the communal legislators hoped to exercise a closer control on bureaucrats administering communal funds.[3] Even more restrictive was a measure enacted in December 1431 that greatly reduced the opportunities of various cashiers to supplement their regular salaries with ancillary earnings made during their term of office. While in the past, communal officials had been allowed to invest surplus funds and personally collect large portions of the interest earned by these transactions, all such dealings were now forbidden and violators were to be punished

2. The regulations for the appointment of these officials are found in a very long provision in *PR*, CXIX, ff. 151r–155v, July 15, 1428. The decision to abandon the method of drawing names from the *borsa* was taken "ut multis vicibus experientia demonstravit quem sorte deputare verissimiliter ydoneum habere non posset."

3. *PR*, CXX, ff. 420r–v, December 23, 1429: "Ne pubblica pecunia immoderata cupiditate lucri ad privatos usus substitutionis pallio convertatur obviare. . . ." The only relatives to whom these posts could be ceded were fathers, sons, grandsons, brothers, and nephews.

severely.[4] Not content to curtail the number of perquisites enjoyed by communal officials, the legislature also ordered a more careful and thorough auditing system, so that misuse of funds could be detected more rapidly and the culprits punished without delay. In December 1426 an audit of all cameral books kept during the previous ten years was ordered, the implication being that errors committed even ten years before could be rectified and the culprits brought to justice.[5] A similar measure was passed in November 1430, at which time one of the Commune's judicial officials, the *esecutore della giustizia,* was empowered to supervise the work of the special auditors.[6] Finally, the audit ordered in June 1431 was to apply to all cameral records dating from the conclusion of the war against Ladislaus of Naples in 1414,[7] while shortly thereafter it was decreed that those found guilty of misappropriating government moneys since the declaration of war (presumably in 1423) would be considered communal rebels.[8]

Savings accumulated by imposing stricter controls over communal officials could be supplemented by reductions in their salaries. Even before the outbreak of war, in March 1420, a commission had been appointed to recommend reductions in the salaries of many officials of the bulging Florentine bureaucracy.[9] Whether the recommendations of this commission were actually applied is not quite known, though a similar measure, affecting two of the major fiscal offices, was enacted soon after

4. *PR,* CXXII, ff. 284v–285r, December 6, 1431.
5. *PR,* CXVI, ff. 228v–229r, December 30, 1426.
6. *PR,* CXXI, ff. 82r–v, November 23, 1430.
7. *PR,* CXXII, ff. 96r–v, June 20, 1431.
8. *PR,* CXXII, ff. 294r–v, December 20, 1431.
9. *PR,* CX, ff. 1r–2v, March 29, 1420.

the outbreak of war, when the salary of a *provveditore della camera* was reduced from 120 to 100 florins per year and that of a Monte official from 80 to 60 florins per year.[10]

It was not until 1425, however, that a special and thorough review of the salary scales of all communal officials was undertaken by a special balìa, appointed *ad risecandum expensas comunis*. The recommendations of this plenipotentiary commission fill an entire volume, and they range from suggestions on curtailing the dining expenses of the priors to actual and severe reductions in the salary of most communal officials. How severe these salary cuts were is suggested by the fact that the salary of a *provveditore della camera* was further reduced from 100 to 80 florins and that of an official of the Monte from 60 to 48 florins per year,[11] while the allowance granted to the *Otto*

10. *PR*, CXIII, ff. 142v–143v, October 1, 1423.

11. *Balie*, XXIII, ff. 3r–4r, December 23, 1425: "Choncio sia cosa che tra gli atti degli huomini humani niuna chosa sia più pretiosa che la libertà la quale in verità da essa natura procede, perchè tutti gli huomini liberi naschono, et con essa desiderabile affectione la conditione della generatione humana quello che la natura insegna con ottima intentione si sforza seguire. E meglio esser si cognosce gli huomini in povero stato liberi vivere che nell'oro e gemme pretiosissime ricchi, et servi e sotto altrui potestà e signoria esser constituti. E però questo, considerati gl'infrascripti honorevoli cittadini fiorentini, per difesa della libertà della loro magnifica città di Firenze, acciò che delle mani del pessimo tiranno sia liberata, e esso tiranno che con suo ardire la libertà si sforza turbare della sua audacia sii confuso, e in pace essa fiorentina città tutti i dì rimanga. Auto rispetto che benchè essa libertà s'assodi per l'ottima unione de'cittadini e questo esser la prima cosa a essa libertà difendere, niente di meno senza alquanta pecunia in parte fare non si può." They appointed the following to serve in the balìa: Giuliano di Tommaso di Guccio Martini, *lanaiolo, uno de'priori*, Angelo di Corso, *calzolaio, de' dodici buonomini*, Giovanni di Tommaso Corbinelli, Antonio di Tedice degli Albizzi, Bartolomeo di Giovanni Carducci, Giovanni d'Andrea Betti Minerbetti, Bartolomeo di Verano Peruzzi, and Rinaldo di Giovanni di Bartolo Gratia, *legnaiolo*. Their task was to examine the fiscal situation in the city, so that Florence might conserve the "celestial dono, cioè Libertà che in questo secolo

di Guardia (a sort of security police) was reduced from 600 to 200 florins per year.[12] The salary of the notarial staff assigned to the priors was now reduced from 100 to 60 florins for each bimonthly priorate, while the annual allowance of the chancellor and his staff could no longer exceed 800 florins.[13] The thoroughness of the review undertaken by the balìa is indicated in the stringency of their recommendations for all governmental agencies: the golden spoons, presented to the new priors upon their assumption of office, which cost the Commune 552 florins per year (92 florins for each bimonthly priorate), could no longer be paid for out of communal funds; priors who wished to obtain these mementos would have to purchase them from the government. The salaries of the *podestà,* the *capitano,* and the *esecutore,* the three highest judicial officials, were considerably reduced, as was the number of scribes, notaries, and soldiers in their retinues. Finally, the ashes of the kitchen of the *Palazzo dei Signori* and the cooked olive oil that was ordinarily given away to the poor would now have to be sold, because, the officials said, "whoever is not master of his own house does not tend to it, and rather is more interested in consuming that

---

nient'è più pretioso, e per la quale conservare non solo desiderar doveremo che a noi fussono diminuiti i salari, provisioni e remunerazioni et in qualunche modo etiamdio con nostro danno l'entrate del comune s'acresciessono, ma i figliuoli e le proprie persone sporre doveremo. E per corroboratione, fortificatione, e aumentatione de'creditori del monte d'esso comune, a'quali crediti ciò che si fa di comodo o utilità, per vigore delle infrascripte deliberationi o capitoli si comprende, cede, e va tutti gli infrascripti salari, provisioni, remunerationi, merciedi, o spese come di sotto . . . è descripto." The references to the Monte officials and to the *provveditori* are found on folio 16r and 17r.

12. *Balie,* XXIII; folio 26v, for the *Otto di Guardia,* and folio 28r for the *Studio.*

13. *Balie,* XXIII; folios 6v–8v for the chancellor, and folio 5r for the notaries.

which he has not earned," and thus cooks and servants would no longer be entrusted with the administration of communal property.[14] It was in a similar spirit that the priors and colleges were instructed to review all communal subsidies traditionally given to lay or ecclesiastical dignitaries and to diminish or abolish them but under no circumstances to augment them.[15] Finally, in a further attempt to curtail unnecessary expenses a provision enacted in the spring of 1431 established the maximum expenditures that could be made for the funerals of office-holders.[16]

The unsettled state of communal finances, reflected in the more stringent supervision of the city's bureaucrats and the reduction of routine expenditures, also resulted in a series of attempts to organize the communal fisc in a more practical and efficient manner. After 1425/26 one discerns a clear effort (even if at times one remains unconvinced about the seriousness of the reform and the willingness of those instigating it to carry it through to its logical conclusions) to organize the Camera more simply, to assign clearer responsibilities in the administration of funds, and even more important, to anticipate the magnitude of communal expenses so as to enable the Florentine legislators to distribute over a longer period of time the taxes to be imposed on the citizenry. Examples of such attempts are numerous and take up large portions of the legislative volumes that have survived until the present.

The agency that traditionally had administered the military

14. *Balie,* XXIII; folio 5r for the priors' spoons, folios 15v–16r for salaries of judges, and folio 14v for the administration of the kitchen in the *Palazzo dei Signori,* in which the members of the balia state "chi non è signore della casa quella non guarda, anzi attende alla consumatione di quello che e' non à ghuadagnato."

15. *PR,* CXV, ff. 176v–177r, October 22, 1425.

16. *PR,* CXXII, ff. 5r–v, April 5, 1431.

budgets of the Commune was the *Capsa Conducte,* known as the condotta, which was a division of the communal Camera. Beginning in January 1425/26 the condotta was divided into two subagencies. The *condotta ordinaria* was entrusted with the administration of the funds for the routine operations and expenses of the government: maintenance of the *Palazzo dei Signori*; salaries for the staff of the priors; expenses for the staffing of certain important fortresses in the contado; pensions granted to retired civil servants; and salaries and equipment for the urban fire department. The *condotta extraordinaria,* to be administered by the *ufficiali del banco,* was empowered to supervise the negotiations with the mercenaries in the Commune's hire and eventually pay their stipends. Each of the two agencies was assigned a specific sum that was considered sufficient to meet its basic expenses (see Table 9): 55,588 florins per annum to the *condotta ordinaria,* 75,288 florins to the *condotta extraordinaria,* with the proviso that the latter would also be authorized to administer all the income from forced loans that was earmarked for military expenses.[17] Similar provisions were enacted on three different occasions before 1433, and no doubt they represent the first attempts to calculate precisely and anticipate the city's expenses. Interestingly, by 1429 the permanent allocation to the *condotta extraordinaria* had been increased from 75,000 to 125,000 florins, a reflection, no doubt, of the increased tempo of military involvement and expenditures.[18] Concurrently, an attempt was made, in 1428, to cal-

17. One word of explanation for the last item listed in the table under the *condotta ordinaria.* The "poor receiving alms for life" were retired civil servants who received a small pension from the government. For this practice, consult Appendix C.

18. *PR,* CXIX, ff. 270v–271r, November 26, 1428; CXX, ff. 400v–403r, December 12, 1429; CXXI, ff. 164v–168v, March 5, 1430/31.

Table 9. Appropriations to *condotta ordinaria* and *condotta extraordinaria*, January 1425/26 (florins per year).

CONDOTTA ORDINARIA	
Mensa dominorum	3,600
Familia dominorum	6,850
Salaries of foreign judges	11,500
Captains of fortresses	15,000
Salary of 300 guards in fortress of Pisa	16,800
Fire department	800
Poveri che anno limosina a vita	1,038
TOTAL	55,588
CONDOTTA EXTRAORDINARIA	
421 lancie permanently in hire, commanded by Cionettino Bastari	54,024
400 foot soldiers (*pedites*)	14,400
8 horsemen (*caballari*)	864
500 florins per month owed to the Monte	6,000
TOTAL	75,288

Source: PR, CXV, ff. 284r–v, January 28, 1425/26.

culate the approximate amount of communal debts to mercenaries and civil servants for back wages. To the surprise and doubtless the annoyance of many, it was found that more than 120,000 florins were still owed for such purposes. The government then instituted an elaborate plan to liquidate this debt, authorizing the officials of the Monte to order the imposition of *tot catasta quot capiet universalis summa et quantitas* until full payment of these old debts had been made.[19]

During 1430 and 1431 some discussions were also held to determine the number of forced loans that would have to be imposed in the near future. In July 1431, for example, when

19. *PR,* CXIX, f. 272r, November 26, 1428.

eight catasti were imposed, experts called in to testify by the priors calculated that the communal expenses from August to December would amount to at least 200,000 florins, so that this large number of forced loans (catasti bearing an interest rate of 8 percent per year) would be required.[20] In the following February, when thirty-six catasti were imposed simultaneously, all bearing an interest rate of 5 percent per year, the preamble of this unusual act explained in some detail the reasoning of the Florentine lawmakers: The Commune needed enormous amounts of money, and only by being assured of its availability could the priors and their advisors properly plan the military and diplomatic actions for the coming year; the citizens, on the other hand, would be aware in advance that a certain number of taxes were required and would have the opportunity to distribute their payments over a longer period of time.[21]

Finally, one observes for the first time in the late 1420's a timid effort toward neutralizing pressures exerted on the government by particular interest groups. The one clear manifestation of this trend was the ban against speculators in the Monte becoming members of that office. Interestingly, the ban was directed not only against the speculators themselves but also against members of their clan (*consorteria*).[22] No doubt, in the eyes of large sections of the Florentine population, the most

20. *PR,* CXXII, f. 131v, July 11, 1431.

21. *PR,* CXXII, ff. 336r–341r, February 6, 1431/32: "Cum ea que certo ordine procedunt finem consequi certiorem soleant, et eo firmius quo maiori ordine et pro longiori tempore stabilita fuerint. Ideo ut et qui solvere onera publica debent se solutioni eorum preparari possint. Et qui recipere de publico debent praesertim in bello presenti facilius expectare vellint. . . ."

22. *PR,* CXVIII, f. 452r, November 25, 1427. *Monte delle graticole,* V, f. 13v: "Quod ementes et vendentes super monte non possit [sic] esse offitialis."

sensitive and important branch of the fiscal administration was the Monte, for almost all citizens had large portions of their tax payments inscribed in it. Those who administered that all-important office, therefore, had to be impartial in the disbursement of the annual interest due to all Monte creditors. On several other occasions during the early 1430's speakers in the communal councils inveighed against the speculators in the Monte, cautioning the governors of the city to ban them from the administration of the public debt.[23]

The greater measure of efficiency injected into the administration of the communal fisc was also reflected in the increasing number of demands that the state was making on its citizens and the insistence with which it could press those demands on them. The most obvious example of such exactitude was the institution of the catasto, which had brought an unprecedented measure of justice and egalitarianism to Florentine taxation policy: After 1427 the main burden of taxation was shifted from the middle ranks of Florentine society, where it had rested since the Trecento, to the more affluent and powerful urban groups. But the harsh regimen instituted in the city as a result of the crisis of the 1420's was also reflected in other governmental initiatives. Communal property that for generations had been appropriated by Florentine families was reclaimed with insistence after 1424: The government often appointed officials to investigate any claims it had against any inhabitant of the city, to collect all back rents and interest, and to guarantee

---

23. Pellegrini, pp. XLI–XLII (from *Consulte e Pratiche*, LI, f. 128r, February 26, 1430/31): "D. Petrus Beccanugi circa officiales montis dixit quod homines erant eligendi cum magna consideratione, ne incidat ut illi qui faciunt mercaturam montis veniant ad idem officium. Ideo limitetur, ut in extractione eius fiat extractio maioris numeri hominum, et postea scrutinentur et eligantur meliores."

the proper administration of all communal properties.[24] Catasto declarations were scrutinized with particular care; endless thought was given to covering all possible loopholes that might allow evasion of proper taxes. Fraudulent transfers of property to tax-exempt individuals or institutions — primarily churches, monasteries, nunneries, and hospitals — were banned in 1431, and the priors authorized the officials of the catasto to detect any such transactions and punish the culprits.[25] The practice of Florentine citizens of taking up residence in the contado so that they might escape the close scrutiny of the urban tax officials was strongly discouraged,[26] while clear procedures for the declaration of capital loaned to others were set forth in a law enacted in 1432.[27] Those who had refused to reach a mutually satisfactory accommodation with the tax officials about the real value of their capital assets were no longer allowed to protract their negotiations with governmental agencies but were now given a brief period in which to reach an agreement; if they refused, the tax officials were asked to impose the tax arbitrarily.[28]

24. *PR*, CXIV, ff. 70r–71v, December 9, 1424; CXV, ff. 173r–175r, October 15, 1425; CXIX, f. 15r, April 28, 1428; CXIX, f. 47v, May 26, 1428.

25. *PR*, CXXII, ff. 227r–v, October 23, 1431. This law was passed in order to eliminate "fraudibus quae in damnum comunis sub alienationis spetie in non subeuntem onera civium."

26. On February 19, 1405/06 the legislature had imposed strict regulations on the authority that tax collectors could wield in the contado. On May 27, 1406 the following entry appears in an administrative enactment: *Camera del Comune — Statuto dei regolatori dell'entrate e spese del comune, volume unico*, ff. 14a r–v (modern pagination in arabic numerals): "Et inteso che molti cittadini dela città di Firenze andarono et vanno ad habitare in contado sotto colore dela decta leggie, acciò che non sieno gravati maximamente così agevolmente, et questo ritorna in danno del decto comune . . ." it was decreed that large fines would be imposed on such evaders. This decree was repeated on numerous occasions in th late 1420's.

27. *PR*, CXXIII, ff. 288r–v, November 22, 1432.

28. *PR*, CXIX, ff. 63v–64r, June 7, 1428: This law was enacted on the

Finally, in order to avoid the loss of valuable revenue, the artificially low exchange rate between silver and gold, which had been allowed to the less affluent when paying their taxes, was revised so as to reflect the new and increased value of gold: While before 1425 those assessed in prestanze less than twenty gold sous could pay in silver coins at the exchange rate of 73 silver sous, 4 deniers, per florin, the exchange rate was thereafter increased to 80 silver sous per florin.[29] A similar provision also established the same exchange rate for the payment of mercenaries' wages, so that even if the florin were to appreciate further, the Commune would be allowed to pay its soldiers at that same rate.[30] Finally, in December 1433, it was decided to curtail all unnecessary expenditures of the Florentine mint. Past debts of that office were not to be paid in full but rather on a percentage basis that would depend on that office's future incomes. The only expenses that, according to this decree, could not be reduced were the wages paid to the workers of the mint.[31]

---

request of the officials of the catasto, who claimed that of the nearly 10,000 catasto returns filed since the passage of the catasto law, about 8,600 had had to be assessed a tax on the basis of negotiations between the government and the individual taxpayers. "Et quod aliqui, sive vitio ingratitudinem erga patriam, sive alio respectu nedum ad compositionem se disponant, sed requisite recusant quicquid ad salutem patrie per compositionem velle subportare . . ." the legislature now established deadlines within which these negotiations had to be completed.

29. *Balie*, XXIII, f. 34v, December 1425. This provision was being enacted to avoid "danno non piccolo del comune di Firenze."

30. *PR*, CXIX, ff. 270v–271r, November 26, 1428.

31. *Zecca*, LXXIX, (*"Il fiorinaio"*), f. 107v: "Dicti domini [zecche] una cum pluribus mercatoribus dictarum artium, videlicet kalismale et cambii, desiderantes honorem et utilitatem dicte zeche tractare fecerunt infrascriptum rapportum, videlicet: Die VI mensis Decembris. Rapporto si fe a voi signori di zeccha ecc. Imprima, che le spese le quali non sono necessarie nel tempo che la zecha non lavora si levino, et le necessarie si paghino lira per soldo secondo l'entrate della detta zecha, et questa dichiaratione de'presenti signiori

With the exception of the institution of the catasto, all these measures could not be considered as having altered fundamentally the structure of communal taxing policies. The catasto itself, rather than being a new tax, was a more judicious way of distributing the old taxes. The remaining measures that have been mentioned in the preceding pages amount to a series of palliatives, one can say, meant to alleviate the most pressing demands made on the state and its governmental structures. No thorough effort was made during the 1420's to refashion the entire fiscal system of the city nor to abandon institutions that, first devised in the course of the thirteenth and early fourteenth centuries, had survived the crises of the Trecento. The innovations and amendments instituted in the course of the 1420's were considered temporary measures, to be abandoned at the conclusion of the war in favor of a return to old and tried institutions. This generally conservative and optimistic attitude of the Florentines could not obscure the constant and serious erosion of the prerogatives that, from the beginning of the Republic, the *grossi e possenti* had arrogated to themselves. Thus, the fiscal crisis of the 1420's and early 1430's had serious institutional and political repercussions which will be discussed later in this monograph.

ECONOMIC EFFECTS

Administrative rearrangements, modest savings in the operations of the government and of its bureaucracy, even the more

---

della zecha non s'intendendo tochare i pregi de'lavoratori della detta zecha. Secondo, che si metta ongni diligentia si può in fare che i mercatanti che mettano oro o ariento nella detta zecha sieno ispacciati il più presto si può non derogando per questo agli ordini della detta zecha che parlano sopra ciò. Tertio, che alla ventura si lasci fare del modo del mettere in zecha nel più et nel meno secondo il temporale."

equitable distribution of taxes did not improve the basic ability of the Florentine merchants and artisans to finance the large and expensive military operations undertaken by the state. Concerted measures were needed to augment the general economic prosperity of the city, to attract foreign capital so as to increase the liquidity of the city's economy, to prevent the flight of Florentine capital abroad, and to protect the city's businessmen from the keen foreign competition offered by Italian and Transalpine entrepreneurs. Many efforts were made during the 1420's to try to attain these goals.

There is little doubt that the first signs of a policy of economic protectionism can be detected in Florence during the last two or three decades of the fourteenth century. In 1393 crippling tariffs on foreign cloth sought to protect the weakening Florentine woolen industry,[32] while shortly thereafter efforts were made to confine the shipment of Florentine goods to boats controlled by the city's merchants.[33] The considerable efforts during the opening years of the fifteenth century to obtain the control of the Pisan port and, in 1421, the port of Livorno, and the speedy development of the Florentine fleet, no doubt reflect this Florentine desire to develop the city's resources to the point where its economy would be able to compete with those of the other major Italian powers.

It was during the 1420's, however, that this policy of protectionism was articulated most forcefully and effectively by the Florentine ruling class. Already in December 1422 the communal legislature had instructed the members of the newly created office of the consuls of the sea (*consoli del mare*) to un-

---

32. *Balie*, XIX, ff. 28v–29r, October 22, 1393.

33. Renato Piattoli, "Le leggi fiorentine sull'assicurazione nel medioevo," *ASI*, XC (1932), 205–257; Guido Bonolis, "Contributo alla storia delle assicurazioni in Firenze," *ASI*, ser. 5a, XXII (1898), 312–321.

dertake a survey of the Florentine economy and suggest what measures need be adopted in order to protect the local industries and introduce new ones to the Florentine domain: ". . . not only how to preserve and strengthen the occupations and trades already practiced in its territory, but also how to attract to it new ones, hitherto not practiced in it, believing that in so doing, infinite benefits would accrue to the polity." This was the express wish of the priors as stated in the preamble of the enactment, and no doubt it contains some rudimentary but essential mercantilistic overtones.[34] The survey, said the

34. *PR,* CXII, ff. 245v–246v, December 29, 1422: "Bonas artes prebere opes et queque exercitia sua consequi premia cognoscentes . . . et ob id opus non solum artes et exercitia in suo dominatu conservare et augere sed etiam novas seu usque in presens ibidem non factas ad suum territorium reducere cupientes cum ex hoc infinita fere comoda rei publice pervenire noscantur," the priors and colleges authorize the *ufficiali del mare* "diligenter examinare omnis et singulas artes et exercitia seu vulgare sumpto vocabulo manifacturas quascunquas que fuint et exercentur in civitate, comitatu, vel distrectu florentie, seu aliquo quocunquo loco in quo dictum comune florentie preheminentiam habet atque custodiam, et investigare, et perquirere quascunquas causas quibus tales artes, exercitia, et manifacture deficerent et quibus verisimiliter ipsa non solum manuteneri et conservari seu augeri possent, si qua augeri posse vel deficere reperirent et etiam examinare artes, exercitiis, et manufacturis et munisteria que in territorio comunis florentie non fuint et investigare et perquirere modos et formas et causas quibus ipsa reduci possent ad ipsum territorium vel in ipso fiant. Et providere et ordinare quicquid utile vel opportunum esse crediderint de jure vel de facto . . . et prout libere voluerint ad hoc maxime ut ipse artes, exercitia et manifacture et ministeria et quodcunque ex eis que in dicta civitate florentie et eius territorio fuint, augeantur et crescant, et qua alibi et non ibi exercentur ad ipsam civitatem et territorium comunis florentie et in ipsis reducantur et fiant etiam declarando ordinando et prohibendo in totum vel in partem res, mercantias, et bona que ad ipsam civitatem et territorium adduci, afferri, vel transire possint, et ad quos effectus et sub quibus observantiis, penis, formis, et cautelis, et quomodo inde extrahi possint, et ad quos effectus et sub quibus observantiis, penis, formis, et cautelis, et quomodo inde extrahi debeant. Et etiam illas res, mercantias et bona qua nullo modo ad ipsam civitatem et

priors, should be complete and should include all the *artes, exercitia, et manifactura, et munisteria* that were not already practiced in the Florentine domain, with specific recommendations for the "ways and means by which they can be introduced into its territory." Not much seems to have been done to fulfill these ambitious behests, and the next year, shortly after the outbreak of war against Milan, the priors renewed their instructions to the consuls of the sea, ordering those who would succeed them in office to proceed with the completion of the survey and attendant recommendations.[35] Unfortunately, the records of the deliberations of the *consoli del mare* contain no references to any discussions held by them on the subject, and one remains uncertain how seriously they might have addressed themselves to such a complex and ambitious task and whether their investigation produced any results.

One new industry whose development was encouraged consistently during the 1420's was silk production. Already by the spring of 1423 leaves of mulberry trees and silkworms (*folia moris et filugellos*) were allowed into the city duty-free in an effort to develop an industry that would be capable of compensating for the gradual decline of the woolen industry.[36] In the fall of 1426, when the regulations for the Florentine fleet were devised, one of the two items whose transport on the communal galleys was prohibited was foreign silk cloth.[37] Later in the decade, as the heavy tax burden tended to drive away from the city a great number of impoverished workers unable

---

territorium adduci possint, seu per ipsa conduci vel transferri directe vel indirecte."

35. *PR*, CXIII, ff. 195r–v, November 27, 1423.

36. *PR*, CXIII, ff. 10r–v, April 29, 1423.

37. *Consoli del Mare*, III, ff. 20r–21v, October 3, 1426.

to pay their taxes and unwilling to end up in prison for their poverty, a special provision was enacted, encouraging any Florentine silk worker who had fled the city because of his tax debts to return. Special concessions were given these workers, and they were offered the chance to pay only one sixth of their debts to the state *ad perdendum*.[38] With the exception of somewhat similar provisions for agricultural workers, no other segment of society — neither artisans nor entrepreneurs — was granted such privileges during those years. Related to the introduction and growth of the silk industry in Florence during the 1420's was the development of the *battiloro* (beaters of gold) craft, which added a greater measure of strength and competitiveness to the Florentine silks in the international market.[39]

Aside from the development of the silk industry, another potentially important economic initiative undertaken in the 1420's was the interest shown by Florentine entrepreneurs who controlled the city's government in developing a strong fleet able to compete with those of Venice and Genoa. Michael Mallett, author of a recent monograph on the history of the Florentine galleys, has concluded that the 1420's, until the eruption of the Lucchese war in 1429, were some of the most active years of Florentine maritime involvement.[40] With galleys plying the Mediterranean to the Levant, and embassies dispatched to secure commercial concessions in Alexandria, Rhodes, and Constantinople, the Florentines made a serious and reasonably succesful bid for their share of the lucrative

38. *PR*, CXX, ff. 303v–304v, August 26, 1429: "tintor serici vel sete, seu pictor drapporum vel alius quicunque laborans florentia de dicta arte seu-Esercitio serici vel sete."

39. Scipione Ammirato, *Istorie fiorentine,* (Florence, 1647), II, 999.

40. Michael Mallett, *The Florentine Galleys in the Fifteenth Century* (Oxford: Oxford University Press, 1967), p. 82.

Mediterranean trade. Similar efforts were expended in developing the maritime traffic to England and Flanders, while, at the same time, important concessions in the form of lower gabelle rates were being offered to Florentine merchants willing to introduce their Levantine or Transalpine merchandise to Italy through the port of Pisa.[41]

Coupled with these early mercantilistic efforts, which were devised to develop an economy dependent as much as possible on the local resources of the city and its domain by preventing the flight of valuable Florentine capital abroad and making possible the introduction of foreign capital in the city, Florentine politicians, beginning in the early 1420's, sought to strengthen the intrinsic value of the Florentine currency so as to place their merchants in an even more competitive position in the international markets. Surely, whatever success could be expected in the campaign to corner a share of an attractive market controlled up till then exclusively by the Venetians, Genoese, and Catalans depended almost entirely on the confidence that the Florentine currency could inspire among the Levantine businessmen with whom the Latin traders negotiated. The Florentine policymakers were keenly aware of this problem. In the diary he kept during his embassy to the Egyptian Sultan, Felice Brancacci relates with relish the many tests to which the Florentine currency was subjected by his hosts. The final and crucial part of the testing took place when, having negotiated the articles of a commercial pact between the Sultan and the Florentine government, the Arabs, before signing the document, insisted on weighing 100 Venetian ducats against 100 florins. "Having weighed them numerous times," said Bran-

41. *PR*, CXX, ff. 503v–504r, February 25, 1429/30.

cacci, "it seemed to them that the florins made a good showing." [42]

When one considers the importance of a strong and respected currency, it is not surprising that the Florentine government took steps during the 1420's to strengthen the florin and improve its intrinsic value. In May 1422 a new gold florin was minted, 6.67 percent more valuable than the old.[43] Exactly ten years later, in May 1432, yet another florin was ordered minted, itself larger and more valuable than that of 1422,[44] so that contemporary Florentines could still boast of having the strongest and most sought-after currency in Europe.[45] The increased value of the florin and the loss of substantial Florentine capital abroad, which was a direct outcome of the city's military involvements, caused the rapid devaluation of the silver currency. As already noted in chapter 1, the "petty currency" had succeeded in maintaining much of its value during the prosperous and more stable decade of the 1410's. Soon after the eruption

42. "Diario di Felice Brancacci," ed. Dante Castellacci, *ASI,* ser. 4, VIII (1881), 175: "E pesato più volte, parve loro ch'e' fiorini rispondesson bene." See also his comments on page 170.

43. *PR,* CXII, f. 17v, May 6, 1422.

44. *PR,* CXXIII, ff. 87r–88r, May 17, 1432; also CXXIV, f. 67v, June 10, 1433: "E fiorini d'oro larghi del conio del comune di Firenze e ducati vinitiani a peso pisano vaglino a ragione di fiorini otto, soldi quindici a oro per centinaio meglio, che viene l'uno soldo uno, danari nove a oro meglio che'l fiorino corrente di sugello vecchio. E ch'e fiorini di camera a peso sanese vaglino meglio a ragione di fiorini sei, soldi cinque a oro per centinaio, che viene l'uno soldo uno danari tre a oro meglio che'l fiorino di sugello vecchio. Gl'altri fiorini nuovi et di camera che sono in sugello presente si restino et spendano nella forma et modo si sono al presente."

45. Biblioteca Nazionale Centrale di Firenze, *Fondo magliabechiano,* lot XI, vol. 119, f. 3r: "Fiorini di Firenze sono meglio perchè sono di carati 24, lo 1/8 di soldi 2 affiorini, che è meglio l'oro fine che l'atro la oncia s. 0, d. 3 affiorino."

of the war in 1423, but particularly after the culmination of the crisis in 1425/26, the exchange rate between silver and gold began fluctuating rapidly, surpassing for the first time in 1429 the rate of 83 silver sous to the florin, and by 1431 reaching the high point of 83 sous, 2 deniers.[46] At this point, the continuous cameral records of the exchange rates between silver and gold cease, but one suspects that this trend persisted well into the 1430's. In order to avert a feeling of revolutionary discontent among the urban workers, who were customarily paid in silver coinage and who obviously suffered most from this continual devaluation of the silver currency, the government ordered in 1431 the minting of new silver coins to the total value of 5,000 florins. Its hope was, of course, that this step would arrest the further deterioration of the silver currency.[47]

In the preceding pages we have been concerned with providing an answer, indirect and fragmented though it has been, to the question posed by Gregorio Dati in his *Istoria di Firenze:* Where would the city find the treasure with which to finance its wars? The measures and policies examined up to this point dealt only indirectly with Dati's query: Administrative reorganization in a society so suspicious of political innovation is significant for reflecting the extent to which the patience and imagination of the Florentines were being tried during those years, but it is clear that the additional income produced could amount only to a small fraction of the disproportionately high military budget of the 1420's. The steps taken to strengthen the foundations of the Florentine economy could, of course,

46. 1424: 81 sous, 1 4/5 deniers. 1425: 80 sous, 9 4/5 deniers. 1426: 81 sous, 8 2/5 deniers. 1427: 82 sous, 6 6/15 deniers. 1428: 82 sous, 11 7/10 deniers. 1429: 83 sous, 1 1/10 deniers. 1430: 82 sous, 11 deniers. 1431: 83 sous, 2 deniers. Consult Appendix D.

47. *PR,* CXXII, ff. 200v–201r, September 26, 1431.

have increased the treasure of the city, but only slowly, after the new industries introduced had been given a chance to develop and attract the skilled labor needed to render them competitive in the international markets, and after the new trade routes had been properly and efficiently exploited. But Dati's imagination had touched upon a more immediate and pressing issue. He had asked about the availability of gold, or as we would put it today, of hard cash. The needs of the Commune escalated so rapidly during the 1420's that its politicians could not afford to wait until the more protectionist economic policies gradually devised and applied during the third decade of the Quattrocento could bear fruit. The mercenaries were pressing their demands, knocking at the Florentine door, as it were, and the city had to respond immediately. Delays could have resulted in a disaster, and even promises were not worth much in the coldly calculating world of the Italian mercenaries. The burning issue of the decade, then, was cash — how to direct it into the state coffers, and more essential, how to attract it into the city.

Gregorio Dati was not alone among his contemporaries in his appreciation of this issue. Deliberations and legislative enactments attest to its immediacy and relevance in the minds of all Florentine statesmen of the 1420's. The state, of course, could try to encourage its citizens to turn over to the mint (*zeccha*) their precious metals, so that these could be converted into currency. Such a step was taken in February 1425/26, when particular inducements in the form of credits were offered to anyone turning in silver (*argento lavorato*), which would then be converted into coins.[48] A similar measure of May 1432 provided that those depositing any silver items in the mint could

48. *PR*, CXV, ff. 300v–301r, February 27, 1425/26.

claim in their catasto returns a deduction equal to the value of the silver deposited.[49] Several speakers during those years proposed in the communal councils that the city seek to import gold and silver from abroad, so that it might increase its ability to hire large numbers of mercenaries.[50]

Equally important was the problem of preventing gold and silver from leaving the Florentine territory. Many measures were taken to that effect, ranging from what we may consider to be serious fiscal policies to somewhat peculiar and futile attempts to control the situation. An enactment in June 1428, for example, claimed that many Florentine citizens were taking their therapeutic baths in locations outside the Florentine territory and in the process spending abroad money that should have remained at home; it then prohibited the use of such baths. In any case, suggested the legislators, *balnearum et aquarum virtutes indictione comunis Florentine existentium . . . ut eorum vigor et bonitas per experientiam cognoscantur.*[51] Even more interesting is a provision dealing with one of the most significant legislative enactments with intellectual and pedagogic overtones instituted in the history of Florence. In the spring of 1428/29, in an attempt to revive the local *Studio* whose decline was due in no small measure to the savings imposed on the Florentine government by the balia of 1425, it was decided to turn over to the *Studio* 1.25 percent of all revenues collected from the imposition of forced loans. Thus, it was hoped that a large number of competent professors would be attracted to the city and that its reputation would be established

49. *PR*, CXXIII, f. 93v, May 27, 1432: "Numerata pecunia maiorem copiam si infrascripta fiant habere credentur. . . ."

50. Pellegrini, P. CVIII–CVIIII (from *Consulte e Pratiche*, LI, f. 157r, May 13, 1431): "Pro quarterio S. Crucis, Alamannus de Salviati [dixit quod] deputentur de civibus valentibus pro providendo ut habeantur pecunie aut aurum vel argentum, etiam de extra territorio nostris."

51. *PR*, CXIX, ff. 91v–92r, June 21, 1428.

in this realm as well. But how could the Florentines allow themselves the luxury of spending money for an educational institution at a time when they could barely raise sufficient revenue with which to pay their mercenaries? The preamble of the act that recreated the *Studio* provides an interesting answer: Because many young men, by necessity, studied in foreign academies and universities, much Florentine money that could otherwise be spent in the city was dispersed abroad. Such a situation could not be allowed to continue, all the more so, because there were about two hundred and fifty such local scholars abroad, spending a total of approximately 5,000 florins per year. It seemed much wiser to keep the money at home, by creating the *casa della sapientia,* which would have the additional merit of attracting foreign scholars and their money to the city. Thus, *tanto sia il fructo delli studi tanto ne segua ornamento della città, tanta commodità della repubblica, tanta conservatione della pecunia civile,* the re-creation and strengthening of the *Studio* was ordered.[52]

These two provisions, though on the surface they might seem rather quaint and a little bizarre, were meant to conserve the resources of the city. Another series of measures instituted during the 1420's and early 1430's was directed toward the same end. In times of peace it was customary to impose severe restrictions on the dealings that private citizens could have with the mercenaries in the city's hire. Above all, the Florentine authorities feared the creation of powerful pressure groups, composed of influential citizens with close relations to the condottieri, who would then be able to manipulate and direct the course of the communal policy. One of the standard restrictions customarily imposed on Florentine citizens was concerned with

52. *PR,* CXX, ff. 41v–42v, March 17, 1428/29: "Et pur alchuni alli strani studii sono mandati e di necessità chelle vostre pecunie per l'altrui terre si spargano, le quali nella vostra città si potrebbono legiermente ritenere. . . ."

the following practice: Often a mercenary, needing money and unable to wait until his pay day, would receive a sum of cash from a local banker, selling to him his future claims against the government, which would now be assumed by the Florentine entrepreneur. Such practices often were very lucrative to bankers and pawnbrokers, who customarily purchased the mercenaries' credits for a fraction of their face value and then exerted pressure on the communal government for their collection. In January 1414/15 citizens speculating in mercenaries' credits were barred from sitting in the priorate or holding any major communal office.[53] In 1424, however, one year after the eruption of the war against Milan, it was discovered that strict adherence to the law of 1414/15 resulted in the exportation of large sums of Florentine capital abroad, by mercenaries serving outside the Florentine domain, possibly in enemy territory. A provision passed in October 1424 therefore rescinded the ban against such transactions. The justification offered for this act of abrogation is interesting: Such a ban, states the enactment, is a useful device in ordinary times, when the city enjoys the fruits of peace, for it directs citizens toward "better dealings" (*meliora exercitia*) than meddling in the affairs of soldiers and adventurers. In periods of war, however, the ban inflicts great damage on the city, for cash (*pecunia numerata*) "is transported to foreign lands, and the city is emptied of its gold." What is more, Florentine citizens, if given a chance to use productively these sums of money, would contribute many useful results to the city, for the mercenaries "whose nature and character is well known, either take their money outside the city, or gamble with it, or they consume it in other ways," with no long-term profit to the economy of the community.[54]

53. *PR*, CIV, ff. 51v–52r, January 30, 1414/15.
54. *PR*, CXIV, f. 30v, October 4, 1424: "Et qualiter tempore ordinario, vi-

A similar provision, permitting Florentine citizens to purchase the credits of the city's mercenaries, was enacted in 1431,
and once again the same justification was offered for its enactment, although in some respects it is even more explicit than
the one offered in 1424: If the law were not enacted, stated the
communal scribe, "public funds would be sent to other places,
from which fact would follow a reduction in the amount of gold
and silver available in the city; if, however, this ban was revoked
during periods of war, numerous advantages to the public weal
and to private citizens would follow." [55] Only a short time before the promulgation of this measure the government had exerted an effort to regulate the substantial profits that private
citizens were reaping from their dealings with the mercenaries,
by declaring that the state would redeem these credits purchased
by private citizens not for their face value but rather for the
purchase value and an annual interest at the rate of 12 percent.[56]
It is interesting that this restriction of the potential profits that

delicet eo quo guerra aliqua non vigeret inter prefatum comune et alium
quecunque, dicte leges perutiles iudicantur, tum quia cives ad meliora exercitia dirigantur, tum quia offensio publica levius esse potest, sed tempore
guerrarum, prout in presenti, dicte leges sine gravissimo incommodo atque
rei publicae danno servari nequeunt cum comune cum pecunia numerata
dumtaxat qua ad forinsecas partes transportatur sua cogitur negotia guber-
nare et civitas auro vacuatur, et non mercantiis de quibus artifices lucrantur.
Et etiam quia persepe stipendiarii qui eiusmodi sunt nature et conditionis
cuius scitur, pecuniam aut recondunt, aut ludo vel alio modo consumunt, et
in eam rem qua egent non convertunt. . . ."

55. *PR*, CXXII, f. 51r, May 29, 1431: "Et quod tempore pacis leges pre-
dicte utiles sunt, ut ad honesta exercitia cives se dedunt, sed tempore belli
inutiles esse prohibentur presertim cum ad aliena loca pecunia publica pro
stipendiis debita mittatur, ex quo sequitur auri, argenti que signati maxima
in civitate diminutio, sed si belli tempore revocentur pro pecuniis res eis
necessarias recipiunt, et civitas habundet pecuniis, et tam publicae quam
privatim emolumenta proveniunt."

56. *PR*, CXIX, ff. 61r–v, June 6, 1428.

could be reaped by Florenine entrepreneurs in their transactions with the mercenaries and with the state was not repeated in the law of 1431, possibly indicating that by the early years of the 1430's the state had to offer its citizens all possible inducements in order to encourage them to cooperate in preventing the flight of capital from the city.

Even more significant than the lifting of the ban against negotiating with mercenaries was a series of measures enacted in the mid- and late 1420's, which created the *Monte delle doti,* universally acknowledged by contemporaries and later commentators as being one of the most significant institutions created in Quattrocento Florence. At a time when the availability of a dowry commensurate to one's social standing was an absolute necessity for marrying off one's daughter, the rising costs of dowries presented serious problems to many of the city's important families. What the state offered to do in the winter of 1424/25 was to guarantee out of its own funds a dowry to every Florentine maiden ready to marry.[57] The system worked as follows: All Florentine fathers were offered an opportunity to deposit with the officials of the Monte a certain sum for each of their children, male or female. The deposit could be made either in cash, which the city officials preferred, or in regular Monte credits (*Monte Comune, Monte de'cinque interi,* etc.) converted according to a predetermined rate. The deposit could be left to mature for periods ranging from five to fifteen years, at which time, if the young man or woman were still alive, he or she could receive the original capital and accumulated com-

57. Gregorio Dati, *Istoria di Firenze,* ed. Luigi Pratesi (Norcia; Tipografia Tonti, 1904), p. 154; L. F. Marks, "The Financial Oligarchy in Florence Under Lorenzo," in *Italian Renaissance Studies,* ed. E. F. Jacob (London: Faber and Faber, 1960), p. 128; Marvin B. Becker, *Florence in Transition* (Baltimore: Johns Hopkins University Press, 1968), II, 236–237.

pound interest. Thus, thanks to the intercession of the city, every young lady of the city could now be promised a dowry, while young men could use this trust fund when they were ready to enter business on their own.[58] If the claimant died before the date of maturity of the deposit, the state and the heirs of the deceased then divided the accumulated sum.

58. *PR*, CXIV, ff. 143r–v, February 23, 1424/25, establishing the *Monte delle doti* for women. The reason for its establishment, according to the *preamble* of the law, was the desire of the city's governors to "debilitatem sexus feminarum adiuvare . . . privilegiis et favoribus infrascriptis ut constituta dote etiam in parva summa secure sint ad honestum et laudabilem vite statum conduci. . . ." The law establishing the *Monte masculorum* is on folios 156r–157r of this same *filza*. In this general context one should also note the creation of trust funds for widows (*PR*, CXIII, f. 229v, December 13, 1423): "Item quod quilibet mulier vidua habilis secundum ordinamenta comunis florentie ad acquirendum de creditis montium dicti comunis possit et sibi liceat suam pecuniam numerata quam voluerit converti facere in diminutionem creditorum montium dicti comunis ad utilitatem et comodum comunis florentie dare et numerare officialibus montis dicti comunis, seu cui datur pecunia pupillorum de quibus infra dicetur. Et scribi debeat talis mulier creditrix dicti comunis in libris et registris dictorum montium in illis et pro illis quantitatibus que realiter de sua expense et converse fuissent in diminutionem predictam eo modo et forma et prout per pupillos observatur. Et eidem mulieri solvi et dari possit et debeat per camerario monti, vel officium representantem pro dono, provisione, et interesse ad rationem florenorum quinque pro quolibet centinario florenorum ipsarum quantitatum pro anno et ad rationem anni, et prout pro pupillis et adultis commissis gubernationi et sub tutela et cura officialibus pupillorum et adultorum comunis florentie de pecunia numerata eorundem qua convertitur in diminutionem creditorum montium dicti comunis fieri consuevit et observatur. Et hoc duret dumtaxat ad voluntatem ipsius vidue seu usque quo vidua steterit seu vixerit et non ultra, quibus casibus evenientibus vel quocunque ex eis et in eventum cuiscunque ex eis dicti camerarii montis seu officium representans eidem mulieri vel eius procuratori seu heredi vel successori legiptimo debeant restituere dictas quantitates in quibus ut dictum est descripta fuerit creditrix. . . . Idem quod statum cessanto viduvate aut per transitum ad secunda vota aut per mortem vel alio quoquo modo, ex tunc pro tali credito nullum interesse vel donum dari aut solvi possit pro tempore et respectu temporis ex tunc secuturi quoquo modo."

There is no question but that the underlying motive and the ultimate aim of the Florentine legislators was to protect the *debilitatem sexus feminarum* of their city and to facilitate the careers of their young men. In this respect the state, to repeat Marvin Becker's recent and quite convincing thesis, became the arbiter of the lives of countless young men and women, and the *Monte delle doti* became the very fulcrum of Florentine political and social life. For the purposes of this monograph, however, it is important to understand the reasons that underlay this decision of the Florentine lawmakers in the middle years of the 1420's. In fact, the short-term effect of this measure was to attract to the state coffers much valuable cash that could be used to fight the wars against Milan. Even if the deposits were not made in cash, but in the form of converted Monte credits of various types, the effect was to reduce the immediate indebtedness of the Commune, thus diminishing the carrying charges of the funded public debt. It is significant, of course, that the *Monte delle doti* was enacted in February 1424/25, at the very moment when the first symptoms of the communal fiscal crisis began making themselves felt. Its institution is interesting for the additional reason that it reveals so great an awareness of the problem in the minds of the Florentines that they sought to resolve it by instituting such a novel and unprecedented measure. The fate of the *Monte delle doti* during the first decade of its life also reveals the increasing tensions and imbalances that were gradually becoming apparent in the communal economy. The bill enacted in 1424/25 provided that a sum of 100 florins left on deposit for fifteen years would be redeemed for a sum of 500 florins at its maturity.[59] By 1428, when the short-

59. *PR*, CXIV, f. 143r, February 23, 1424/25: "Quod si quantitas data fuerit pro dotte et sub nomine filie vel puelle pro quindecim annis quod elapsis ipsis quindecim annis officiales et camerarii montis vel exercens pro

age of cash had become more acute, the state was promising a higher rate of return: 75 florins deposited for fifteen years now matured into 500 florins,[60] while by 1433 the initial deposit, for a sum maturing after a period of fifteen years into 500 florins, was further reduced to 60 florins.[61] Thus, within less than a decade the promised rate of return on deposits in the *Monte delle doti* was nearly doubled, an additional indication that the principal problem of the 1420's and early 1430's was that of attracting cash into the state coffers so that the city's mercenaries might be paid promptly and in full. Even though in fiscal terms the effects of this policy tended to create problems for the future, in its immediate consequences it helped considerably to alleviate the shortage of cash and to ensure the viability of the state.

Yet another course that could be followed by the Florentine government in order to attract more capital into the city and have it deposited directly into the state coffers was to allow for-

---

eis teneantur et debeant etiam sine alia apodixa, licentia, stantiamento subscriptione, vel actu, et sine alia solemnitate vel substantialitate servanda de quacunque pecunia sui camerariatus etiam deputata vel deputanda tam pro solutione interesse cuiscunque montis, quam etiam pro diminutione vere sortis cuiuscunque crediti montis restituere, dare, numerare, atque solvere pro dote talis puelle seu filie marito seu viro ipsius puelle seu filie seu cui idem vir voluerit pro restitutione quantitatis solute pro dote et usque in quantitatem receptam pro dote talis puelle vel filie et solutionem facere dumtaxat statim postquam vir consumaverit matrimonium et non ante, quincuplum, videlicet pro florenis centum datis ut supra pro quindecim annis florenos quingentos auri et non plures. . . . Et si datio facta fuerit pro septem annis et sex mensibus quod elapso dicto tempore . . . debeant . . . restituere . . . duplum cum dimidio quantitatis date, videlicet pro quibuslibet florenis centum florenos ducentos quinquaginta auri."

60. *PR,* CXIX, f. 300r, December 20, 1428.

61. *Balie,* XXIV, ff. 49v–50v, November 10, 1433, and *PR,* CXXIV, ff. 27v–29v, April 24, 1433. After December 1433 every sixty florins deposited were registered as sixty-five (*PR,* CXXIII, ff. 297v–298r).

eigners to invest their money in the communal Monte. The history of the many communal public debts established in Italy starting with the early years of the fourteenth century has received insufficient attention by students of economic history. Nevertheless, it seems clear enough that these public debts, particularly in northern and central Italy, served as a source of investment for various noble and landholding families, which were not interested in engaging in any kind of entrepreneurial activities: Genoese aristocrats, members of northern and central Italian families of condottieri, foreign mercenaries, ecclesiastical prelates, and the like considered with good reason that investments in the Genoese, Venetian, or Florentine public debts were reasonably safe and lucrative, since the governments of these cities, for fear of retaliations, promptly disbursed the interest on investments made by such important clients. The communal governments, on the other hand, sought to secure the friendship of various lords, lay or ecclesiastical, by allowing them to invest in their public debts, a policy that could not only result in diplomatic advantages but also one that made available in the city quantities of gold, which was always in short supply during those decades.[62] The Florentine Monte had attracted sporadic foreign investments during the second half of the fourteenth century, but the policy of the communal statesmen seems to have been somewhat eclectic, for not many foreigners' names appear in the few registers of the Monte that are currently available for consultation.

62. On the investments of the Genoese family Adorno in the Florentine Monte, see John Day's article, "I conti privati della famiglia Adorno (1401–1408), *Miscellanea di storia ligure,*" I (1958), pp. 43–120. See also Gino Luzzatto, *Il debito pubblico della repubblica di Venezia* (Milan; Istituto editoriale cisalpino, 1963), and Heinrich Sieveking, *Genuenser Finanzwesen mit besonderer Berücksichtigung der casa S. Giorgio* (Freiburg, 1898–1899).

The situation, however, was altered in the 1420's, when the acute cash shortage brought about by the exorbitant military expenditures caused the flight of much Florentine capital out of the city. One easy and productive way to balance this loss would have been for the Commune to encourage more foreigners to deposit their cash with the Florentine state. Although it does not seem that an actual legislative enactment was passed fostering this policy, one observes the names of numerous foreigners being granted special permission by the Signory and the legislature to become investors in the Monte. And as the decade progressed, and the crisis became more acute, the numbers of such petitions increased considerably, while concurrently the Florentines, competing as they were in the tight Italian money market of those times, were forced to offer these foreign investors much higher returns for their deposits. Moreover, as the demands of the mercenaries also became higher, the Commune often was forced to pay their salaries in Monte credits, for which they were offered interest rates 50 to 100 percent higher than those offered to regular citizen investors.

In the decade separating the conclusion of the war against Naples and the outbreak of hostilities against Milan in 1423 the Florentines had compensated mercenaries in their service with Monte credits only twice. Interestingly, the interest rate offered them for their credits was identical with that offered citizens, a fact which probably indicates that the arrangement was basically political in nature and was not dictated by financial shortages in the city.[63] By the mid-1420's, however, the Commune was seeking to pay large portions of mercenaries'

63. *PR*, CVIII, ff. 22v–24v, April 21, 1418, in which Braccio de'Forte-bracci was inscribed as creditor of the Monte for 18,000 florins, a sum equal to his back wages; and CXII, ff. 184v–186v, November 21, 1422, when Count Guidantonio of Urbino was made a Monte creditor for 13,195 florins.

salaries with the credits of the public debt. The members of the de'Flisco or Fieschi, a large and enterprising family of Genoese lords and condottieri serving Florence, were paid in such "paper currency" twice in the late years of the decade,[64] while in early 1429 Marchionne Estense, lord of Ferrara and a Florentine mercenary, was given a credit of 60,000 florins in the *Monte Comune* for back wages amounting to 30,000 florins, thus receiving actual interest of 7.5 percent on his investment, twice that received by citizens.[65] Three years later, for yet another sum of money owed him, Marchionne Estense received a Monte credit equal in value to twice his overdue wages,[66] while other important mercenaries also received the same kind of payment, among them both Niccolò da Tolentino and Antonio Alberigo.[67] The advantages of adopting such a policy vis-à-vis the mercenaries was not lost on Florentine statesmen, who often decreed that sums already allocated for the payment of mercenaries and subsequently not expended because payment was made in Monte credits should be used to reduce the public indebtedness by repurchasing the credits of Florentine citizens.[68]

Even more important advantages could be reaped by the

64. *PR*, CXVII, ff. 31r–33r, May 5, 1427, and CXIX, ff. 144v–145r, July 7, 1428, both dealing with Giovanni di Luigi da Pontremoli de'Flisco, CXIX, ff. 146r–148v, July 7, 1428, for Niccolao di Antonio de'Flisco; also CXXII, ff. 18v–19r, April 11, 1431.

65. *PR*, CXX, ff. 66r–70r, March 23, 1428/29.

66. *PR*, CXXIII, ff. 290v–294v, December 1, 1432. His back wages amounted to 20,000 florins. His Monte credit was set at 40,000 florins.

67. *DSSp Aut.*, XXII, ff. 111v–112r, July 17, 1432, for Niccolò da Tolentino; *PR*, CXXIV, ff. 131r–133v, July 22, 1433, for Antonio Alberigo. Other examples: *PR*, CXXIII, ff. 168v–170r, August 5, 1432, for Jacopo Accatabriga; CXXIV, ff. 32v–35r, April 24, 1433, for Giovanni di Leonardo Cipolla de Orbinga, for whom a trust fund was established, with payments to be made after his death to his widow and children.

68. For example, see the provision regarding Niccolò da Tolentino in note 67.

Commune by encouraging foreigners to send to the city their cash for deposit in the Monte. A law of 1415 outlined the procedure to be followed upon receiving requests of foreigners for permission to make deposits in the Monte. The petitioner, according to that law, was required to deposit 10 percent of the sum he wished to invest with the officials of the Monte, and only then could the legislative chambers, which were entrusted with ultimate jurisdiction over this matter, vote on the issue.[69] Shortly thereafter, Jacopo Appiano, lord of Piombino, was allowed to deposit a sum not exceeding 12,000 florins in the Monte, for which he was promised a rate of return equivalent to that paid to the citizens of the state.[70] Appiano was the last foreigner allowed to invest in the Monte until five years later, when Tommaso di Campofregoso, Doge of Genoa and lord of Livorno, received a portion of the payment for his sale of Livorno to Florence in the form of Monte credits.[71] A short time later, Francesco Carmagnola, the famous Milanese mercenary who was soon to pass into Venetian service, was allowed to invest up to 30,000 florins on condition that the deposit not be withdrawn before five years. The promised rate of return was 4 percent per annum, only slightly more than that received by the citizens of Florence.[72] Once more before the eruption of the hostilities with Milan, a foreigner was permitted to invest in the Monte, but this was the rather special case of Tommaso di Campofregoso, who was still awaiting the full payment for his

69. *PR*, CV, ff. 266r–267v, December 30, 1415.

70. *PR*, CVI, ff. 142r–143r, September 9, 1416.

71. The price of Livorno was 100,000 florins, of which Florence was to pay 90,000 florins in cash and the remaining 10,000 florins with 16,500 florins of *Monte Comune* credits. *PR*, CXI, ff. 31r–35r, May 28, 1421, and ff. 197r–198r, November 28, 1421.

72. *PR*, CXI, ff. 52v–54r, June 23, 1421. A subsequent provision, *PR*, CXIII, f. 227r, reveals that he actually deposited only 15,000 florins.

sale of Livorno to Florence and who was invited to deposit a sum of no more than 35,000 florins, for which he would be paid interest of 3.75 percent on a face value of 57,750 florins. In essence, then, he was promised interest on 165 florins for every 100 florins that he deposited. The important Genoese investor, however, could not deposit more than 10,000 florins at a time but was required to schedule his deposits according to the instructions of the Monte officials, "so that by such a division a greater use and comfort may accrue to the Commune of Florence." This statement reveals that the Florentines were well aware of the economic advantages that could be reaped by such deposits, and in the case of Campofregoso's investment they specified how the Monte officials were to spend the money: 20,000 florins were to be used for the city's military budget, while the remaining 15,000 florins should be assigned to the officials charged with amortizing the communal debt.[73]

With the outbreak of war the number of petitions submitted to the Signory by foreigners for permission to invest in the Florentine Monte increased substantially, reflecting the active effort of the city's government to solicit these deposits. While in the entire decade 1413–1423 no more than five such permissions had been granted, from 1423 through 1433 the number increased to thirty-five, often involving very respectable sums. Table 10 illustrates this trend, making it clear that by the early 1430's the Florentine budget was strengthened substantially by these deposits.

What is evident from this table is that the number of authori-

73. *PR*, CXII, ff. 89v–91r, July 31, 1422: ". . . ut ex tali divisione maior commoditas et utilitas comunis florentie pervenire posse." See also *PR*, CXIII, ff. 10v–11v, April 29, 1423, when Tommaso and his brothers were granted Florentine citizenship and were allowed to pay their forced loans at special rates.

Table 10. Foreign investments in the Florentine Monte (values expressed in florins rounded off to nearest complete figure. Silver currencies converted to gold at current exchange rates, for which consult Appendix D).

Year	Number of Petitions	Actual Value	Face Value
1423	3	5,000	8,250[a]
1424	0	0	0
1425	1	10,000	14,500[a]
1426	1	20,000	20,000[b]
1427	3	120,000	240,000[a]
1428	0	0	0
1429	2	16,000	16,000[a]
1430	0	0	0
1431	2	14,000	24,000[a]
1432	7	63,340	82,850[a]
1433	16	57,610	109,840[a]

Sources: 1423: *PR*, CXIII, ff. 230v, 227r. 1425: *PR*, CXV, ff. 34v–38r. 1426: *PR*, CXVI, ff. 198v–201r. 1427: *PR*, CXVII, ff. 268r–270r, 270v–272r, 272v–274v. 1429: *PR*, CXX, ff. 30v–33r, 279r–282r. 1431: *PR*, CXXI, ff. 134v–135v, 149v–152r. 1432: *PR*, CXXII, ff. 310v–311r, 383v–385v; CXXIII, ff. 226r–228v. *DSSp Aut.*, XXII, ff. 129v, 162r, 162v–163r; XXIII, ff. 6v–7r. 1433: *PR*, CXXIV, ff. 187v–189v. *Balie*, XXIV, ff. 27v–28v. *DSSp Aut.*, XXII, ff. 168v–169r; XXIII, ff. 4v–5r, 6r–6v, 14r, 14v, 20r–v, 28v–29r, 35r–v, 39v–40r, 42r–v, 54r–v, 76v.

[a] Interest rate promised: 3 percent of face value.
[b] Interest rate promised: 10 percent of face value.

zations to foreigners increased considerably during the last two years of the war, and that the gap between the actual value invested and the amount on which interest was paid became much more noticeable, a rather clear indication that the communal efforts to solicit such deposits could bear fruit only if the promised rate of return was consistently high. Among the Commune's clients were several lords and condottieri of central Italy and also important personages of those years, like

Pope Martin V's nephews, Antonio Colonna, Prince of Salerno, and his brothers, who in 1427 were allowed to deposit 100,000 florins and receive a return of 6 percent per annum; and the councillor of the French crown Jean Bellevue (Giovanni di Carardo Bellevisis), who in 1426 was invited to deposit 20,000 florins in the Monte, for which he would receive 5 percent per year or, in case he settled in the city *familiariter,* 1 percent more.

One should emphasize at this point that the arrangements with these foreign lords should not be viewed solely from the perspective of the city's financial needs. As already indicated, the advantages were reciprocal to Florence and her investors, and in most cases permission to invest in the Monte could be considered as a useful diplomatic tool in the hands of the Florentine statesmen and diplomats. Alliances and friendships could be fortified, hurt feelings placated, good intentions proved by allowing certain foreigners to invest in the Monte, and the Florentine lawmakers were well aware of these aspects. Often citizenship was conferred on those to whom permission was granted to invest in the Monte, as was the case with Jean Bellevue; Martin V's nephews; two of the Pope's councillors; members of the Malaspina family who were mercenaries in the hire of Florence; the chancellor of the marquis Este of Ferrara; and many others. Our knowledge of the juridical and political meanings of late medieval citizenship is so vague that one is not quite certain what to make of the association between permission to invest in the public debt and bestowal of Florentine citizenship. On the surface, it would seem that these were simply honorific gestures, meant to consolidate even further the political ties binding Florence and some of her important allies.[74]

74. This suspicion is reinforced by a scribe's marginal notation on a scrapbook, in which there is a reference to foreign investors in the Monte. The scribe described them as *ficti cives. Monte delle graticole,* V, f. 138r.

The political and diplomatic advantages gained by the Commune by this procedure were important, but it is probably true that had the financial need not arisen, gradually reaching such extremely serious proportions, so many foreigners would not have been granted such advantageous terms for depositing their savings in the Monte. In the long run, the purely economic price that Florence paid for this policy was substantial, as the annual interest the city was obliged to pay for the deposits made by foreigners between 1423 and 1433 amounted to nearly 40,000 florins! The willingness of the Florentine government to disburse such a substantial sum at a time when the city's normal expenditures were already inflated is somewhat more easily understandable if it is viewed from the perspective of the immediate financial advantages accruing to the *Camera fiscale* and the Florentine economy in general. As the shortage of cash was the immediate issue, the preambles of provisions dealing with foreign investments in the Monte make the explicit connection between the request of the petitioner and the communal needs. The priors considered a proposal to allow one of their mercenaries to invest in the Monte "above all, so that the city may abound in gold and silver, and so that it may be more able to meet its needs." [75] The same language reappears in several of the other provisions dealing with the issue.[76] In 1428 the officials of the Monte had been instructed to accept the deposits of any foreigners, paying no more than 5 percent per annum, although the provision does not specify whether this interest was to be paid on the actual value invested or on some fictitious

75. *DSSp Aut.*, XXII, ff. 155r–v, October 20, 1432: "Maxime ut civitas magis habundet auro, argento que signato, et ut necessitatibus habilius provideri possit."

76. For another example, see *DSSp Aut.*, XXII, ff. 168r–169r, January 27, 1432/33: ". . . ut pecunia numerata maior copia in civitate remaneret, et maxime tempore belli. . . ."

sum agreed upon by the investor and the communal authorities. This privilege was to be granted to foreigners leaving their deposits for at least one year.[77] By the early 1430's the situation had deteriorated so rapidly that, in a provision unprecedented in the annals of Florentine history, the Monte officials were instructed to sell to foreigners Monte credits amounting to at most 300,000 florins. This sum, which in times of peace was nearly equal to the annual budget of the city, was to be used to amortize the communal debt to its citizens, thus releasing money usually assigned to the carrying charges of the Monte for the payment of mercenaries.[78] This provision was repeated once again by the balia of 1433, which exiled Cosimo de'Medici, and during its enforcement some 130,000 florins of foreign capital were attracted to the city.[79]

The various tables appearing in this monograph make it abundantly clear that the most acute time of crisis for the Florentine fisc was in the early 1430's. Although the first signs had already appeared as early as 1424/25, the combination of disasters in the military and diplomatic fields and the steady erosion of the financial bases of the Commune's policies produced visible psychological and nervous tensions in the Florentine society. The effort to convince foreigners of the wisdom of investing their money in the Florentine Monte (*et certe valor talis est, ut optimi redditus exinde percipiantur,* an official scribe wrote to Carmagnola in January 1431/32)[80] was only partly successful, and the communal leaders were forced to look else-

77. *PR*, CXIX, ff. 277r–v, November 22, 1428, and ff. 302r–v, December 20, 1428.

78. *PR*, CXXII, ff. 48r–v, May 29, 1431, and ff. 273r–v, November 17, 1431.

79. *Balie*, XXIV, ff. 62r–v, December 4, 1433.

80. Angelo Fabronio, "Adnotationes et monumenta," *Magni Cosmi medicei vita* (Pisa, 1789), pp. 64–65.

where for additional sources of capital. This is why, in June 1430, at the time of a plague that was adding to the troubles of the city, the Florentines, imitating the example of the subjects in the contado, enacted a law that for the first time admitted the Jews to the city. The logic explaining the adoption of this measure reveals many of the same arguments that the contadini and *distrittualles* had used in the 1390's and early 1400's, when petitioning the Florentine Signory for permission to admit the Jewish moneylenders to their own lands: *Ne pauperes Florentine urbis tam gravi fenore presertim hoc pestis tempore pessundentur, sed ut leviori onere cum necessitas eos impulerit rebus suis providere possint. . . .*[81] Thus, in a sense, the Florentines were now being paid in the same currency as their subjects had been. A consistent policy of financial bleeding had forced the contadini to rely partially on the resources that Jewish moneylenders could bring into their territories; and an equally consistent policy of reckless military involvement and expenditures had imposed the same necessity upon the Florentines. Once again moral precepts were becoming adjusted to the economic exigencies of the moment. Shortly after the enactment of the original measure the Signory set the maximum allowable rate of interest that Jewish moneylenders could charge in the city at 20 percent per annum (4 deniers per lira per month), a rate that seems suspiciously low in light of the interest charged by Florentine bankers for loans they advanced to the subject villages and communities of the city.[82] The effec-

81. *PR,* CXXI, ff. 15v–16r, June 12, 1430. See also the statement of Manettus Tucci Scambrilli in a communal deliberation in Pellegrini, p. CLII (from *Consulte e Pratiche,* LI, f. 180v, August 3, 1431): "Tollantur tasse a Judeis pro 5 annis, ut veniant ad prestantum hic; et ferrent multas pecunias."

82. *PR,* CXXI, ff. 80v–81r, November 14, 1430, and CXXII, ff. 49v–50r, May 29, 1431.

tiveness of this measure in introducing large quantities of capital into the city are rather difficult to measure, particularly because there seems to be no evidence that any Jews actually accepted the invitation to settle in the city. The first such moneylenders to offer their services in Florence arrived in 1437, well after the chronological limits of this study.[83]

83. Umberto Cassuto, *Gli ebrei a Firenze nell'età del Rinascimento* (Florence: Galletti e Cocci, 1918), pp. 20–21.

6

THE FISCAL CRISIS, 1431–1433

Legislation of the kind described in the previous two chapters — limiting the movements of Florentines and their capital; and abrogating old and venerable laws, such as those dealing with the relations between Florentines and mercenaries and banning foreigners from holding credits in the Monte — as well as the accommodation of moral principles to the financial needs of the Commune are clear indications that the Florentine economy of the 1420's and early 1430's was suffering from a potentially crippling lack of liquid capital. Already by 1425 there had been bankruptcies involving several banking firms, among which were those of Palla di Palla Strozzi, Niccolò d'Agnolo Serragli, Salamone di Carlo Strozzi, and others.[1] In no small measure these bankruptcies were a result of the inability of the *Dieci di balia* to repay these bankers for short-term

---

1. Biblioteca Nazionale Centrale di Firenze, *Conventi Soppressi,* C.4.895. *Cronica di Piero* Pietribuoni, f. 115r: "A tempo de'detti priori, del mese di Novembre et Dicembre 1425 fallì in Firenze: Giovanni di Matteo Corsini, banchiere di fiorini . . . ,

Messer Palla di messer Palla degli Strozzi ⎫ banchieri di fiorini . . . ,
Giovanni di Francesco dell'Orto ⎭

Bartolomeo di Tommaso d'Ugholino di Vieri ⎫ fondachai di fiorini . . . ,
Francesco di Ghuidetto di Jacopo Ghuidetti ⎭

Salamone di Carlo degli Strozzi ⎫ e compagni, banchieri di
Giovanni di Jacopo di Latino de'Pilli ⎭ fiorini . . . ,

Nicholò d'Agnolo Serragli ⎫ e compagni, banchieri di
Ghoro d'Antonio di ser Niccholò Serragli ⎭ fiorini . . . ,

Luigi d'Antonio di Pagholo Chovoni ⎫ e compagni, mercatanti di
. . . di Tommaso dell'Acierito ⎭ fiorini . . . .

See also Ugo Procacci, "Sulla cronologia delle opere di Masaccio e di Masolino," *Rivisto d'arte,* XXVIII (1953), 16, n. 29. For the case of Niccolò de'Serragli, and for a petition dealing with his bankruptcy of 1425, see *PR,* CXXII, ff. 65r–66r, May 29, 1431.

loans that they had advanced that office in order to enable it to pay the mercenaries in the Florentine hire.[2] By the end of the decade and the opening years of the next the situation seems to have deteriorated substantially, with references to the shortage of cash found in private and public documents alike. Francesco Tornabuoni informed Averardo de'Medici in April 1431 that business conditions were bad and that it was impossible to collect any debts from anyone.[3] Only shortly before, in an attempt to avoid additional expenditures, the government had recalled one of its ambassadors to Venice, Bernardo Guadagni, inspiring a caustic remark on Cosimo de'Medici's part about the shamefulness of having to take such a step.[4] Alamanno Salviati, writing to Averardo de'Medici in the fall of 1431, despaired of the seriousness of the situation, which was caused "by a greater scarcity of money than is necessary, and things get worse as time advances. Here everyone is predicting his own destruction, without an end or an improvement in sight, and with ruin overtaking [all] fairly rapidly."[5] References to the

2. See later in this chapter.

3. Pellegrini, p. LVII (from *Mediceo avanti il principato*, III, no. 74), letter from Francesco Tornabuoni to Averardo de'Medici, dated April 6, 1431: "A Nicholò ò scritto e scriverò che facia ciò che può per assotiglar la tua ragone, ma e' mi dice ch'è una gran chosa, che non si può risquotere da persona; vogla Dio non ci pericholate; in tutto farò mia possa d'asotiglare el debito, che so mi quoce tropo. Idio provegha el meglio."

4. Pellegrini, p. XIX (from *Mediceo avanti il principato*, II, no. 588), letter from Cosimo de'Medici to Averardo de'Medici, dated October 21, 1430: "La rivochazione di Bernardo [Guadagni] non so intendere, sennon per masserizia, che è verghognia del Chomune."

5. Pellegrini, p. CLXXIV (from *Mediceo avanti il principato*, III, no. 656), letter from Alamanno Salviati to Averardo de'Medici, dated November 4, 1431: "Et tutto è nato e nascie, perchè v'è suto et è più stremità di danari, che non sare'bisogno, e quanto più va inanzi ogni dì fia maggiore, et è pericholo non piccholo che non agranchiano sotto la soma. Acci molti, che fanno il loro debito, et altri che non si vogliono schonciare sotto nome di non

tight money conditions abound in the public documents of the period, reinforcing the impression that large numbers of Florentine entrepreneurs were becoming alarmed by the situation. Paolo di Vanni Rucellai deplored the "lack of cash" (*mancamento del danaio*),[6] while a commission appointed to investigate the general economic and fiscal situation in July 1431 reached the rather unoriginal but readily acceptable conclusion that the city's troubles stemmed from the *mancamento del credito che è ne' mercatanti*.[7] This was also the conclusion of one of the many councillors requested to testify in a public meeting: if only Florentines could reconcile their private feuds, and the state coffers be replenished, said Antonio di Bernardo

---

potere, et forse è vero. . . . Qui si vede ogniuno la sua destruzione, o pocho a pocho loghorarsi, sanza speranza di fine o di meglio, o chon assai presta ruina; et acci chillo cognosce e chi no, che anchora ci à delle pazzie usate et assai più non credetti. Il fine lascio pensare a voi."

6. Pellegrini, p. CXLVII (from *Consulte e pratiche*, LI, f. 174v, July 21, 1431): "Paulus Vannis de Oricellariis, pro se et aliis de pratica retulit: Quod, inteso il bisogno dei Dieci della balìa, del quale ci pare che con ogni modo possibile si debba provedere, perchè tutto consiste in aparechiare danari, et gran somma; et veduto che per l'adrieto il Comune s'è governato in gran parte per via d'acatto; et considerato il mancamento del danaio ed i costi agri che al presente corrono, et il peso che i cittadini che sono acti a fare simile achatti ano del passato; ci pare che per ora questa via non sia possibile tenere. . . ."

7. Pellegrini, p. CXLI (from *Consulte e pratiche*, LI, f. 173r, July 5, 1431): "Paulus Vanni Oricellari, Jannozus Janfiglazi, Jacobus Baroncelli, et Bancus Sandri, *coltriciarius*, pro se et aliis de pratica [dixerunt quod]: Et perchè, volendo provedere al bisogno sopradecto per la via ordinaria de'catasti, bisognerebbe incorrere de'due inconvenienti in uno: o veramente pel bisogno presente por nuovi catasti sopra agl'altri posti ne'decti 4 mesi, la qual cosa sarebbe graveza intollerabile et da far fuggire i citadini dal pagamento; o veramente porre per lo tempo avenire in su mesi che non anno graveza, cioè da Dicembre in là, et per mezo degli uficiali del banco acattare in su'cambi i decti danari; a qual cosa, oltr'a l'essere impossibile per lo mancamento del credito che è ne'mercatanti, ne seguiterebbe grandissimo danno al Comune et a'privati citadini, per cagione degl'interessi de'decti danari."

Ligi somewhat piously and naïvely, Florence would have no difficulty in vanquishing any foe and overcoming any obstacle.[8] Continual and ardent appeals to the patriotic spirit of the Florentines, who were implored to bring forth their *pecunias absconsas*,[9] seemed to produce no result. By 1431 the strain of the situation became so great that one observes for the first time speakers suggesting, apparently not in jest, that although bankers and merchants were short of funds, the workers and artisans had made such substantial profits during the war that they had accumulated large patrimonies, which they were hiding from the inquisitive eyes of the communal tax officials.[10] The *strettezza del denaio* that plagued the Florentine economy during the late 1420's and early 1430's became a memory

8. Pellegrini, p. LII (from *Consulte e pratiche*, LI, f. 134r, April 1, 1431): "Antonius Bernardi Ligi, allegavit Cecchum de Esculo: *Tempore felici etc.* Civitas nostra numquam fuit in peiori termino: huius causa sunt primo, divisio intrinseca, unde remedium esset unire cives nostros. Alia causa est defectus pecuniarum. Provideatur igitur pratica quedam civium intelligentium, qui habeant cogitare et ponere remedia."

9. Pellegrini, pp. CVII–CVIII (from *Consulte e pratiche*, LI, f. 157r, May 13, 1431): "Pro officialibus banchi, Andreas de Pazis [dixit quod] debet quilibet se preparare ad subveniendum Communi, cum casus mereantur in presentiarum. Et ipsi ad posse fecerunt. Non sunt presentes officiales idonei, prout erant precessores in officio; et rationes assignavit. Obtulit tamen usque ad posse cum personis et substantia ad subveniendum, recordans fuisse taliter factas solutiones per alios Decem, que nunc bene ostenditur, quia florenus valebat 1. 4 s. 3, et nunc descendit satis. Dixit non esse possibile facere solutiones occurrentes, nisi iam qui habet pecunias absconsas patefaceret illas. Tangere bursas de sighillo esset pericholosum pro reputatione."

10. Pellegrini, p. CVIII (from *Consulte e pratiche*, LI, f. 157v, May 13, 1431): "Pro sex mercantie, Nicolaus Bartolomei Valori: Pecunia deficit, et pars maxima in manus artificum debet esse. Deputentur qui praticent que via esset ad inveniendum ut pecunia veniat in communi; et se ad posse obtulerunt subvenire Communi." Valori's claim was altogether false. If anything, the well-being of the workers was being greatly compromised by the constant devaluation of the silver currency in which they received their wages.

deeply engraved in the minds of numerous Florentines. Some thirty years later Giovanni di Paolo Rucellai, author of a recently published *Zibaldone,* commented upon it, and suggested that many of the economic difficulties experienced by Florentines during the second quarter of the fifteenth century were a direct result of the very heavy tax burden imposed on the citizenry during the 1420's and of the flight of capital that took place during those years.[11]

The predicament of Palla di Nofri Strozzi (not to be confused with his cousin Palla di Palla Strozzi, whose bank had failed in 1425) must have been shared by many other Florentines, businessmen and artisans alike. What makes Strozzi's case outstanding was that at the beginning of the 1420's he had been among the wealthiest citizens of Florence.[12] In a lengthy and poignant petition submitted to the Signory in 1431 he explained his case: His assessment in the catasto of 1427 had been 506 florins, 14 gold sous, 4 deniers; in that of 1431, 329 florins, 8 gold sous. Considering the frequency with which catasti were being imposed during those years, this meant that Strozzi had been asked to pay several thousand florins in taxes. What was more, continued Strozzi, in the course of the previous eight years, in order to pay his taxes, he had been forced to borrow large sums at high interest. Now he found himself having investments in land and in the Monte only; he had no part in any business firm nor did he have any cash. His creditors were losing patience and had been clamoring for the repayment of their capital. To satisfy them, Strozzi had tried to sell some

11. *Giovanni di Pagolo Rucellai ed il suo Zibaldone,* I. *Il Zibaldone Quaresimale,* ed. Alessandro Perosa (London: Warburg Institute, 1960), p. 62.

12. *Ibid.,* pp. 63–64. This thumbnail biography of Palla di Nofri Strozzi has now been translated into English in my anthology *Economic and Social Foundations of the Italian Renaissance* (New York: Wiley, 1969), p. 200.

of his real estate, but, to his chagrin, he had discovered that because of "the war and the nature of the times" such a sale was not possible. He had then tried to redeem some of his Monte credits with the officials of the Monte, but they had responded that they had no cash available with which to buy these credits back from him. Nor did he have any greater success in his attempt to sell his Monte credits in the open market, for there was nobody willing to buy them. He was, therefore, asking the priors' permission to sell credits in the Monte for a value not exceeding 100,000 florins to foreigners, who, as already noted, were not allowed to invest in the Monte without obtaining the government's approval. This was the only possible solution to his predicament, and unless such permission were granted, he concluded, he would find it entirely impossible to continue paying taxes in the future. Almost as an afterthought, he explained why the priors should be pleased with the proposed solution: no Florentine capital would be leaving the city; on the contrary, a goodly sum would be imported into it as a result of the sale, "and those from whom he had borrowed would receive their money, from which thing there would be a greater abundance of cash in the city." [13] Although

13. *PR*, CXXII, ff. 16r–v, April 10, 1431: "Quod secundum ratam sibi impositam in distributionibus onerum vestre civitatis ipse omni diligentia conatus est solvere, satisfacere comuni vestro. Et quod ab annis octo citra per multiplicationem onerorum non sufficientibus fructibus et redditibus suis ad predicta coactus fuit acquirere mutuo in depositum et ad cambium a pluribus personis non paucas quantitates pecunie ad magnum et grave interesse. Et quod volens providere circa solutionem onerorum pro futuro et se liberare ab interesse et cambiis suprascriptis substantiam suam reperit consistere in possessionibus et creditis montium. Et quod cognoscit ut predicta facere possit necesse sibi esse vendere de creditis predictis aut de suis possessionibus. Et quod respectu temporis et belli presentis videt venditionem possessionum suarum non esse ad presens possibilem. Et quod propterea restat eidem dumtaxat vendere de creditis montium. Et quod querens promutare de dictis

the Signory granted Strozzi's request, his endeavors to sell his credits were not entirely successful. When allowing the sale to the foreigners, the catasto officials had calculated Strozzi's new tax assessment on the basis of sale values that the Monte credits presumably were going to fetch in the open market. Their calculations, however, proved exaggerated, because the market for Monte credits, inside and outside of Florence, was depressed, for obvious reasons. Once again, therefore, Strozzi was forced to petition the Signory, informing them that he had sold his credits in the *Monte Comune* not for 30 percent of their face value, as the officials had calculated, but for only 27 percent; the credits in the *Monte de'prestanzoni,* not for 50 percent, but only for 31 percent, of par; and the credits in the *Monte de'cinque interi,* for 25 percent, instead of 37 percent, of face value. He implored that his new tax assessment be reduced to take into consideration the actual, rather than the presumed, income derived from the sale of his Monte credits, and he concluded by saying that from 1423, when the war against Milan

creditis in officiales montis respondetur sibi ab eis non posse emptioni creditorum suorum vacare. Et quod etiam querens promutare in cives vestros non invenit emptores nisi de parvis quantitatibus que non sufficerent sibi etiam pro minima parte quo ad predicta. Et quod revolvens in animo quonam modo de suo posset pro futuro solvere onera et liberare se ab interesse et cambiis occurrerit infrascriptu modus alienandi de creditis montium in forenses. Et quod examinans modum predictum credit sibi utilem fore quia sperat emptores invenire et hac via conservabit se solventem onera, et poterit comode se liberare ab interesse et debitis suprascriptis. Et quod putat etiam utilem esse civitati quia extrinsecos afferetur pecunia pro emptione creditorum predictorum qua remanebit in civitate et ex hoc sequetur quod illius copia maior erit in civitate predicta. Et etiam quod debentes ab eo recipere recuperabiunt pecunias suas. Ex qua re maior habundantia pecunie etiam erit in civitate, et considerato quod ipse ab octo annis citra soluit circa florenos centum duodecim milia. Et quod alium modum non habet sine eius gravissiomo danno. Ideo petit de gratia spetiali id quod inferius dicetur. . . ." Final approval for his request was granted on June 15, 1431, f. 99r.

had first erupted, he had paid between 118,000 and 120,000 florins in forced loans and about 38,000 florins in interest for loans taken to pay his tax assessments, so that in the previous eight years he had paid out (*de suis manibus exierunt*) about 158,000 florins.[14]

While sums of this magnitude must be considered exceptional, if not unique, in the annals of Florentine taxation, Strozzi's predicament was shared by many of his contemporaries. Petitions similar to that of Palla Strozzi were submitted by several other Florentines. One of them, Domenico di Antonio Allegri, requested permission to sell 12,000 florins of Monte credits to foreigners, because "having inquired among those citizens who are entitled to purchase such credits, at present, because of the shortage of money that afflicts us all," he was unable to locate any purchasers, neither for the sum at which he desired to sell nor even for a minimal fraction of it.[15]

14. *PR*, CXXIII, ff. 69v–71v, April 25, 1432, reveals the following information: In the first *catasto* of 1427 Palla had been assessed 507 florins, 14 gold sous, 4 deniers; his assessment of 1431 had been reduced to 329 florins, 8 sous. But he disputed this assessment on two grounds. In 1427 he had 380,000 florins in Monte credits, which had been valued at 50 percent of par, for 190,000 florins. This same sum, however, in 1431 was assessed at 35 percent of par, but the catasto officials had computed his new assessment on the basis of a presumed sale value of these Monte credits of 170,000 florins. Strozzi contended that the figure should have been 120,000 florins. (Actually, his calculation also is mistaken, for 35 percent of 380,000 florins is 133,000 florins.) Moreover, in his sales of Monte credits he had realized 15,317 florins, 19 gold sous, 2 deniers, less than the catasto officials had calculated in assessing his new tax. On the basis of these two arguments he petitioned for a reduction of his assessment. Moreover he stated that he still owed six catasti of the previous distribution, and seventeen of the present one, for a total of 8,639 florins, 17 gold sous, 4 deniers. He concluded by saying that from 1423 to 1433 he had spent 158,000 florins in paying his taxes and in disbursing interest for loans he had taken to pay his taxes.

15. *PR*, CXXII, ff. 63v–64r, May 15, 1431: "Et querens civibus vestris ad acquirendum de ipsis creditis, habilibus vendere et promutare, ad praesens

In this context, one may recall the examples of Matteo Palmieri and of the Medici family, already cited in chapter 4. In both cases, large portions of their incomes were being used to honor their fiscal obligations to the Florentine government.

The constant complaint found in catasto returns of 1430 and 1433 was that business conditions were severely depressed, and although one must treat the complaints of Florentines with a measure of scepticism, there is no question but that the pitch of complaining was much higher in the early 1430's than it had been in 1427. A careful study of the Florentine economy in the first half of the Quattrocento, though it would be extremely useful, still remains to be done. One possible indicator of the general economic and business trends of the third and fourth decades of the fifteenth century might be the demand for, and the value of, Monte credits. In fact, an examination of the market values commanded by those negotiable government credits reveals an interesting trend: Starting in the middle years of the 1420's, and continuing into the early 1430's, there was a steady and occasionally precipitous decline. In 1427, for example, for purposes of computing a catasto return, credits in the *Monte Comune* were assessed at 50 percent of their face value, and one must assume that, as usual, there was a margin between official and actual values of these credits.[16] Although credits of the *Monte Comune* had fallen to such low levels in the past,[17]

---

oppressione pecunie omnis comuniter invadente, emptores non reperit nedum pro quantitate oportuna, sed nec pro minima parte." Authorization was granted to him on June 21, 1431, f. 104r. See also folios 99v–100r, June 20, 1431, for the case of Francesco di Simone and Filippo di Filippo Tornabuoni.

16. *Catasto,* 15 (*Santo Spirito, Scala*), f. 57r.

17. *Carte strozziane,* II, vol. 4, f. 97r. *Ricordanze di Paolo di Alessandro Sassetti:* "Ricordanza ch'io Paolo conperai per la Sandra nostra serocchia, da Giovanni di Bartolo Biliotti, prochuratore di messer Cristofano degli Spini, fiorini 106 iscritti nel monte nuovo delle prestanze, a ragione di fiorini 46

hardly ever before had they consistently remained at such low levels. Almost always, even when reaching levels below 30 percent of par, they had quickly rebounded into the high thirties and low forties.[18] By 1431, however, the quotations for these credits were fluctuating between 24 and 27 percent of par,[19] while by 1433 they had fallen to 15 percent, possibly their lowest value since the institution of the Monte nearly one hundred years before.[20] The same general trend is evident in the market prices of other types of Monte credits, and although one must emphasize again that Monte credits are only one type of economic indicator, they reveal a trend that it would not be surprising to find in other economic developments of those years.

The decline in the market value of Monte credits was undoubtedly related to the inability of the Monte officials to disburse interest to the credit owners promptly and to the lack of

---

per ciento, carta per mano di ser Roma Bartoli da Sommaia, dì xxvi di Settembre, anno 1387, sensale il Lanza."

18. Armando Sapori, *Studi di storia economica* (Florence: Sansoni, 1955), I, 347–352, in which Sapori reproduces the pages of an account book belonging to Francesco di Iacopo del Bene that deal with his speculations in Monte credits from 1361 to 1371.

19. Pellegrini, pp. CLXXIII–CLXXIIII (from *Mediceo avanti il principato,* III, no. 633), letter from Antonio Salvestri Serristori to Averardo de'Medici, dated November 12, [1431]: "I denari del monte da 27 o più torna' a 24, et d'onde abiamo la speranza d' avere il caldo ci è dubi di fredura, et niuna cosa ci grana tra mano, se non in contradio. Et andando le cose come vanno, non vegho, traendose i danari di poche borse, come fa, come ci possiamo risistere al paghare."

20. On June 12, 1433, Barduccio Cherichini reported having sold 11,140 florins of *Monte Comune* credits for 1,686 florins (*PR,* CXXIV, f. 89v). To prevent large losses of communal revenue by the fall of Monte prices, the catasto officials declared that for the purpose of assessing catasti no Monte credits could be declared at less than 32 percent of face value (*Balie,* XXIV, f. 47r, November 3, 1433).

demand for the purchase of these credits. Thus, one can suggest the reasonable hypothesis that economic conditions from the mid-1420's to the mid-1430's were characterized by both these phenomena, which in turn resulted from the heavy military expenditures of the city, the flight of capital from it, and the resulting shortage of cash in it. It is a fact that the most difficult period in the history of the Medici bank was experienced in the opening years of the 1430's, when, according to the evidence contained in the *libri segreti,* the Medici had to employ all their profits from other branches of the bank in order to offset the large losses being incurred by the Florentine *tavola.*[21]

The fiscal and economic crisis of the early 1430's exacerbated the tensions and problems that had always existed within the Florentine Camera and the other administrative branches charged with the city's fiscal policy. The main problem, as one might expect, was how to collect already imposed forced loans and how to come up with substantial amounts of cash to pay the city's expensive but valuable mercenaries. Forced loans, whether they were prestanze, prestanzoni, or catasti, were ordinarily assessed in order to meet specific needs of the city, and their prompt collection was essential, particularly when they were earmarked for military expenditures. Yet, as already noted, the collection of taxes was a slow process. Individual citizens procrastinated in paying their assessments, often having recourse to the right of appeal and claiming, as Palla Strozzi did, that the assessments were unfair or that they were unable to meet the deadline established by the tax authorities. Thus, before a forced loan could be collected in full, weeks and even months elapsed. In the meantime, the officials charged with financing

21. Raymond de Roover, *The Rise and Decline of the Medici Bank* (Cambridge, Mass.: Harvard University Press, 1963), p. 230.

the conduct of war were forced to devise other methods for raising the needed cash while waiting for the collection of the regular tax revenues.

Clearly, this problem was not new in the early 1430's. Communal officials charged with implementing Florentine tax policy had confronted the same difficulty in the past. During the late fourteenth and early fifteenth centuries the *Dieci di balia* (the ten officials entrusted with the overall administration of communal military affairs), were authorized to take short-term loans from local bankers, using as collateral the anticipated revenue of taxes already imposed but not yet collected, and promising their creditors an interest rate commensurate to that quoted in the open market for private loans. Thus the tradition of the state operating in the open money market in order to secure its financial needs was firmly established by the late fourteenth century; possibly it was common well before then. Unfortunately, the volumes in which the accountants of the Dieci recorded these transactions seem to have been lost, and precise calculations of the sums and individuals involved are difficult to make. From a seventeenth-century manuscript compilation of miscellaneous facts about the history of Trecento Florence, however, we learn that from 1390 through 1392, that is, during the first stage of the war against Giangaleazzo Visconti, the Dieci borrowed some 206,000 florins from eighty-three affluent citizens, repaying each within brief periods of time and offering as compensation an interest rate of 5 percent per annum.[22] Although records for later decades, until 1425, apparently do not exist, there is little doubt that this practice was followed during subsequent periods of war and fiscal crisis.

22. Biblioteca Nazionale Centrale di Firenze, Fondo nazionale, II-II-196, pp. 104–107. The precise sum involved was 825,460 lire, with the largest individual transaction not exceeding 40,000 lire.

The Dieci must have borrowed exceedingly large sums during the first two years of the war against Filippo Maria Visconti, for in mid-1425 they found themselves indebted to several Florentine bankers for a sum nearly 200,000 florins in excess of the anticipated communal incomes from prestanze (*non est designata quantitas pro restitutione talium quantitatum ut supra acceptarum.*)[23] In the wake of the disastrous military defeats that Florentine forces had suffered during those first two years of war, the discontent of large segments of the populace was reflected in the unwillingness of many citizens to pay their taxes. Thus the Dieci found themselves in the difficult position of having borrowed sums in excess of their anticipated income while also not being able to collect those taxes that had already been imposed on the city.[24] Therefore, unable to satisfy their

23. *PR*, CXV, ff. 268r–v, December 30, 1425: "Qualiter officium decem balie prefati comunis, mutuo seu ad cambium seu vulgo sumpto vocabulo pe'llire di grossi seu in depositum pro gravissimis necessitatibus rei publice florentine et ut ipsis necessitatibus respondere valeret, accepit a pluribus, variis, et diversis personis multa milia florenorum, pro quorum restitutionem dictum officium seu officiales eiusdem propriis nominibus eorumdem, seu dictum comune florentie dicuntur effectualiter obligati. Et hodie restare debitores earumdem personarum in florenis centum octuaginta milibus auri vel circha, prout tam de nominibus creditorum, quam quantitatibus et alius circa predicta dicitur in quaterno capserii camere dicti comunis, seriosius atque clarius apparere. Et qualiter pro eo quia non est designata quantitas pro restitutione talium quantitatum ut supra acceptarum aliqua sunt orta inconvenientia et de gravioribus dubitatur nisi provisione sit oportunum reparatum. . . ."

24. Nero di Gino Capponi, *Commentarii*, in *Rerum Italicarum Scriptores*, (Milan, 1723–1751), XVIII, 1164-C: "E trovandosi i Dieci di Balìa debito dugento trentadue migliaia di fiorini in su'cambi, et essendo chiarissimi, il Popolo rugghiava, e' Dieci perderono il credito, e tolsonlo a tutti i mercatanti, che gli aveano serviti con disfacimento di parte di loro. Pure provvide il Comune di dare loro ogni mese fiorini 10 mila de'primi danari si risquoteranno di qualunque gravezza: e cancellossi in fine il debito e diessi xii per 100."

creditors, the Dieci defaulted on their debts, causing the collapse, as already noted, of several banking houses. At that point the Signory and the legislature intervened, assuming the responsibility of the Dieci and offering to compensate their creditors over a period of several years, also promising them a return of 12 percent per year on their capital.[25]

The bankruptcy and discrediting of the Dieci brought about a drastic realignment of authority within the communal government. Authority to administer funds related to the military effort was withdrawn from the Dieci, who for the next few years were to be entrusted solely with military and defense matters: negotiations of contracts with mercenaries, supervision of fortifications in the contado, and the like. Funds related to the military effort were to be administered by an office that, though first created in the mid-fourteenth century, was entirely revitalized after 1425: The *ufficiali del banco* (officials of the bank) had usually administered the operations of a pawnshop from which mercenaries were allowed to borrow money, and sometimes they had been entrusted with making the actual payments of wages to Florentine soldiers.[26] After 1425, however, the officials of the bank, who almost always were recruited from among the most prominent bankers and businessmen of the city, played a crucial role in the administration of communal finances. Originally, they were assigned the task of borrowing money from private Florentines, much in the same manner in which the Dieci had done, offering their creditors interest rates

25. The interest set in the provision quoted in note 23 was 15 percent per annum. Later it was reduced to 12 percent (*PR,* CXVI, ff. 197r–198r, December 12, 1426). Earlier in that same year (ff. 22v–25r, April 12, 1426) these creditors were allowed to apply their outstanding credits with the Commune toward the payment of forced loans assessed on them.

26. *LF,* XLIV, f. 151r, and *PR,* LXXXII, ff. 221v–222v, December 12, 1394.

deemed sufficiently attractive to procure the necessary funds: *nomine comunis florentie et pro suis necessitatibus mutuo tam ad cambium quam ad depositum seu alio quocunque modo acquirere possunt.*[27] Soon, however, their activities encompassed wider spheres of the fiscal realm. Authorized to collect all unpaid prestanze and catasti, they also had the right to diminish or completely eliminate any communal expenses that they considered unnecessary or superfluous, while also supervising all expenditures for the fortification of garrisons in the Florentine domain.[28] Shortly thereafter the cashiers (*camarlinghi*) entrusted with the collection of forced loans were placed directly under the jurisdiction of the officials of the bank, so that these latter might be in a position of having precise and accurate knowledge of the amount of cash entering the communal Treasury.[29]

A large measure of the special status and particular importance that the officials of the bank came to enjoy was determined by a requirement established for obtaining membership in that office: All these officials, during their tenure, were asked to advance loans from their own private patrimonies to the state. Those unwilling or unable to do so were removed from their posts and also rendered ineligible to hold any other governmental office (by having their names inserted in the *specchio*).[30] Sometimes, even before assuming their posts, the of-

27. *PR,* CXVI, ff. 168r–170r, September 24, 1426.

28. *PR,* CXXII, ff. 192r–v, September 10, 1431: "Predicti officiales . . . possint quotiens voluerint quascunquas expensas dumtaxat belli presentis que eis inutiles aut superflue viderentur removere seu minuere in totum vel in partem." They were also authorized to supervise the maintenance of rural fortifications.

29. *PR,* CXXII, ff. 201v–202r, September 26, 1431.

30. *PR,* CXXII, ff. 331v–333v, January 23, 1431/32: "Quilibet dictorum offiitialium teneatur solvere quacunqua onera tam imposita quam imponenda

ficials of the bank were required to lend certain sums to the Commune. This was the case in May 1432, when the priors and the colleges ordered the twenty-two new officials of the bank to lend the government a total of 80,000 florins, concurrently determining the share of this sum for which each new officeholder would be responsible: from Cosimo de'Medici's share of 7,500 florins and Andrea di Guglielmino de'Pazzi's 3,750 florins to the rather modest requirements made on Cante di Giovanni Compagni and the historian Domenico di Leonardo Buoninsegni, each of whom was asked to lend the government 430 florins.[31] On occasion, the need for modest sums of cash

durante eorum officio. . . ." Those not paying within one month to be inscribed in the *specchio*.

31. *DSSp Aut.*, XXII ff. 106r–v, May 27, 1432, in which the following *ufficiali del banco* were required to lend certain sums to the government:

Cosimo di Giovanni de'Medici	7,500 florins
Andrea di Guglielmino de'Pazzi	3,750 "
Giannozzo di Bernardo Manetti	3,250 "
Bernardo di Domenico Lamberteschi	3,250 "
Vanni di Nicolao di ser Vanni /Castellani/	1,250 "
Luti di Michele	2,000 "
Jacopo de'Villani	2,500 "
Andrea di Lipaccio de'Bardi	2,500 "
Bianco di Agostino del Bene	2,500 "
Francesco di Jacopo Ventura	1,500 "
Bernardo d'Antonio Uzzano	3,225 "
Mariotto di Dinozzo di Stefano Lippi	1,750 "
Antonio di Silvestro di ser Ristoro	3,225 "
Francesco d'Altobianco Alberti	3,763 "
Pierozzo di Francesco della Luna	2,150 "
Cante di Giovanni Compagni	430 "
Domenico di Leonardo Buoninsegni	430 "
Taddeo di Zanobi Gaddi	1,612 "
Jacopo di Giovanni Bischeri	1,705 "
Stefano Nelli di ser Bartolomeo	1,612 "
Bartolomeo di Luca di Piero Rinieri	2,150 "
Adoardo Giachinotti	1,750 "

could be met by the appointment of new officials of the bank, who, upon assuming their positions, were asked to advance to the government, often to the accountants of their own office, the needed money.[32] Thus, the officials of the bank, because of their extraordinary power and the special requests made upon them, came to play an increasingly important, one can say even crucial, function in the maintenance of the fiscal and military viability of the Commune. The authority to borrow large sums of cash, to determine the interest rates at which these transactions were concluded, to allocate communal revenues as they saw fit, to repay debts assumed by their office at their discretion, and to administer their own loans to the Commune — all these privileges made them important, and rather special, figures in the arena of communal politics. In moments of particularly acute crises it was the officials of the bank who were looked to for direction and help. During such a time, in May 1431, a communal councillor, Lipozus de'Mangioni, exclaimed in the course of what must have been an agitated meeting: "Before the ten officials of the bank leave this room they must be compelled to provide the funds needed by the government. If those in office now are unable to do so, additional men must be appointed to it." [33] The inference in Mangioni's dry and pointed remark is clear: The only officials in the city capable, because of their own private wealth and the influence that in-

32. *PR*, CXXIII, ff. 41r–v, April 15, 1432: "Cum quantitas paranda pecunie ratione novi temporis augeri debeat duplicare, expedit eos qui a mutuandi et ab aliis querendi onus suscepere . . ." they appoint 12 more officials of the bank.

33. Pellegrini, p. CVI (from *Consulte e pratiche*, LI, ff. 156v, May 13, 1431): "Lipozus de Mangionibus: Pericula exigunt celerem provisionem; ideo antequam X banchi exeant de ista sala, compellantur providere; et si ipsi non possunt, quod credo, det eis Domini socios alios cives quinpossint; et in hoc Domini faciant viriliter, et provideant isto modo."

dividually and collectively they enjoyed, of contributing to the alleviation of the Commune's fiscal needs and the correction of such imbalances were the officials of the bank. Thus the members of that office became an important élite, able through its particular position in the governmental structure and the specific role it was called upon to play in the administration of communal affairs to determine the course of policy and of many citizens' private fortunes.

Given the large and constantly expanding needs of the Florentine government, and the acutely depressed business conditions prevailing in the city during the late 1420's and early 1430's, how could the *ufficiali del banco* convince the important businessmen to lend their office substantial sums of money? And why would any Florentine, considering these conditions, be attracted to serve as a member of that office while also being required to advance substantial sums to the government? References to the patriotic spirit of the Florentine citizens would be woefully inadequate to explain these circumstances for, as already noted, one of the principal, and most urgent, problems confronting every Florentine government during that period was the collection of duly assessed taxes. The reluctance of Florentines to part with their money was indeed proverbial, and perfectly understandable in that of all the commodities available in the world of these merchants the most difficult to obtain was liquid cash. Even those Florentine statesmen who constantly urged their compatriots to act selflessly and magnanimously toward the government invariably drew the line at advancing large sums of their own money to the state. Giovanni di Mico Capponi, a man well known for his fiery and patriotic speeches, in an oration delivered in April 1432 exhorted his fellow citizens to be patriotic, selfless, brave, and honest, but then added: "I do not have much money. And I also have an older daughter, for whom I shall have to provide a dowry. Nevertheless, I offer [to the government] all my substance, as long as its demands take into account my condition." [34] Patriotic rhetoric alone would not convince hardened Florentine businessmen to part with their money. More concrete incentives were needed, and these, in fact, were offered by the communal policymakers in order to attract to the government's coffers the capital of its great entrepreneurs. [35]

Fortunately, several of the records kept by the scribes and accountants of the officials of the bank after 1425 have survived and provide particularly important information on the entire *modus operandi* of these officials. Although the records are not continuous, offering information only for the period from November 1427 until the end of 1428, and from December 1430 to August 1432, their contents reveal one of the most interesting aspects of the operation of the Florentine government during the early Quattrocento. [36]

34. Pellegrini, p. LII (from *Consulte e pratiche*, LI, f. 134v, April 1, 1431): "Johannes Michi Capponi: Omnes cives debent moveri cum personis et pecuniis ad succurrendum Rempublicam. Ego offero me dispositum ad omnia circa unionem; persona autem mea non est acta armis, propter etatem et propter dissuetudinem; pecunias non habeo multas et habeo filiam grandem, cui danda est dos. Tamen omnia offero, iuxta possibilitatem."

35. In this context one should recall the oft-quoted remark of Giovanni di Pagolo Morelli in his *Ricordi* (ed. Vittore Branca [Florence: Le Monnier, 1956], pp. 252–253, 265): "E dove elle [le gravezze] non valessono e trovassiti pure nelle gravezze grandi, le quai fussono sofficienti a disfarti, non le pagare. Rubellati dal Comune, acconcia il tuo in forma non ti possa essere tolto."

36. Two other volumes, although they have survived, were unavailable for consultation, having been in the restoration laboratory of the *Archivio di Stato* for the entire duration of my Florentine sojourn. These two volumes, nos. 21 and 22 in the *PCUB*, deal with the years 1425–1428.

Loans from individual entrepreneurs to the officials of the bank involved the principle of dry exchange, "a spurious exchange transaction that was actually a cloak for a straight loan." [37] The object of this procedure was to conceal the payment of interest, which in cases of loans from individuals to the state was often very high. Dry exchange involved the advancement of a loan quoted by the creditor in a foreign currency at a given exchange rate. Repayment of the loan was made on the basis of the exchange rate between the local and foreign currencies at the time of the bill's maturity. Essentially, then, by engaging in transactions involving dry exchange (*cambium secum*) one speculated on the values of various currencies in the international money market. High profits for the creditor, however, could be guaranteed if at the time of the conclusion of the original bill the exchange rates were established in advance in favor of the creditor.

One example extracted from the books of the *ufficiali del banco* will suffice to illustrate the procedure. (It should be noted that all transactions undertaken by these officials quoted exchange rates between the florin and the lira di grossi, a Venetian money of account.) On March 8, 1425/26, Tommaso di Giacomino & Co. advanced to the officials of the bank 635 florins, 13 silver sous, 8 deniers, in the form of 60 lire di grossi, at an exchange rate of 15 lire, 7 sous affiorino, per lira di grossi. On April 30 of that same year the Commune repaid that loan of 60 lire di grossi at an exchange rate of 15 lire, 16 sous, 8⅔ deniers affiorino per lira di grossi, which in turn amounted to 655 florins, 1 lira, 3 silver sous. Thus, the firm of Tommaso di Giacomino had earned 20 florins on a 635-florin loan issued

37. Raymond de Roover, *The Medici Bank: Its Organization, Management, Operations and Decline* (New York: New York University Press, 1948), pp. 38, 82–84.

for a period of almost eight weeks, or an interest rate of nearly 20 percent per year.[38]

The surviving volumes of the *ufficiali del banco* record dozens of such transactions, some for sums of a few hundred florins, others for several thousand. What is interesting is that under normal circumstances the use of dry exchange was strictly prohibited in transactions between the state and its creditors, for such a procedure was considered by the Church as involving the practice of usury. But, as was the case with the relations between Florence and the Jewish moneylenders, the normal and accepted ethical guidelines of the age were somewhat obscured by the financial exigencies of the moment. In 1429, for example, in an apparent attempt to prevent the loss of vital communal revenue for the payment of excessive interest rates charged by the city's bankers for their loans to the officials of the bank, a provision reiterated the long-standing prohibition of dry exchange on the grounds that such a practice diverted money from honest commercial ventures and that it tended to subvert high standards of ethical behavior (*bonisque moribus contraria mercatorum honestas semper censuit*).[39] Soon, however, under the pressure of events, the prohibition was retracted,

38. *PCUB*, XXI, f. 37v: "Tomaso di Giachomino e chonpagni deono dare a dì XXX d'Aprile 1426 fiorini secento cinquantacinque s. viii, d. iiii larghi. Ebono da Ghualtieri Biliotti, chamarlingho in questo a c. 217, sono per lire 60, rendemo a lire 15 s. 16 d. 8⅔ per lira. Sono fiorini 655 l. 1 s. 3." f. 38r: "Tomaso di Giachomino e chonpagni deono avere a dì viii di Marzo fiorini secento trentacinque, soldi 5 larghi, die a Ghualtieri Biliotti, charmarlingho, deba dare in questo a c. 20, sono per lire 60 di grossi, tolsono per noi a chanbio a lire 15 s. 7. Sono fiorini 653, lire — , s. 13, d. 8.

39. *PR*, CXX, ff. 249r–v, July 15, 1429: "Nequis cupiditate amplioris questio ab honesto et laudabili exercitio mercature se suamque pecunia retrahat, et ad ea se ucetat que inutilia reipublica, bonisque moribus contraria mercatorum honestas semper censuit, salutari remedio ire obviam desiderantes. . . ."

because, says the provision abrogating the ban, many citizens had advised the government that only by allowing the use of dry exchange would the Commune be able to raise sufficient sums of cash to proceed with the war.[40] The abrogation of the law of 1429, which was to have been in effect for two years, was subsequently reiterated twice more — an indication that only thus could the Commune continue fighting its war against Lucca.[41]

In 1426 the firm of Tommaso di Giacomino & Co., as mentioned above, earned interest on its loan to the state at the rate of about 20 percent per annum. Such rates were rather common during that first phase of the war against Milan, although one must consider these as quite high even by the standards of that age. After all, when Jews were finally admitted into the city in 1431, they were not allowed to charge more than 20 percent per annum, a rate that must have been considered usurious.[42] With the deterioration of the military and economic situation, however, the interest rates paid by the government in 1425 and 1426 were low compared with those charged in the years 1431, 1432, and 1433. Antonio di Salvestro Serristori, for example, earned 89 florins, 17 silver sous, 2 deniers, on a three-month loan of 1,041 florins issued in December 1430 and collected in March 1431, or an interest rate of 34 percent per annum.[43] Cosimo de'Medici & Co. re-

40. *PR*, CXXI, ff. 106r–v, December 8, 1430: "Et quod secundum relationes plurium civium utile esset ordinamentum predictum mutare, vel ad presens irritare pro pecunia paranda, qua pro necessitatibus instantis belli requiritur."

41. *PR*, CXXIII, ff. 2r–v, March 31, 1432; *Balie*, XXIV, f. 16r, September 22, 1433.

42. One should point out, however, that the short-term loans issued by moneylenders were meant for consumption, while loans taken on dry exchange were almost invariably business loans.

43. *PCUB*, XXIV, f. 1r.

ceived an interest payment of 724 florins, 4 silver sous, on a three-month bill of 6,563 florins, 12 silver sous, 4 deniers, issued in May 1431 and collected the following August. This amounted to slightly more than 33 percent per year.[44] Without having analyzed the details of each of the numerous transactions recorded in the account books of the officials of the bank, it seems safe to suggest that by the years 1431 and 1432 the average interest rates at which these bills were issued exceeded 30 percent per annum. The most profitable such loan that I found recorded (among the few dozen that I analyzed) bore an interest rate of slightly more than 46 percent per annum. It involved a loan of 545 florins issued by Ridolfo di Bonifazio Peruzzi for three months, for which he collected an interest of 64 florins.[45]

Interest rates of this magnitude could be justified on the basis of the extreme scarcity of cash in the Florentine, and for that matter the Italian, economy during those years. Yet, justifiable though they may have been, they were not palatable to many strata of the Florentine society whose members were not in a position to engage in such transactions and could not enjoy the profits and prestige reaped by their more affluent compatriots.

Undoubtedly such a reliance on the private fortunes of the wealthiest and most successful Florentine businessmen added a considerable burden to the Florentine budget. Now, in addition to the nearly 200,000 florins expended annually for the carrying charges of the funded public debt, a considerable sum, whose precise magnitude it is impossible to calculate but which must have amounted to several thousand florins each year, had to be spent for the interest charges of the floating debt, into which were inscribed the short-term loans issued by

44. *PCUB,* XXV, ff. 158r, 175r.
45. *PCUB,* ff. 113r, 169r. He collected 64 florins on a three-month bill of 545 florins.

the bankers to the state.[46] Thus an unusually complex system of deficit financing was being created, based on the creation of two categories of creditors. The first category, composed of large segments of the populace, received a return of $3\frac{1}{2}$ to 8 percent per year on their investments, which, however, they made reluctantly and under duress. The second category of creditors, whose investments fetched them a return of 20 to 40 percent per year, advanced their money to the state only on the understanding that the collateral for their loans, as well as the funds from which their interest would be paid, would come from assured forced investments in the Monte in the form of catasto payments on the part of the regular middle-rank bourgeois. In a very real sense the particular economic and fiscal situation in which Florence found itself during the late 1420's and early 1430's contributed to the forging of a fiscal structure whose maintenance depended on the continued exploitation, as it were, of the rank-and-file bourgeois by the grand entrepreneurs of the age. The overwhelming majority of Florentines were losing entire patrimonies during those years because of the oppressive tax burden. Yet, concurrently, their very tax payments were being used, partially but consistently, to pay the interest owed by the government to those few citizens fortunate enough to have large sums of cash available that they could loan to the state.

It would be tempting to conclude from these comments that the high, and on the surface lucrative, interest rates being charged to the government represented the profits collected by those few members of the *haute bourgeoisie* sufficiently affluent

46. At the conclusion of the second peace of Ferrara, in April 1433, the government owed 42,000 florins to various merchants, as well as the interest on various other loans that it had already amortized. Pellegrini, p. CCLII (from *Consulte e pratiche*, LII, f. 78v, July 3, 1433).

to engage in such transactions. Unfortunately, the evidence on this point is not entirely clear. No account books of those large firms that were the most consistent lenders to the government seem to have survived. Even for the Medici, our knowledge is limited to the few statements that Giovanni and Cosimo inserted in their catasto returns of 1427 and 1433. The picture that emerges from these fragments of evidence seems to suggest a rather surprising trend. While it may be altogether plausible that until 1430, possibly even until the first few months of 1431, Cosimo de'Medici was profiting from his dealings with the *ufficiali del banco,* it seems clear that after the first few months of 1431, and until the peace of Ferrara was signed in the spring of 1433, he may have actually been losing money from these transactions. There is some evidence to suggest that in 1432–1433, in order to advance the loans that the officials of the bank had requested from him, Cosimo, through the Florentine branch of his firm, had to borrow money in the Venetian money market, presumably at high interest rates. This is the only possible explanation of a debt exceeding 32,000 florins that the Florentine *tavola* of the Medici firm had incurred shortly before Cosimo filed his catasto return in 1433.[47] Moreover, the personal *libro segreto* of Cosimo reveals quite convincingly that the most hard-pressed branch of his firm during those years was the Florentine bank, which was, without question, running in the red.[48] Cosimo himself, when filing his catasto return, had attributed his bank's difficulties to the large sums that he had been forced to lend the government. It would thus seem that by the concluding phases of the war against Lucca the economic hardships that the policy of Florentine expansionism had first

47. de Roover, *The Rise and Decline of the Medici Bank,* pp. 230; 452, n.11, 12 (from *Catasto,* 470 [*San Giovanni, Leon d'Oro*], f. 539r).

48. *Mediceo avanti il principato,* CLIII, no. 2, ff. 73r, 76r.

imposed on the inhabitants of the contado had gradually come to be felt even by the most affluent members of the Florentine society.

While the above conclusion cannot be supported by definitive and entirely convincing evidence, it is clear that during the years of economic, military, and fiscal crisis a restricted and easily defined group of Florentine entrepreneurs were gradually being allowed to acquire an overwhelming share in the development of Florentine politics, for the reason that their resources were the only ones available to the government for the successful continuation of its military and political programs. What is interesting (this topic, while not closely examined here, nevertheless merits careful study) is that the opposition to the war against Lucca was entirely ineffectual. The majority of Florentine citizens, although opposed to the crushing burden of taxation, seemed unwilling to bring it to an end. A kind of schizophrenia, entirely foreign to the normal businesslike attitude of the Florentines, seemed to have completely overwhelmed most citizens involved in the political deliberations of those years, with the result that the long-range political consequences of their course were realized only belatedly, at a point when it became impossible to reverse events that led to the erosion of much-cherished traditional, constitutional, and political liberties.

The political and constitutional dangers inherent in such a policy remained unidentified until late in the war, but the immediate economic pressures were recognized all too clearly, and some efforts were made to limit the large interest rates that the important bankers and industrialists were charging the state during the conduct of the war. These efforts became concentrated during the spring and summer months of 1431, when a legislative proposal was introduced to limit the amount of interest charged the state by individuals to 15 percent per year.[49] Though the proposal was defeated, its presentation to the Camera del Comune brought about a heated discussion. It is not good to set a limit on the interest to be charged, said Bartolomeo di Giovanni Carducci, "for wherever there is little money, there is bound to be even less" (*quia ubi sunt pauce pecunie essent etiam paucores*). Better to try to locate and import into the city additional gold and silver. Andrea di Guglielmino de'Pazzi, one of the great bankers of those years, added that he served the Commune as best he could. If interest rates increased, he continued, *non fuit culpa nostra*. He concluded by deploring the intolerable costs of the war, offered to change places with any citizen accusing him of having made excessive profits during the war's duration, and assured his audience that those claiming that he was making a profit of 100 percent on his loans to the state did not know what they were talking about.[50] A month earlier, another prominent politician, Lipozzo de'Mangioni, had suggested that the officials of the bank seek to limit the interest they paid to their creditors to no more than 60 percent per annum.[51] All these efforts failed, as they were

49. *LF, LV*, f. 160v, August 4, 1431: "Provisionem [continentem] limitationem cambiorum pro uno anno a die consigli comuni, quod non excedant ad rationem florenorum xv pro centenario, ad rationem anni; et auctoritatem in Sex Mercantie circa providendum ne aurum exportetur extra civitatem Florentie; et providendum quod civibus debitoribus aliorum civium non detur nimia molestia. Displicuit."

50. Pellegrini, p. CLI (from *Consulte e pratiche*, LI, f. 180r, August 3, 1431): "Andreas Guiglelmini de Pazis dixit servisse in periculo Communis, et habiliori modo quam potuit. Si cambia ascenderunt, non fuit culpa nostra. Quando servivimus, valebant 15 per centinario, et non ultra; quare non dicat aliquis de 100 pr centinario, quia libenter haberem propriam sortem meam."

51. Pellegrini, p. CXXXIII (from *Consulte e pratiche*, LI, f. 169v, July 3, 1431): "Lipozzus de Mangionibus . . . et retinebunt cambia, ne ascendant ad 60 per 100."

bound to. Extending charity to the government was not characteristic of Florentine entrepreneurs, and the only possible manner of alleviating the situation would have been a cessation of the war against Lucca. That course was advocated neither by the affluent bankers and industrialists nor by the rank-and-file members of the Florentine patriciate, whose rhetoric during those years was replete with references to the honor of the Commune and the need to defend it stoutly against the aggression of the Lucchese.[52]

Who, then, were these entrepreneurs on whose initiative came to depend the fate of Florentine politics during the late 1420's and early 1430's? The records of the *ufficiali del banco,* as already noted, are not complete. Those that I was able to consult cover a total of thirty-four discontinuous months, although they offer a continuous record of these transactions from the end of 1430 until mid-August 1432. During that period the officials of the bank borrowed from the great capitalists of the city a total of 561,098 florins, an average of slightly more than 16.500 florins per month. The total number of Florentines whose funds were used by the officials of the bank during these months was sixty-four, some lending modest sums of a few hundred florins each, others advancing to the government amounts of money unprecedented in the fiscal history of Florence, possibly in the history of any Italian commune of the Trecento and Quattrocento. Table 11 lists the names of those entrepreneurs who each advanced to the officials of the bank a sum exceeding 10,000 florins. The total credit of these eleven citizens, each of whom was backed by enormous resources of family and business connections, amounted to 436,942 florins.

52. Mrs. Dale Kent, a doctoral candidate at the University of London, is currently preparing a dissertation on the political disputes and alliances of the years 1433 and 1434.

Table 11. Creditors of the *ufficiali del banco* for more than 10,000 florins (values expressed in florins rounded off to nearest complete figure. Silver currencies converted to gold at current exchange rates, for which consult Appendix D).

Name	Sum Lent (Florins)	Reference in *PCUB*
Cosimo & Lorenzo de Medici & Co.	155,887	XXIII, 92r, 232r; XXIV, 16r; XXV, 150r, 158r; XXVII, 7r, 20r; XXVIII, 9r
Andrea d'Ugolino de' Pazzi & Co.	58,524	XXIII, 156r; XXIV, 5r, 18r; XXV, 81r; XXVII, 8r, 19r; XXVIII, 18r
Bernardo di Lamberto Lamberteschi & Co.	34,825	XXIII, 257r; XXIV, 44r; XXV, 105r; XXVIII, 3r
Lorenzo di messer Palla di Nofri Strozzi & Co.	33,951	XXIII, 20r
Pierozzo di Francesco della Luna	27,156	XXIII, 93r; XXIV, 42r; XXV, 106r; XXVIII, 25r
Antonio di Salvestro Serristori	26,527	XXIII, 157r; XXIV, 22r; XXVII, 9r; XXVIII, 25r
Donato d'Ugolino de'Bonsi & Co.	26,405	XXIII, 91r; XXV, 87r; XXVI, 12r
Antonio di Jacopo Pitti	26,106	XXIII, 2r
Jacopo di Piero Baroncelli & Co.	18,362	XXIII, 19r; XXIV, 43r
Gianozzo & Filippo di Bernardo Manetti	15,345	XXIV, 9r; XXV, 84r; XXVIII, 4r, 32r
Bernardo d'Antonio da Uzzano & Co.	13,854	XXV, 85r; XXVI, 10r; XXVIII, 37r

Moreover, while these eleven accounted for slightly more than 75 percent of the total sum borrowed by the officials of the bank, the firm of Cosimo and Lorenzo de'Medici alone had lent to the government fully 27 percent of the 560,000 florins that the state had needed during that period. It is interesting to note in this context that by the late 1420's and early 1430's the increased needs of the government and the adverse economic conditions plaguing the city, which had eroded the well-being of numerous Florentine families, had contributed to reducing the number of Florentines capable of assisting the government by lending it money, with the result that a smaller number of citizens was now being called upon to bear this particular responsibility — concurrently enjoying whatever economic and political profits accrued from it. The *Dieci di balia* had borrowed, as already noted, a total of some 206,000 florins from 1390 to 1392. Eighty-three citizens had then been asked to contribute, the average share of each being slightly less than 2,500 florins. Moreover, the single highest contribution was that of Gucciozzo & Uguciozzo di Vincenzo de'Ricci & Sons, and it amounted to only 10,000 florins, or less than 5 percent of the total. In the late 1420's and early 1430's, however, the average contribution of each creditor exceeded 8,700 florins, or more than three times what it had been earlier, and even more significantly, the largest contribution, that of the Medici, was more than one quarter of the total sum borrowed by the officials of the bank.[53]

53. Consult Appendix E for the names of all these creditors and the sums they advanced to the government.

7

CONCLUSION

In this monograph we have examined the fiscal situation that had developed in Florence during the first three and a half decades of the fifteenth century, paying particular attention to the decade 1423–1433. While some of the reasons for the economic crisis that arose, and some of the government's countermeasures (ineffective though they may have been) have been analyzed, our inquiry raises several unanswered questions. The answers lie well beyond the scope of this monograph, for to find them would require much additional study among other archival collections. However, these questions will at least be enunciated and possible avenues of investigation suggested in the hope that at some future time these queries may be resolved.

How, then, in a period of economic hardship, were certain Florentine entrepreneurs able to command large reserves of cash that they could lend the government? What were the sources of profit of these firms? Where did they earn their money, and why were they able to continue earning it while most other businessmen could do no better than preserve their patrimonies, often having to liquidate investments in real estate and government bonds? We know surprisingly little about the structure of the Florentine economy during the first half of the fifteenth century, even less about the operations and fortunes of individual business firms. An examination of surviving business records of those decades might reveal a great deal about the secrets of their strengths and weaknesses. An example of the kind of inquiry that should be undertaken is Raymond de Roover's exhaustive study of the structure and operations of the Medici bank.[1] With the help of de Roover's findings one can,

1. Raymond de Roover, *The Rise and Decline of the Medici Bank* (Cambridge, Mass.: Harvard University Press, 1963). Much interesting informa-

in fact, begin to understand the sources of the enormous economic power the Medici were able to wield during those years. Of all the branches of the Medici bank, the most profitable during the second and third quarters of the fifteenth century was that of Rome. Consistently, according to de Roover's calculations, the Rome branch produced profits far exceeding those of the other branches,[2] and what is interesting is that during the late 1420's and early 1430's most of these profits were invested in the central company of Florence.[3] Might it not be plausible to suggest that the source of the abundant cash reserves that the Medici made available to the officials of the bank was the profits they derived from their position as papal bankers?[4] If the answer to this question is affirmative, then the connections between the Medici and the Papacy in the fifteenth century, or in any case during the third and fourth decades of the Quattrocento, would merit careful study. But even if we can ascertain without much doubt that the Roman connections of the Medici were important, what of the Lamberteschi, della Luna, Serristori, Pitti, and other important bankers of the time? What was the source of their funds? [5]

Even more intriguing would be the investigation of the politi-

---

tion also appears in Richard Goldthwaite's recent *Private Wealth in Renaissance Florence* (Princeton: Princeton University Press, 1969).

2. de Roover, *The Rise and Decline of the Medici Bank,* p. 47, Table 8, and p. 54, Table 11.

3. *Ibid.,* p. 208, Table 34.

4. On the background of the success of the Medici in assuming their position as papal bankers, see George Holmes, "How the Medici Became the Pope's Bankers," in *Florentine Studies,* ed. Nicolai Rubinstein (London: Faber and Faber, 1968), pp. 357–380.

5. It is also interesting to note that the Pazzi were papal bankers during that period, but to the best of my knowledge there exists no study devoted to their role in the papal finances, or for that matter, to their precise economic position within Florence.

cal and social consequences of the fiscal situation already described. One can begin by suggesting that a condition of such prolonged and vast crisis could not but have serious results, not only on the fiscal structure of the city but on its constitutional and institutional framework as well. The lack of funds, the obvious inability of the Florentine government to devise satisfactory and well-accepted modes of raising them, led to the creation of governmental agencies capable of acting without much regard to established procedures or existing lines of command and authority. The *ufficiali del banco* represented a trend in such a direction. By being able to supervise large areas of the fiscal administration, by being responsible for the location of the necessary funds without which the entire diplomatic and military policy could not be sustained, they assumed a particularly interesting and important position in the framework of the government. But that same trend is also evident elsewhere. Authority to assess forced loans, be they prestanze or catasti, gradually passed into the hands of special plenipotentiary commissions (*balie*), which periodically were appointed and entrusted with the task. In the process, of course, the traditional authority of the legislature was undermined.[6] It would be interesting to try to assess the degree to which the failure of existing institutions to satisfy the needs created by the wars of that decade contributed to the discrediting of the entire régime of the 1420's and early 1430's. Can one, in other words, attribute the great changes that transformed the bases of Florentine politics in

6. For legislation of this kind, *PR*, CXIII, ff. 33r–v, May 28, 1423; CXIV, ff. 114v–115v, January 9, 1424/25; CXV, f. 283r, January 28, 1425/26; CXVI, ff. 265v–267r, February 16, 1426/27; CXVIII, ff. 592v–593v, March 15, 1427/28; CXXI, ff. 139v–140v January 9, 1430/31. For an examination of this trend during an earlier period, see my article "The Florentine Oligarchy and the *Balie* of the Late Trecento," *Speculum*, XLIII (1968), 23–51.

1434 to the dislocations created by the fiscal crisis? The immediate temptation would be to answer the question affirmatively,
for there are sufficient indications that during those years there
developed a clear realization among Florentines that the only
possible solution to their problems lay in the continued reliance
on balìe staffed by experts. Deploring the chaos of the communal fisc and the deep factional disputes agitating the Florentine government, Giovenco della Filicaia said on February 21,
1430/31: "They should therefore, elect a small number of dis-
passionate men, among those who do not speculate in the public
well-being, and who do not thrive in factionalism." [7] A series
of discussions held in July and August of 1431 was the occasion
for the airing of several views on this same subject. The motion
before the legislature provided for the appointment of a small
plenipotentiary commission over fiscal matters to serve for the
duration of the war. The bill was rejected twice,[8] but numerous
orators spoke up in favor of its adoption, one — Antonio di
Ghezzo della Casa — invoking the example of the Venetians,
who through the *Consiglio dei Pregadi* seemed to have found
a satisfactory solution to the problems of distribution of power
and the decision-making process.[9] Obviously, recommendations

7. Pellegrini, p. XXXVIII (from *Consulte e pratiche*, LI, f. 125v, February
21, 1430/31): "Pro Capitaneis partis Guelfe, Jovencus de Filicaria . . .
eligantur ergo cives in parvo numero et non passionati, vel minus quam
potest, et qui non faciant mercaturam de re publica et non nutriantur in
divisionibus."

8. *LF*, LV, ff. 163v, 164r, August 23 and 24, 1431.

9. Pellegrini, p. CLIII (from *Consulte e pratiche*, LI, f. 180v, August 3,
1431): Antonius Ghezi de Casa . . . ut autem tollatur molestia circa con-
silia habenda, ideo deputetur pratica hominum, qui habeant vigilare circa
ista; et si non sufficit una pratica, deputentur due, et praticata mictantur
executioni. Venetiis est consilium centum, quod habet baliam circa provisionem onerum et impositionem pecuniarum, etc. Alias fuit relatum per
praticam de civibus 48 deputandis, nec erat incoveniens quod praticatis
redderetur fabe per dominos et collegia."

to rely on the more efficient balie had often been made in the Florentine past. In other times of danger, such as in the 1390's, balie had been used extensively, but then, the danger overcome, they had been abandoned in favor of the traditional system. In the 1420's and early 1430's, however, the crisis was so deep and its consequences so far-reaching that despite the clear knowledge that the appointment of balie was very unpopular (*i popoli sono mal vaghi di dar balia*)[10] the city proved incapable of avoiding rule by plenipotentiary commission after 1434. It seems that the erosion of constitutional controls and the very cavalier handling they received in the hands of the régime installed in 1434 are two phenomena not entirely unrelated to each other.

Continuing along the same lines of investigation, one might wish to know more about the role that, because of the new fiscal situation, Cosimo de'Medici and his friends were called upon to play on the stage of communal politics. Table 11 suggests the power of Cosimo could wield. He alone was in a position to continue assisting the government in its quest to overcome Lucca. What was the price that one of his capacity and ambition would exact for such extraordinary service? Did he really

10. Pellegrini, p. CL, n. 1 (from *Consulte e pratiche*, LI, f. 176v, July 23, 1431): "Alla seconda [parte] del dar balia, diciamo che i popoli sono mal vaghi di dar balìa, et per questo ci pare, et così riportiamo, che di nuovo, o per quelli medesimi della pratica, o per altri che paresse alla Signoria, si disamini in che parte questa balìa s'abbia ad extendere; et poichè fia dichiarato et inteso le parti in che s'abbia la balìa, si potrà procedere più oltre al darle effecto." Giovanni di Jacopo Morelli, shortly after the outbreak of war against Lucca, wrote in his *Ricordi*: "Diessi balìa al porre danari, et soldare genti d'arme, et molto si limitò la balìa a'Dieci, et tutto si fecie per induciere el popolo sotto il giogo. Il fine fu, s'allargò ogni balìa in brevissimo tempo; et come disse Cristo, chi ha orecchi oda, et intendano gl'intelletti humani" (from *Delizie degli erudi toscani,* ed. Fr. Ildelfonso di San Luigi [Florence, 1770–1789], XIX, 87).

seek the new role, trying to exploit the political advantages he enjoyed as a result of his economic power, or was it thrust upon him by the force of circumstance? His contemporaries were well aware of the enormous power his financial position enabled him to wield. Is there possibly any relation between his exile in 1433 and the antagonisms his financial dealings with the government of the city must have created? At the very moment of his exile Cosimo delivered a speech before the *Signory,* referring to the numerous occasions in the past when at the moment of dire financial need the Commune had come to him and asked him for help. "Ask your soldiers how many times they were paid with my own funds, the Commune subsequently repaying me when it was able to do so," he exclaimed, hoping that the recollection of these past gestures would be interpreted favorably by his listeners.[11] But his enemies held a somewhat different view of his activities. In the testimony against Cosimo which Niccolò Tinucci presented to the Florentine authorities shortly after the great banker's exile there is one recurring theme: Cosimo, his relatives and friends were profiting from the continued prosecution of the war at the expense of large segments of the populace. Tinucci graphically depicts a carefully laid plan whose details enabled Cosimo to increase his wealth and establish his political primacy in the city. It would be important to know if the details of Tinucci's deposition are correct. But even without that knowledge one can suggest that Cosimo's all too particular position in the city was well recognized by his friends and enemies alike. "Often I heard Cosimo and Averardo [de'Medici]," said Tinucci, "proclaim that the only time when

11. Angelo Fabronio, *Magni Cosmi Medicei Vita. Adnotationes et Monumenta* (Pisa, 1789), pp. 74–75: "Dimandisene i vostri soldati quante volte da me per lo Comune sono stati pagati di mio proprio, e poi satisfattimi, quando il Comune è suto più abile."

one could become great in the city was during war, by providing for the military needs of the city, lending money to the Commune, for these loans provided no risk and were very profitable, while at the same time the people would imagine that they were being helped by them." [12] It was the Medici, said Tinucci, who favored the war against Lucca, for it gave them a grand chance to make large profits and to improve their status in the city. By insisting on high military expenditures, thus augmenting the burden of taxation, continued Tinucci, they drove to bankruptcy many of their political enemies, who were disfranchised for not being able to pay their taxes.[13] By corrupting mercenaries, subverting the foundations of the government, feigning to be indispensible to the survival of the city, the Medici, according to Tinucci, had created and sought to take advantage of the fiscal crisis that plagued the city during those years.

It would undoubtedly be a little naïve to accept all of Tinucci's accusations at their face value. There are enough indications that the motivating forces behind the Florentine expedition against Lucca were not the Medici, but rather their principal opponents, Rinaldo degli Albizzi and his friends. But even so, the Medici and the other great entrepreneurs who advanced

12. Niccolò Tinucci, "Esamina," published in the appendix of Giovanni Cavalcanti, *Istorie fiorentine,* ed. I. Polidori (Florence, 1838–1839), II, 400: "Senti' molte volte dire a Chosimo e Averardo, che'l modo a mantenersi grande era lo stare in ghuerra, e'l merchato nuovo fornire in ghuerra, e poi prestare al Chomune, che erano sichuri, e di ghuadagnio grande, e al popolo parrebbe essere sovvenuto da loro; sicchè a loro seghuirebbe utile e onore e grandezza e altezza."

13. *Ibid.,* p. 405: "E condussono [the Medici] poi Niccholò da Tollentino e Micheletto, per essere signori dell'arme, e tenere i cittadini in tale spesa che convenisse che del loro non si potessono aiutare, nè da loro non fussono atati, e perdessono lo stato: chome voi vedete, che è avvenuto a molti, che di continovo sono stati allo specchio, e anchora vi sono."

substantial loans to the state did extract large quantities of money from the government for interest on their loans. It is interesting to note that of the eleven men listed in Table 11, ten were represented in the balia of 1434 either personally or by immediate relatives (father, sons, or grandsons). The only one of the eleven unrepresented was Bernardo Lamberteschi; he and Lorenzo Strozzi were the only two of that group exiled from the city in 1434.[14] Can one, therefore, refer to the existence of what today we would call a lobby, whose members, whether or not they had originally favored the war against Lucca, sought to influence communal policy along certain lines favorable to their own interests? Interestingly, shortly before his exile from Florence, Cosimo sent substantial quantities of cash found in the local *tavola* to Venice, a fact that suggests he was clearly aware that one of his major political weapons in the city in the past had been the cash he had lent to the government.[15] Nor was Cosimo alone in realizing this. Even his enemies knew that as long as Cosimo controlled the vast quantities of wealth that he did, he was bound to exercise a substantial, if not always direct, influence in communal politics. A bitterly anti-Medicean publicist, in a poem composed during Cosimo's Venetian sojourn, complained that the Medici were emptying the great treasure of their city into "the bosom of Mark." [16]

Granting that the war against Lucca had consequences of disastrous proportions for the ruling class of the 1420's, and

14. Check the inventory of the members of the balia of 1434 printed in Nicolai Rubinstein, *The Government of Florence under the Medici (1434 to 1494)* (Oxford: Oxford University Press, 1966), pp. 244–253.

15. de Roover, *The Rise and Decline of the Medici Bank,* p. 54.

16. Curt Gutkind, *Cosimo de'Medici il vecchio* (Florence: Marzocco, 1940), p. 414: "Per costui ti verrà di dì in dì meno/ la forza e'l senno; e del tuo gran tesoro/ ti vôta sempre, et empie a Marco il seno."

also that the tax burden proved impossible to support by all but a most restricted minority, why was it not ended earlier, before it resulted in the complete discrediting of the politicians, policies, and institutions of the city? The Albizzi and the Uzzano, the Strozzi and the Ridolfi, members of families that had gained their favored political status after the restoration of the patrician government of 1382, had determined the communal policy during the 1420's. At what point during the war can one say that the breakdown of governmental structures became irreversible, forcing men to follow rather than to lead events? [17]

These are not rhetorical questions. They demand of the historian patient and exhaustive, and sometimes exhausting, work. The material in the Florentine archives is abundant, and its careful examination would help illuminate one of the most dramatic and fateful moments in the history of Florence. Giovanni Cavalcanti reports in his *Istorie fiorentine* a speech that Rinaldo degli Albizzi delivered in 1423 at the very outset of the war against Milan. We have the men and the resources, said the Florentine statesman, to fight and win this war. What we need to do is to open our purses and let our money flow to the state as if it were a strong and powerful stream. By doing that we shall win.[18] Provided that the speech is correct, one can suggest that not in his wildest dreams could Rinaldo degli Albizzi have imagined in 1423 that the stream to which he graphically referred

17. See the discussions of January 1432/33 recorded in the *Consulte e pratiche*, LII, f. 29r, in which Bernardo de'Guadagni and Rinaldo degli Albizzi oppose the terms of the peace that was then being negotiated in Ferrara.

18. Giovanni Cavalcanti, *Istorie fiorentine*, ed. Guido di Pino (Milan: Polidori, 1944), p. 11: "Allora la spada si cavi del fodero, e le borse si sciolgano, e i denari si versino; de'quali nasca un fiume che inebrii i soldati delle nostre richezze."

would become a powerful river sweeping in its path the entire political leadership of the city. The essential question, then, may be this: Why did not Rinaldo and his advisers realize that they were being swept away, carried to exile, by a powerful movement that they themselves had helped to initiate?

APPENDICES AND INDEX

APPENDIX A

THE RECORDS OF THE CAMERA DEL COMUNE —

PROVVEDITORI — ENTRATA E USCITA

Charles M. de la Roncière in his recent study of the Florentine gabelles during the first three quarters of the fourteenth century ("Indirect Taxes or 'Gabelles' at Florence in the Fourteenth Century: The Evolution of Tariffs and Problems of Collection," in *Florentine Studies,* ed. Nicolai Rubinstein (London: Faber and Faber, 1968), pp. 140–192) suggests that the records of the Florentine Camera del Comune do not always contain accurate and complete information on the state of communal finances. According to de la Roncière (p. 163, n. 1), scribes of the communal Camera did not record all the incomes received by the government, but rather only those channeled through the Camera itself. As he clearly demonstrates in his essay, often during the first three quarters of the Trecento such governmental agencies as the Monte, the *ufficio delle condotte,* and others, were assigned the incomes from certain gabelles they collected, and spent them without availing themselves of the machinery of the Camera. The result was said to be that the cameral records reflect no more than the financial position of the Camera alone, and not that of the Commune as a whole.

De la Roncière's argument is entirely convincing for the years preceding 1384. Beginning in that year, however, the office of the *provveditori della camera del comune,* which had existed for several decades before, assumed the responsibility of preparing a set of books that were to present an overall picture of the government's financial standing by recording abstracts of all of the city's numerous incomes and expenditures. The decision to initiate such a system must have resulted from an internal administrative decision taken by the officials of the Camera itself, for neither the *Libri Fabarum* nor the *Provvisioni* contain any reference to it. In any case, I have been unable to locate any kind of decree initiating this practice, either in the deliberations of the *signori* and *collegi* or in the few surviving records of the cameral deliberations. Therefore, the possibility should not be discounted that the officials serving in 1384 undertook to prepare such a book on their own initiative and that those who succeded them in office continued the practice.

The *Camera del Comune — Provveditori — Entrata e Uscita* consists of fifty-one volumes, each covering one year, with the exception of the last two, each of which is devoted to special incomes and expenditures over long periods of time. The fact that the attempt of the *provveditori* was to present a synopsis of the city's financial standing should be made clear from the following transcription of entries selected from various volumes of the series.

PC, I (1384), f. 1r: "Al nome di Dio, Amen. Questo libro si chiama Specchio, libro primo segnato. A. il quale io, Leonardo di Niccolò Beccanugi, provveditore della Camera, terrò e farò tenere, et in esso si schriverà tutta entrata e uscita della chamera del Comune di Firenze, e cascheduna ragione di per se, e appresso tutte entrate e uscite delle gabelle del detto comune di Firenze, e ogn'altra cosa che mi parà che bisogno sia a chiarezza di potere vedere quanto sarà di bisogno intorno alle rendite e uscite del detto comune, comminciando in kalende di Gennaio anni mccclxxxiii e finendo a dì ultimo di Dicembre 1384. Idio ch'è padre e signore ne conceda grazia di fare si che sia sua laude e reverenzia, e bene e utile del detto comune di Firenze, e mio onore."

PC, V (1388), f. 1r: "Questo libro è del chomune di Firenze e chiamasi libro biancho sechondo, segnato. E. dello specchio, il quale libro si terrà per Jachopo di Francesco Arighi, e per Nigi di Nerone di Nigi, uficiali diputati per lo chomune di Firenze per uno anno prossimo che dee venire, per provveditori della chamera del detto chomune, in sul quale libro si scriverà ordinatamente tutte l'entrate del chomune di Firenze, e onde dette entrate venghono, e chosì tutte l'uscite del detto chomune. E dove e a chui i detti denari si daranno, si chè chiaro si mostrerà per questo libro tutti i fatti del chomune e della detta chamera, appartenenti a entrata e uscita del chomune.

PC, XI (1395), f. 223v: Prestanze. "Qui appresso scriveremo quello s'è rischosso di prestanze e di residui per tutti chamarlinghi da dì iiii° di Genaio mccclxxxxiiii° a dì iiii° di Genaio mccclxxxxv."

PC, XV (1400), f. 104v: "Qui apresso scriveremo tutta l'entrata della ghabella delle porti da dì iiii° di Genaio 1399 a tutto dì iiii° di Genaio 1400."

PC, XXVIII (1420), f. lr: "Questo libro è di Bartolomeo di Verano Peruzzi e di Ghuccio d'Andrea da Sommaia, proveditori della chamera del chomune di Firenze, e chiamosi champione biancho signato RR, carte 450, tenuto per me Rinieri Baronci, scrivano di sopradetti proveditori, in sul quale si scrive lo stato del Magnificho chomune di Firenze."

PC, XXXI (1427), f. 50r: "Tutta l'entrata della ghabella delle porti in quest' anno, cioè da dì primo di Febraio 1426 per infino e tutto il mese di Gienaio 1427, come si vede adrieto in questo, fiorini 100,490."

All these entries, and they are but a representative fraction of many others one can locate in these volumes, clearly indicate that the preoccupation of the *provveditori* and of their scribes was to record all the income of all the agencies of the communal government. Additional evidence reinforcing this suggestion lies in the fact that when striking the balances for the various gabelles, these scribes took into account the administrative expenses incurred by the officials in charge of the gabelles. This fact would indicate that all income from the gabelle was accounted for (whether or not it was sent to the Camera) and that from it were deducted these administrative expenses, thus producing the total net income from each gabelle.

APPENDIX B. FOLIO REFERENCES IN THE *PCUB* FOR PRINCIPAL ITEMS OF INCOME AND EXPENDITURE, 1402–1433

Year	Vol-ume	Gp	Gs	Gc	Gv	C	P	Cond.	M
1402	17	104v	120r	137r	151r	166v, 177r, 186v, 195r, 202v, 371r, 303v, 304r, 368v, 376v	226r	51r	271r
1403	18	114r	120r	137v	151r	166v, 177r, 187r, 195r, 207r, 202v, 305v, 306r, 358r, 376v	229r	53r	269r
1404	19	104r	122v	138r	151r	166v, 177r, 186v, 195r, 205v, 213v, 306v, 307r	227v	52r	269r
1405	20	104r	120r	137v	151r	167r, 177r, 187r, 195r, 204r, 207v, 290r–298r, 300r–302r, 376v, 388r–393v	228v	49r	269v
1407	21	90r–93r	108r–109r	122r–124r	134r–135r	145r, 155r–156v, 164r, 173r–174r, 181r–183r, 201r–208r, 284r, 376r	220r–225v	22v, 26r, 29v, 32v, 36v, 40v	250r–253v, 259r–260r, 261r–264r, 267r, 268r
1408	22	90r–93r	108r–109r	122r–123r	134r–136r	173r–174r, 181r–183r, 201r–208r, 308v–309r, 375r–376r	220r–224r	20r–42v	250r–254v, 259r–260r, 261r–265v, 267r, 268r
1409	23	90r–93r	108r–109r	133r	134r–135r	170r–171r, 178r–180r, 200r, 201r–208r, 306r–308v, 375r–376v	220r–225r	20r–47v	250r–254r, 257v–259r, 260v, 263r–266v, 267r–v, 268r–v
1411	24	90r–93r	108r–109r	122v–123v	134r–135r	170v–171r, 178r–181r, 198v–207r, 306r–309r, 375r–376r	220r–224v	20r–50r	251r–254v, 257r–258v, 259r, 261r–262v, 267r, 268r
1414	25	97r–99v	111r–112r	123r–125r	134r–135r	148r–149r, 158r–162v, 178r–180r, 202v–208r, 305r–v, 308r–v, 375r–v	220r–227v	20r–43r	251r–255r, 256r–258r, 259r–v, 261r–v, 263r, 266r, 266v–267r, 268r–v, 270r–v
1416	26	101v	112v	125r	135v	60r–63v, 159v, 163r–165r, 181r, 208r, 214r–215v, 284r	230r–v	21v–32r, 40r–59v, 93r–95v	251r–255v, 274r–276v, 285r–286v, 256r–257v, 261r–262r, 282v–283r, 259r–260r, 263r–264v, 265r, 265v–266v, 279v, 267r–v, 269r, 270r–271r, 281r, 271v, 278v
1419	27	74v	93v	111v	121v	30r–31v, 139v, 151v, 163r, 182r, 322v, 294r, 311v	194r–201v	45r–v, 52r, 56v, 60r, 65r	220v, 233v, 239v, 241r, 242v, 249r, 253r, 254r, 256r, 258r, 260v, 263r, 266r, 269r, 272r, 273r

Appendix B. (*Continued*)

1420	28	75r	91v	105r	117v	139v, 146v, 152v, 182r, 295r, 308r, 372r, 388v, 403r, 278r, 414v-415r	203v	30r-63r	227v, 231r, 234r, 237r, 240r, 241v, 242r, 244v, 246v, 248v, 250v, 252v, 254v, 257v, 258v, 260v
1424	29	86r, 345r	102v	117v	131r	156r, 164v, 172v, 185v, 242v, 318v, 338v, 339r	204r	34r-79v	269r, 274v, 276r, 277r, 278r, 283v, 285r, 288r, 290r
1426	30	60r	76r	89r	102v	122r, 131v, 137v, 146v, 227r-v, 255r	154r-165v, 178r-180r	26r-41v, 262r-265v	214r-215r, 217v, 229r, 220r-v, 223v, 226v, 266r-268v
1427	31	50r	66v	81r	95r	116v, 125v, 132r, 140v, 159r, 228v, 232v, 238r, 323v	148r-158r	24r-31v, 40r-43r, 32r-39r, 239r-242v	172r-189r, 192r-v, 196r-198v, 200r-v, 202r-v, 206r, 244r-246v, 248r
1429	32	54r-56v, 69r-v	70r-73r, 83r-84v	85r-87r, 97r-v	98r-101v, 111r	117r-119v, 127r-128r, 135r-v, 140r-v, 154r-158v, 165r, 166r-169v, 174r, 249r-v	175r-185v, 226r-227v	28r-32v, 44r-51v, 265r-269v	35r-40v, 190r-202r, 206r-v, 207r, 209r-213r, 214r-v, 216r-217r, 218r-219r
1430	33	52r-56r, 69r	70r-72v, 83r	85r-87r, 97r	98r-100r, 111r	117r-119r, 127r-128v, 135r-v, 140r-v, 154r-157r, 165r, 166r-168v, 174r	175r-185v	25r-29v, 44r-47r, 48r-51v, 265r-267r	190r-199r, 206r-v, 225r, 207r-208v, 209r-212r, 214r-v, 216r-217r, 218r-219r
1431	34	56r-59r, 73r	75r-77r, 91r	92r-93v, 105r	106r-107v, 113r	130r-131r, 140r-v, 150r-v, 158r-v, 180r-182r, 191r	202r-211v	25r-28r, 45r-48r, 50r-53v	222r-226v, 246r-v, 250r-252r, 256r, 258r-v, 262r-263r
1432	35	52r-56v, 69r	70r-74r, 84r	85r-87v, 97r	98v-100v, 111r	127r-129r, 135r-136r, 140r-v, 154r-158r, 165r, 166r-168r, 174r, 249r	171v-184v	29r, 44r-47v, 202r	190r-201v, 209r-212v, 214r-215r, 216r-v, 218r, 222r-223r
1433	36	58r-61r, 79r	75r-78r, 91r	92r-94r, 105r	106r-108r, 113r	140r-141r, 150r-v, 180r-182v, 192r-194r	None	None	None

Abbreviations: *gabella delle porte* (Gp); *gabella del sale* (Gs); *gabella dei contratti* (Gc); *gabella del vino al minuto* (Gv); *contado* (C); *prestanze* or *catasto* (P); *condotta* (Cond.); *Monte* (M).

APPENDIX C

GENERAL EXENDITURES IN THE BUDGET OF 1401

What follows is a detailed breakdown of the general expenditures listed in the Florentine budget for the year 1401. Not included here are the military expenditures which invariably were considered extraordinary and which were accounted for in different ways. The expenses listed here, therefore, were those that the Commune could expect to meet any given year, regardless of circumstances. While the headings of each entry have been copied as they appear in *PC*, XVI, the description of the entry has been condensed. Folio references in parentheses follow each entry.

Spese ordinarie de'signiori per loro mensa (f. 324r): *3,614 florins, 21 lire.*

Spese straordinarie de'signiori, cioè spesi nella mensa oltre all'ordinario (f. 326r): *2,273 florins, 14 lire.*

Spese ordinarie della chamera dell'arme (f. 328r): *1,990 florins, 943 lire.*

Spese straordinarie della chamera dell'arme (f. 330r): *total of 758 florins, 3,247 lire. (Among these expenses are listed the items following.)*

220 florins, 140 lire, a frate Donato per lo squitinio generale fatto d'Ottobre 1400.

550 lire a frate Donato per spese fatte in più cose per fare venire la tavola di Santa Maria Inpruneta del mese di Magio 1400.

452 florins, 2,430 lire, a frate Donato per spese fatte in onorare i rettori e drapelloni de'chollegi morti, e charte e ciera, per riformagione fatta d'Aprile 1400.

86 florins a frate Bartolo Bencucci per spese fatte in drappo, e dipigniere e altre chose per fare il ghonfalone della giustizia.

Spese di fanti e comandatori e chapitano de'fanti de'signiori (f. 331v): total of 11,300 lire.

Two captains are listed: Berna di Luperello da Sa'Miniato (25 lire per month) and Bartoluccio d'Agnoluccio da Monte Migiano "chapitano de'fanti" (35 lire per month).

94 fanti (10 lire per month each); six comandanti (15 lire per month each); and Matteo di Gianni "comandatore de'signiori" (5 lire per month).

Spese de'mazieri de'signiori (f. 333r): total of 60 florins, 1,440 lire.

12 mazieri (10 lire per month each).

60 florins per le veste ch'arendeono per la festa di San Giovanni di Giugnio 1401.

Spese di donzelli, chuochi e chanpanai de'signiori (f. 334v): total of 278 florins, 922 lire.

9 donzelli (5 lire per month each).

Stefano di Lapo, chuocho de'signiori, e due conpagni (12 lire, 10 sous, per month for all).

4 chanpanai (16 lire per month for all).

117 florins a frate Nichola Bartholomei e VIIII° conpagni donzelli de'signiori per le robe deono avere per la festa di San Giovanni Batesta di Giugnio 1401.

A Stefano di Lapo, chuocho de'signiori per la vesta de'avere per la detta festa, 6 florins.

16 florins a Bartolo di Giovanni e tre conpagni chanpanai per le veste deono avere per detta festa.

A frate Nicola Bartolomei e 9 conpagni donzelli de'signiori per le robbe debbono avere per la pascha di Natale di Dicenbre, 117 florins.

22 florins to the cuocho and the chanpanai for the same reason.

Spese di ser Viviano e di ser Choluccio, e di tutti sonatori, e aprova-tori, e bufone de'signiori (f. 337r): total of 597 florins, 1,861 lire.

Nanni di Masino e Nicholò di Nicholò, piferi per uno anno per le robe deono avere per la pasqua di Natale, lire 36.

The salaries of the above (4 florins per month to Nanni and 3 florins per month to Nicholò).

Ser Viviani Neri, notaio delle riformagioni, con salario di lire 250 l'anno per lui, e fiorini 50 per uno aiutatore, e lire 100 per anno per uno famiglio.

Ser Cholucio Pieri, 140 florins per year.

Messer Antonio di Piero Freani, chavaliere di corte de'signiori, 10 lire per month.

Lionardo d'Andrea e quatro conpagni, tronbetti del comune (4 florins per month each).

Matteo di Marco e cinque conpagni, banditori e aprovatori del comune di Firenze (8 lire, 4 sous, per month each).

Domenico di Baldo e 7 conpagni, tronbadori, nacherini, e tenbame-lai, 40 lire per month for all.

Loci di Cristofano da Firenze, chantore de'signiori, 4 lire, 10 sous, per month.

A Dino di Bondi e quattro chonpagni, tronbetti, per le robe ch'aren-deono per la festa di San Giovanni di Giugnio 1401, a ragione di lire 20, soldi 10, per uno, e per penoncielli ch'arendeono per la detta festa, fiorini 34. In tutto fiorini 34, lire 102, soldi 10.

A Nanni e Bartolome, pifferi, per le robe ch'arendeono per la festa di San Giovanni di Giugnio 1401 a ragione di lire 20, soldi 10, per uno, e per penoncielli ch'arendeono per la detta festa, lire 10, soldi 17.

Ai 6 banditori e aprovatori per le robe e vestimenta ch'arendeono per San Giovanni Battista di Giugnio 1401, fiorini 40.

92 lire ai cinque tronbetti per le robe che arendeono per la pasqua di Natale del presente mese di Dicenbre.

Spese di messi e lanternieri del comune (f. *339v*) : *total of 1,121 lire.*

15 messi de'ghonfalonieri (3 lire, 12 sous, 6 deniers, per month each).

25 messi e lanternieri de'rettori di Firenze (2 lire, 10 sous, 3 deniers, per month each).

1 messo del podestà, 2 lire, 10 sous, 1 denier, per month.

1 messo della condotta, 15 lire, 15 sous, 6 deniers, for four months.

1 messo a'difetti, 20 lire for four months.

Spese generali del comune (f. *343v*) : *total of 2,090 florins, 2,152 lire.*

2 Savi del comune (4 florins per month each).

A Giovanni Federighi, magiore del sagro, 25 florins per month.

Notaio dello specchio, 6 florins per month.

Quattro della moneta (4 florins per month each).

Ser Giovanni di Bartolo Gherardini, notaio de'ghonfalonieri, 13 lire, 6 sous, 8 deniers, for four months.

Nicholò di Michele, tessitore de'drapi, eletto a ghovernare l'oriolo, 3 florins per month.

1° sindacho minore, 4 florins per month.

Domenicho di Matteo Moni, scrivano de'reghulatori, 6 florins per month.

A Betto Bernardi, massaio della chamera, per spese fatte oltre all'ordinario nel palio di San Giovanni di Giugnio 1400, fiorini 22, soldi 10, denari 9, per riformagione fatta d'Aprile 1401.

1° scrivano de'regholatori, 6 florins per month.

A ser Cristofano di Niccolò, notaio fiorentino, diputato a scrivere le deliberagione degl'uficiali posti a porre le prestanze, che sono XX uficiali, 6 florins per month.

A Richardo di Nicholò di Nome, e a Gherardo di Boninsegna Machiavelli eletti per regholatori ragioneri a rivedere la ragione di Gianozo Strada, e di Jacopo Risaliti, uficiali del banco del comune di Firenze (10 florins each).

A Betto Bernardi, massaio della chamera, per veluto, e vaio, fregio, banda, frangia, e manifatura per fare il palio di San Giovanni di Giugnio 1401, fiorini 200.

1° ragioniere de'regholatori, 60 florins per year.

A Giovanni d'Andrea da Fucechio, famiglio degl'otto per dare e paghare nelle spese fatte in ricevere il Chastello di Monte Lungho della Berardengha del mese d'Ottobre 1399, 196 florins, 1,692 lire, 10 deniers.

Spese fatte oltre al ordinario nel palio si San Giovanni di Giugnio 1401, 87 florins.

Spese fatte per onorare Gianni Orsini, anbasciadore del Re Lancislao del mese di Settenbre 1399, in chavalli, drappi, ariento a lui donate, fiorini 730, soldi 9, denari 9 a oro.

Ad Anichino di Segliri da San Gimignano il quale a dì 3 di Febraio 1400/01 diede preso a Franceschino, asecutore, Tomaso d'Agnolo, vochato Mazocchio da Tolano, di Valdigrieve sbandito del chomune di Firenze nell'avere e nella persona, a dì 12 di Magio 1400, del quale si fecie esechuzione, lire 250.

A frate Donato Fancelli per spese fatte in racociare la chanpana Magiore del palagio de'signiori in feramento, legniame, e maestero, per riformagione fatta d'Aprile 1401, fiorini 67, lire 104, soldi 6, denari 4.

A Lodovicho di messer Maligio per pigione d'uno anno comminciato a dì 4 d'Ottobre 1401, dove si fu gella, fiorini 60.

Per spese fatte nel palio di San Bernaba di Giugnio 1401, e di Santa Leperata del mese d'Ottobre 1401, in tutto chostano amendue i detti pali fiorini 44, lire 35, soldi 10, denari 8.

Spese di vichari e podestà di Bargha (f. 346v), including the territories of Valdinievole, Anghiari, Firenzuola, Podere, Bargha, Valdarno di Sopra, Pescia: 362 florins, 17,030 lire.

Spese della chamera de chomune di Firenze (f. *349r*): *total of 667 florins, 943 lire.*

Due frati, chamarlinghi della chamera del chomune (10 lire per month each).

1° scrivano all'entrata, e 1° scrivano all'uscita (10 florins per month each).

1° notaio all'entrata, 10 lire per month.

2 messi della chamera (4 lire per month each).

1° massaio della chamera, 8 lire per month.

Al masaio per spese fatte in pane, vino, confetti, ciera, cierotti, chandelle di sevo e di ciera, inchiostro, e spese per oche di Ognisanti, 148 lire, 8 sous, 4 deniers.

Al masaio per dare a quelli che portano lupi (8 lupi), 18 lire, 11 sous.

Al massaio per dare a'poveri di Christo, 44 lire.

Al massaio per spese fatte in esecuzioni corporali fatte per rettori di Firenze, 29 lire, 1 soldo.

1° chassiere della chamera, 6 florins per month.

A Bartolo di Tuccio, chartolaio, per due libri grandi choverti di cuoio per lo notaio e scrivano de'proveditori, e altri libri e carte di pecora e di banbagia, lire 47, soldi 13, denari 6.

A Giovanni di Michele, chartolaio, per charte di pechora e di chavretto datte al notaio dell'uscita, e [per] leghare i libri agli atti, lire 32, soldi 2.

A Bartolo di Tuccio, chartolaio, per libri e charte di pechora e di banbagia, lire 34, soldi 6.

A Jacopo di Bino, chartolaio, lire 36, soldi 10, denari 8.

A Bartolo di Tuccio, chartolaio, lire 41.

1° provveditore della chamera, for previous year's salary, at 12 florins, 2 lire, per month.

2 provveditori della chamera (12 florins, 2 lire, per month for each).

Per pigione d'una chasa si tiene per le masserizie del palio di San Giovanni ed altre chose, 2 florins per year.

Spese di tutti i rettori di Firenze (f. 354r): total of 533 florins, 55,934 lire.

1° giudice del podestà per sindachare messer Cristofano degli Spini, vichario d'Anghiari, lire 40.

Salary of esecutore della giustizia, 500 lire per month.

Salary of the bargello, 600 lire per month.

Salary of podestà, 1,607 lire, 17 sous, 4 deniers, per month.

Salary of the giudice di grascia, 12 florins, 170 lire, per month.

To the above for ciera, fogli, charte, inchiostro, 5 lire.

Salary of the notaio dell'esecutore, 35 lire per month.

Salary of the notaio del podestà, 35 lire per month.

A'sindachi che andarono a'legere l'asecutore del mese di Febraio 1399/1400, lire 270.

A'sindachi che andarono a'legere il podestà di Magio 1400, lire 270.

A'sindachi che andarono a'legere l'asecutore del mese di Giugnio 1400, lire 270.

A messer Piero da Bologna, giudice del podestà, per andare a sendachare il vechario del Podere, lire 30.

A'sindachi che andorono a'legere l'asecutore, del mese di Febraio 1400/01, lire 270.

Al notaio del podestà per diritto di lire 67, soldi 10, di chondanagione rischosse de'chastellani, a soldi ii per lira, lire 6, soldi 15.

A messer lo podestà per diritto di lire 53 di consiglio rischossi nel primo uficio a soldi ii per lira, montano lire 5, soldi 6.

A messer lo podestà, perchè prese Andrea e Piero, figliuoli di messer Gualderotto da Pisa, sbanditi del chomune di Firenze nell'avere e nella persona, ebe per ordine del chomune di Firenze, lire 100.

Salary of the notaio del chapitano di balia, 35 lire per month.

4 notai forestieri (10 florins per month each).

Salary of the chapitani di balia, 1,566 lire, 16 sous, 8 deniers, per month.

Al giudice del presente podestà per andare a sindachare Messer Filippo Maghalotti, vichario di Firenzuola, lire 30.

Al esecutore per charta, ciera e inchiostro, lire 5.

Al giudice della grascia per charta, ciera, e inchiostro, lire 5.

A Betto Bernardi, massaio della chamera, per danari avea paghati Francescho di Feduccio, chasiere, a messer Giovanni Ghabrieli, chapitano di balia, il quale morì a dì 4 d'Aghosto 1400, lire 5,174, soldi 15, denari 8.

Al notaio del podestà per diritto di lire 320, soldi 15, di chondanagioni rischossi de'chastellani per lui fatte nel suo uficio, lire 32, soldi 2, denari 6.

Al notaio della rassegna del chapitano per diritto di lire 201, soldi 5, di chondanagioni rischossi de'chastellani nel suo uficio, lire 20, soldi 2, denari 6.

Al podestà passato per diritto di'puntature, lire 2, soldi 16, denari 6.

Al giudice del podestà eletto a'ndare a sindachare Bartolomeo del Panochia, vichario di Firenzuola, lire 30.

Spese di soprastanti, notai, ghuardie delle stinche e del conte provveditore (f. 356v): total of 468 florins, 125 lire.

Salary of notaio alle stinche, 4 florins per month.

5 soprastanti alle stinche (6 florins per month each).

3 ghuardie alle stinche (4 florins per month each).

1 provveditore alle stinche, 8 lire, 6 sous, 4 deniers, per month.

Spese d'anbasciadori di Firenze mandati in ogni parte, e rassegnatori de'soldati (f. 361r): 4,093 florins, 636 lire.

Spese di ragionieri ordinari e del loro messo (f. 364v): total of 179 florins, 77 lire.

4 ragionieri (6 florins per month each).

1 messo, 8 lire per month.

Danari dati a'fanti e altri famigli de'signori che si dà loro per limo-

sina, o danari dati ala famiglia de'signori che sono chassi, e dassi loro per limosina (f. 367r): 52 florins, 450 lire. (This was essentially a form of retirement pay given to civil servants. It varies from 5 lire to 2 florins per month.)

Spese di tutti provisionati del comune di Firenze che non servono (ff. 372r–373v): 5,356 florins, 170 lire.

APPENDIX D

RATE OF *FIORINO DI SUGGELLO* IN *MONETA DI PICCIOLI* (SILVER SOUS AND DENIERS), 1389–1432

The *fondo Miscellanea repubblicana,* vol. XXXIII, contains four small notebooks in which are recorded the daily exchange rates between the florin and the silver currency from 1389 until January 1432/33. For every day on which business transactions were conducted, the scribe recorded both the high and low exchange rates. More often than not, he also offered the weekly and monthly averages. In the following table are listed the monthly averages from January 1388/89 through January 1431/32, when the notebooks stop offering this valuable information. Values are expressed in *soldi di piccioli* (sous) and *denari di piccioli* (deniers).

Month	1389	1390	1391	1392
I	74.11	75.2$\frac{1}{2}$	75.11$\frac{1}{5}$	75.1
II	74.7	75.2	75.10$\frac{1}{2}$	75.$\frac{1}{2}$
III	74.8	74.9$\frac{1}{2}$	75.5$\frac{3}{5}$	75.0
IV	74.5	75.4$\frac{1}{2}$	75.5$\frac{1}{5}$	75.$\frac{7}{10}$
V	74.6	76.2$\frac{4}{5}$	75.3	75.2$\frac{1}{15}$
VI	73.10	76.6$\frac{1}{2}$	74.6$\frac{1}{4}$	75.0
VII	74.0	75.8	74.6$\frac{1}{4}$	75.$\frac{1}{3}$
VIII	73.7$\frac{1}{2}$	74.10$\frac{1}{4}$	74.1	75.1$\frac{1}{10}$
IX	74.2	74.10$\frac{1}{2}$	74.$\frac{3}{5}$	75.1$\frac{4}{5}$
X	74.5	75.7$\frac{1}{4}$	74.5$\frac{3}{5}$	75.9$\frac{3}{5}$
XI	74.3$\frac{1}{2}$	75.6$\frac{2}{5}$	74.2$\frac{1}{3}$	76.1
XII	75.$\frac{1}{3}$	75.6$\frac{4}{5}$	74.11$\frac{4}{5}$	76.8$\frac{1}{4}$

Month	1393	1394	1395	1396
I	76.5$\frac{9}{10}$	76.8$\frac{19}{38}$	77.6	77.1$\frac{17}{20}$
II	76.4$\frac{1}{3}$	76.10$\frac{2}{5}$	77.4$\frac{1}{3}$	76.10$\frac{44}{95}$
III	75.7$\frac{3}{5}$	76.10$\frac{1}{2}$	77.$\frac{2}{5}$	76.10$\frac{49}{100}$

IV	$75.9\frac{2}{5}$	$76.9\frac{8}{20}$	$76.10\frac{1}{19}$	$77.2\frac{1}{5}$
V	$76.2\frac{3}{7}$	$76.9\frac{4}{22}$	$76.9\frac{2}{19}$	$77.\frac{1}{5}$
VI	$75.3\frac{3}{4}$	$76.9\frac{10}{19}$	$76.5\frac{5}{8}$	$76.6\frac{21}{22}$
VII	$75.2\frac{11}{13}$	$76.2\frac{5}{12}$	$76.3\frac{19}{24}$	$76.5\frac{12}{22}$
VIII	74.10	$76.\frac{3}{8}$	$76.2\frac{16}{19}$	$76.4\frac{1}{2}$
IX	75.0	$75.10\frac{3}{17}$	$76.3\frac{14}{21}$	$76.6\frac{3}{4}$
X	$75.11\frac{7}{10}$	$76.9\frac{18}{25}$	$76.7\frac{6}{22}$	$76.11\frac{1}{5}$
XI	$76.2\frac{8}{21}$	$77.\frac{9}{20}$	$76.6\frac{8}{19}$	76.11
XII	$76.7\frac{2}{19}$	$77.\frac{3}{4}$	$77.1\frac{4}{19}$	$77.2\frac{8}{18}$

Month	1397	1398	1399	1400
I	$77.4\frac{8}{22}$	$77.11\frac{13}{24}$	$77.5\frac{4}{22}$	$77.8\frac{1}{22}$
II	77.4	$77.9\frac{17}{21}$	$77.3\frac{9}{25}$	$77.6\frac{12}{14}$
III	77.2	$77.\frac{22}{115}$	$77.2\frac{1}{5}$	$76.11\frac{21}{33}$
IV	$77.3\frac{3}{4}$	$77.1\frac{6}{19}$	$77.3\frac{1}{2}$	$76.6\frac{7}{19}$
V	$77.7\frac{3}{4}$	$76.10\frac{4}{5}$	$76.10\frac{1}{2}$	$76.9\frac{6}{20}$
VI	$77.10\frac{74}{105}$	$76.8\frac{7}{25}$	$76.8\frac{83}{95}$	$76.7\frac{2}{3}$
VII	$77.7\frac{15}{22}$	$76.1\frac{37}{40}$	$76.8\frac{47}{115}$	$76.2\frac{1}{3}$[b]
VIII	$77.5\frac{1}{40}$	76.4	$76.5\frac{4}{15}$	76.1[b]
IX	$77.5\frac{18}{20}$	$77.1\frac{1}{4}$	$76.5\frac{15}{17}$[a]	76.8
X	$77.8\frac{19}{24}$	$77.1\frac{6}{23}$	$76.10\frac{7}{22}$	$76.10\frac{13}{22}$
XI	$77.9\frac{3}{21}$	$77.2\frac{15}{19}$	$77.3\frac{13}{21}$	$76.10\frac{11}{20}$
XII	$77.10\frac{9}{10}$	$77.6\frac{8}{17}$	$77.9\frac{7}{19}$	$76.11\frac{11}{18}$

Month	1401	1402	1403	1404
I	$77.1\frac{4}{21}$	$76.5\frac{3}{20}$	$77.3\frac{11}{1}$	$76.8\frac{23}{25}$
II	$76.8\frac{10}{14}$	$76.2\frac{3}{5}$	$76.11\frac{6}{17}$	$76.3\frac{11}{25}$
III	$76.8\frac{5}{22}$	$76.\frac{3}{5}$	$76.11\frac{11}{25}$	$75.10\frac{23}{25}$
IV	$76.7\frac{1}{6}$	$76.6\frac{21}{23}$	76.11	$76.2\frac{1}{2}$
V	$76.4\frac{13}{14}$	$76.\frac{3}{5}$	$76.11\frac{2}{5}$	$76.1\frac{2}{3}$
VI	$75.10\frac{7}{8}$	$76.5\frac{12}{23}$	$76.9\frac{1}{3}$	$76.3\frac{1}{2}$
VII	$75.3\frac{3}{4}$	$75.8\frac{8}{21}$	$76.7\frac{4}{5}$	$76.3\frac{1}{3}$
VIII	$75.1\frac{13}{18}$	$75.9\frac{17}{19}$	$76.10\frac{2}{15}$	$75.11\frac{3}{5}$
IX	$75.\frac{19}{22}$	$76.1\frac{1}{11}$	$77.\frac{1}{5}$	$76.2\frac{4}{5}$
X	75.8	$76.7\frac{12}{22}$	$76.10\frac{24}{25}$	$76.8\frac{1}{5}$
XI	$76.5\frac{3}{5}$	$76.9\frac{18}{19}$	$76.10\frac{1}{5}$	$77.1\frac{3}{10}$
XII	$76.9\frac{1}{5}$	$77.\frac{1}{17}$	$76.9\frac{21}{25}$	$77.1\frac{3}{8}$

Month	1405	1406	1407	1408
I	77.2$\frac{2}{3}$	77.7$\frac{19}{21}$	77.10$\frac{1}{2}$	77.8$\frac{1}{3}$
II	76.11$\frac{3}{8}$	77.3$\frac{11}{21}$	77.11$\frac{15}{19}$	77.6$\frac{5}{8}$
III	76.11$\frac{16}{21}$	77.1$\frac{1}{4}$	78.1$\frac{1}{8}$	77.7$\frac{10}{23}$
IV	76.7$\frac{1}{4}$	76.7$\frac{4}{5}$	78.3$\frac{1}{3}$	77.3$\frac{17}{19}$
V	76.6$\frac{2}{3}$	76.11$\frac{1}{3}$	77.10$\frac{7}{8}$	77.5$\frac{2}{3}$
VI	76.2$\frac{7}{9}$	76.4$\frac{1}{47}$	77.11$\frac{1}{4}$	77.1$\frac{5}{6}$
VII	76.3$\frac{5}{28}$	76.8$\frac{17}{22}$	77.4$\frac{1}{4}$	77.1$\frac{21}{19}$
VIII	76.4$\frac{7}{8}$	77.7$\frac{14}{19}$	77.6$\frac{1}{10}$	77.5$\frac{1}{19}$
IX	77.3$\frac{1}{55}$	77.11$\frac{8}{11}$	77.5$\frac{1}{4}$	77.7$\frac{4}{5}$
X	77.5$\frac{7}{8}$	78.$\frac{39}{40}$	77.5$\frac{15}{22}$	77.9$\frac{14}{28}$
XI	77.9$\frac{14}{10}$	77.8$\frac{2}{3}$	77.4$\frac{7}{9}$	77.11
XII	77.8$\frac{14}{95}$	78.1$\frac{5}{6}$	77.6$\frac{10}{19}$	78.2

Month	1409	1410	1411	1412
I	78.2$\frac{1}{6}$	80.2$\frac{5}{8}$	80.2$\frac{1}{2}$	80.11$\frac{3}{7}$
II	78.1$\frac{13}{20}$	80.4$\frac{2}{21}$	79.11$\frac{4}{19}$	80.11$\frac{2}{5}$
III	78.1$\frac{7}{7}$	79.11$\frac{3}{20}$	80.0	80.7$\frac{23}{23}$
IV	77.7$\frac{3}{7}$	79.4$\frac{11}{12}$	79.9$\frac{3}{8}$	79.8$\frac{3}{20}$
V	77.11$\frac{2}{7}$	79.2$\frac{16}{21}$	79.11$\frac{13}{22}$	79.3$\frac{87}{120}$
VI	77.10$\frac{1}{7}$	78.9$\frac{3}{7}$	79.9$\frac{14}{19}$	79.9$\frac{1}{5}$
VII	77.11	78.10$\frac{1}{12}$	79.3$\frac{2}{3}$	80.1
VIII	78.3$\frac{12}{7}$	79.3$\frac{14}{19}$	79.3$\frac{23}{45}$	80.1$\frac{1}{4}$
IX	78.7$\frac{3}{7}$	79.10$\frac{7}{24}$	79.7$\frac{4}{21}$	80.4$\frac{13}{21}$
X	79.1$\frac{3}{10}$	80.2$\frac{10}{11}$	80.3$\frac{1}{3}$	80.6$\frac{8}{11}$
XI	79.3$\frac{13}{19}$	80.3$\frac{1}{8}$	80.7$\frac{1}{10}$	80.8$\frac{17}{18}$
XII	80.1$\frac{2}{3}$	80.4$\frac{4}{5}$	80.8$\frac{12}{13}$	80.11$\frac{17}{18}$

Month	1413	1414	1415	1416
I	80.10$\frac{1}{4}$	80.11$\frac{19}{20}$	81.2$\frac{3}{5}$	80.9$\frac{3}{5}$
II	80.$\frac{3}{7}$	80.11$\frac{7}{8}$	81.2$\frac{11}{12}$	80.8$\frac{3}{4}$
III	80.4$\frac{4}{11}$	81.$\frac{23}{26}$	80.11$\frac{1}{2}$	80.9$\frac{5}{6}$
IV	79.8$\frac{2}{7}$	81.1$\frac{2}{3}$	80.11$\frac{1}{3}$	80.5$\frac{1}{3}$
V	79.5$\frac{1}{2}$	81.1$\frac{7}{10}$	80.5$\frac{24}{25}$	80.3$\frac{1}{4}$
VI	79.8$\frac{7}{8}$	80.11	80.2$\frac{4}{15}$	80.1$\frac{1}{2}$
VII	80.5$\frac{10}{13}$	80.8$\frac{1}{2}$	80.2$\frac{10}{13}$	79.8$\frac{3}{5}$

VIII	$80.3\frac{1}{10}$	$80.\frac{5}{6}$	$80.3\frac{1}{2}$	$78.7\frac{3}{4}$
IX	$80.4\frac{5}{13}$	$79.11\frac{1}{20}$	$80.4\frac{2}{3}$	$79.\frac{6}{7}$
X	$80.5\frac{11}{13}$	$80.2\frac{12}{19}$	$80.3\frac{14}{15}$	$79.11\frac{7}{8}$
XI	$80.7\frac{1}{6}$	$80.9\frac{17}{20}$	$79.8\frac{1}{2}$	$80.4\frac{1}{6}$
XII	$80.9\frac{4}{5}$	$81.1\frac{17}{30}$	$80.5\frac{4}{5}$	$80.11\frac{1}{2}$

Month	1417	1418	1419	1420
I	80.11	$81.3\frac{7}{10}$	$81.8\frac{3}{4}$	$79.9\frac{1}{2}$
II	$80.10\frac{21}{23}$	$81.9\frac{1}{3}$	$80.7\frac{1}{8}$	$79.9\frac{2}{5}$
III	$80.10\frac{2}{5}$	$82.5\frac{1}{3}$	$79.10\frac{1}{3}$	$79.11\frac{1}{4}$
IV	$80.5\frac{2}{5}$	$82.2\frac{3}{5}$	$80.1\frac{1}{4}$	$79.11\frac{3}{5}$
V	$80.3\frac{5}{9}$	$81.10\frac{1}{5}$	$79.8\frac{3}{10}$	$79.9\frac{1}{2}$
VI	$80.3\frac{1}{3}$	$80.10\frac{2}{5}$	$78.11\frac{1}{5}$	79.4
VII	$80.2\frac{2}{3}$	$80.11\frac{2}{5}$	$78.11\frac{1}{4}$	79.4
VIII	$79.9\frac{1}{4}$	$80.9\frac{5}{6}$	$77.8\frac{3}{5}$	$79.5\frac{1}{4}$
IX	80.6	80.9	$78.3\frac{1}{2}$	79.5
X	$80.10\frac{1}{3}$	81.3	$78.8\frac{2}{3}$	$80.1\frac{1}{4}$
XI	$80.7\frac{2}{3}$	$81.5\frac{1}{2}$	79.5	80.3
XII	$81.2\frac{3}{4}$	$81.8\frac{1}{5}$	79.9	$80.6\frac{7}{8}$

Month	1421	1422	1423	1424
I	$80.9\frac{1}{2}$	81.4	$81.1\frac{1}{5}$	$81.4\frac{3}{10}$
II	80.8	$81.1\frac{1}{2}$	$80.10\frac{4}{5}$	$81.5\frac{2}{5}$
III	80.7	$80.11\frac{1}{2}$	$80.6\frac{2}{3}$	81.2
IV	$80.7\frac{4}{5}$	$80.8\frac{4}{5}$	$80.4\frac{2}{3}$	$81.4\frac{2}{5}$
V	$80.5\frac{4}{5}$	$80.4\frac{2}{5}$	$80.1\frac{2}{3}$	$81.2\frac{4}{5}$
VI	$80.3\frac{5}{6}$	$79.4\frac{1}{2}$	79.8	81.0
VII	$80.6\frac{4}{5}$	$79.6\frac{4}{5}$	80.3	$81.1\frac{4}{5}$
VIII	$80.5\frac{1}{3}$	$79.5\frac{1}{2}$	80.2	$80.6\frac{4}{5}$
IX	80.7	$79.4\frac{3}{4}$	$80.8\frac{1}{2}$	$80.2\frac{4}{5}$
X	$80.11\frac{3}{4}$	$79.11\frac{1}{3}$	80.10	80.8
XI	$81.\frac{1}{8}$	$80.8\frac{7}{8}$	81.4	$81.1\frac{1}{2}$
XII	$81.4\frac{1}{6}$	$80.10\frac{1}{6}$	$81.3\frac{1}{5}$	81.3

Month	1425	1426	1427	1428
I	$81.4\frac{5}{14}$	$81.6\frac{2}{5}$	$82.11\frac{1}{2}$	$83.8\frac{3}{8}$
II	$81.4\frac{13}{15}$	81.7	$82.11\frac{3}{5}$	$83.7\frac{2}{5}$

III	$81.3\frac{4}{5}$	$81.5\frac{3}{5}$	$82.6\frac{2}{3}$	$83.7\frac{2}{5}$
IV	$80.8\frac{1}{2}$	$81.4\frac{2}{5}$	$82.4\frac{7}{8}$	82.9
V	80.5	$81.7\frac{4}{5}$	$82.6\frac{1}{5}$	82.10
VI	$80.\frac{2}{3}$	$81.6\frac{9}{10}$	82.1	$82.4\frac{3}{5}$
VII	$80.4\frac{4}{5}$	$81.9\frac{4}{5}$	$82.1\frac{9}{10}$	$82.4\frac{1}{5}$
VIII	$80.\frac{3}{5}$	$82.1\frac{2}{5}$	$82.4\frac{3}{5}$	82.9
IX	$80.2\frac{4}{5}$	$82.1\frac{1}{8}$	82.6	$82.11\frac{7}{10}$
X	$81.\frac{3}{5}$	$82.1\frac{1}{4}$	$82.9\frac{1}{8}$	$82.11\frac{7}{10}$
XI	$81.2\frac{4}{5}$	$82.1\frac{1}{5}$	$83.1\frac{1}{6}$	$83.5\frac{2}{3}$
XII	$80.10\frac{1}{4}$	82.6	$83.8\frac{1}{4}$	$83.9\frac{1}{2}$

Month	1429	1430	1431	1432
I	83.8	$83.8\frac{7}{25}$	$83.4\frac{1}{105}$	$83.11\frac{1}{5}$
II	$83.3\frac{2}{3}$	$83.8\frac{8}{13}$	$82.11\frac{14}{15}$	
III	$83.2\frac{1}{5}$	$83.7\frac{5}{24}$	83.4	
IV	83.0	$83.2\frac{1}{4}$	$82.2\frac{4}{11}$	
V	$82.10\frac{1}{4}$	$82.11\frac{3}{5}$	$81.2\frac{21}{93}$	
VI	$82.7\frac{3}{8}$	$82.5\frac{3}{4}$	$81.10\frac{4}{13}$	
VII	82.10	$82.5\frac{3}{8}$	$82.10\frac{6}{25}$	
VIII	$82.9\frac{27}{45}$	$82.3\frac{1}{4}$	$83.5\frac{8}{25}$	
IX	$82.10\frac{12}{35}$	$82.5\frac{1}{4}$	$83.5\frac{1}{2}$	
X	$82.10\frac{67}{110}$	$82.7\frac{5}{23}$	$82.8\frac{9}{23}$	
XI	$83.3\frac{31}{90}$	$82.10\frac{1}{2}$	$83.6\frac{13}{100}$	
XII	$83.8\frac{82}{85}$	$83.3\frac{1}{2}$	$83.10\frac{11}{80}$	

[a] For the first week of September 1399 one reads the following entry: "Non si potè avere la valuta che le tavole stettono serate per la festa de bianchi, che ogni persona si vestì di biancho."

[b] For the last two weeks of July 1400 and the first two weeks of August 1400 one reads: "Non si potè avere la valuta pe'l fatto della moria, e'provveditori vollono si disse a'chamarlinghi a s. 76 il fiorino."

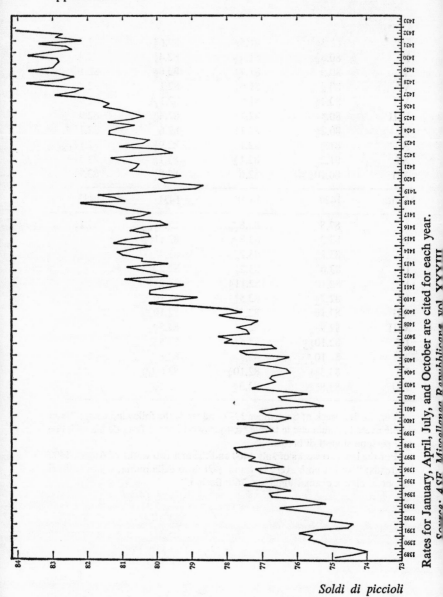

Rates for January, April, July, and October are cited for each year.

Soldi di piccioli

APPENDIX E

CREDITORS OF THE *UFFICIALI DEL BANCO,*
NOVEMBER 27, 1427 TO JUNE 14, 1434

Name	Sum Lent (Florins)	Reference in *PCUB*
Alberti, Benedetto degli, & Co.	2,390	XXIV, 47r
Alberti, Francesco d'Altobianco degli, & Co.	6,339	XXVII, 20r; XXVIII, 22r
Alberti, Gianozzo & Antonio degli	600	XXV, 149r
Agli, Filippo & Domenico, & Co.	649	XXIII, 158r
Agli, Jacopo di Barnaba	210	XXIV, 46r
Barbadoro, Giovanni, & Co.	434	XXIII, 159r
Barbadoro, Niccolò di Donato, & Co.	1,120	XXIII, 160r; XXIV, 44r
Bardi, Andrea di Lipaccio	1,938	XXVIII, 33r
Bardi, Bardo de', & Co.	651	XXIII, 157r
Bardi, Ubertino de'	264	XXIV, 47r
Baroncelli, Jacopo di Piero, & Co.	18,362	XXIII, 19r; XXIV, 43r
Bellaccio, Niccolò & Giovanni del	1,649	XXIII, 159r; XXIV, 42r
Bindi, Guglielmo di Guglielmo	200	XXIV, 47r
Bischeri, Jacopo di Jacopo	1,687	XXIV, 47r; XXVIII, 27r
Bonciani, Niccola di Filippo	105	XXIV, 46r
Bonsi, Donato d'Ugolino de', & Co.	26,405	XXIII, 91r; XXV, 87r; XXVI, 12r
Bischeri, Giovanni di Nofri	5,639	XXIII, 25r
Bischeri, Jacopo di Giovanni	1,259	XXV, 86r
Bonciani, Niccola di Filippo	550	XXVI, 13r
Boscoli, Francesco, & Co.	3,256	XXVII, 20r
Buoninsegni, Domenico di Lionardo	562	XXVIII, 24r
Buonromei, Gabriello, & Co.	541	XXIII, 159r
Buonromei, Galeazzo, & Co.	1,086	XXIII, 157r

Appendix E. (*Continued*)

Name	Sum Lent (Florins)	Reference in *PCUB*
Canigiani, Antonio, & Co.	2,292	XXIII, 23r
Carnesechi, Bernardo, & Co.	3,294	XXIII, 158r; XXIV, 45r; XXVIII, 12r
Cinti, Pagolo di Niccolò	211	XXIV, 46r
Compagni, Cante di Giovanni, & Co.	807	XXIV, 45r; XXVIII, 23r
Della Luna, Giovanni di Francesco, & Co.	2,862	XXVII, 10r
Della Luna, Pierozzo di Francesco	27,156	XXIII, 93r; XXIV, 42r; XXV, 106r; XXVIII, 25r
Domenico di Piero, *medico*	100	XXIV, 46r
Fanti, Lorenzo di Bartolomeo di ser	217	XXIII, 158r
Gaddi, Agnolo di Zanobi, & Co.	758	XXV, 85r
Gaddi, Taddeo di Zanobi	2,523	XXIV, 42r; XXVIII, 22r
Giachinotti, Adoardo & Cambini Niccolò, & Co.	2,821	XXIV, 43r; XXV, 86r; XXVII, 19r; XXVIII, 23r
Gondi, Simone di Salvestro	465	XXIV, 44r; XXVIII, 26r
Guicciardini, Giovanni di Niccolò, & Co.	433	XXIII, 160r
Guidotti, Migliorini, & Co.	217	XXIII, 157r
Lamberteschi, Bernardo di Lamberto, & Co.	34,825	XXIII, 257r; XXIV, 44r; XXV, 105r; XXVIII, 3r
Lapi, Salvestro di Michele	1,664	XXV, 113r
Ligi, Antonio di Bernardo	324	XXIII, 160r
Luti, Luti di Michele di, & Co.	8,876	XXIV, 43r; XXV, 106r; XXVIII, 4r, 35r
Macinghi, Carlo di Niccolò	216	XXIII, 156r
Macinghi, Giovachino di Niccolò	217	XXIII, 160r
Manetti, Bernardo	541	XXIII, 159r
Manetti, Gianozzo & Filippo di Bernardo	15,345	XXIV, 9r; XXV, 84r; XXVIII, 4r, 32r
Medici, Averardo de', & Co.	5,498	XXIII, 158r; XXIV, 41r; XXV, 85r; XXVIII, 6r
Medici, Cosimo & Lorenzo de', & Co.	155,887	XXIII, 92r, 232r; XXIV, 16r; XXV, 150r, 158r;

Appendix E. (*Continued*)

Name	Sum Lent (Florins)	Reference in *PCUB*
		XXVII, 7r, 20r; XXVIII, 9r
Nelli, Stefano di Nello	2,112	XXVIII, 26r
Panciatichi, Giovanni di Bartolomeo	3,472	XXIV, 43r; XXV, 80r
Panciatichi, Piero di Giovanni	1,721	XXVI, 9r
Pazzi, Andrea d'Ugolino de', & Co.	58,524	XXIII, 156r; XXIV, 5r, 18r; XXV, 81r; XXVIII, 8r, 19r; XXVIII, 18r
Peruzzi, Ridolfo, & Co.	2,831	XXIII, 159r; XXIV, 42r; XXV, 113r
Pitti, Antonio di Jacopo	26,106	XXIII, 2r
Rede di Antonio di ser Bartolomeo di ser Nello & Co.	855	XXIII, 158r; XXIV, 43r
Rede di Giovanni Quaratesi & Co.	7,602	XXIV, 6r; XXV, 87r; XXVIII, 5r
Ricci, Corso de', & Co.	217	XXIII, 157r
Rinieri, Bartolomeo di Luca di Piero	7,495	XXV, 86r; XXVI, 8r; XXVIII, 24r
Rinieri, Luca di Piero, & Co.	1,626	XXIII, 156r
Rinuccini, Francesco di Cino	1,662	XXV, 150r; XXVI, 11r
Salvestro, Lionardo di, *brigliaio*	2,589	XXIII, 146r; XXIV, 45r
Salviati, Bernardo di Jacopo	1,085	XXIV, 41r
Serristori, Antonio di Salvestro	26,527	XXIII, 157r; XXIV, 22r; XXVII, 9r; XXVIII, 25r
Spinelli, Bianco d'Agostino	8,636	XXVIII, 11r
Strozzi, Lorenzo di messer Palla di Nofri, & Co.	33,951	XXIII, 20r
Uzzano, Bernardo d'Antonio da, & Co.	13,854	XXV, 85r; XXVI, 10r; XXVIII, 37r
Uzzano, Niccolò da, & Co.	4,708	XXIII, 156r; XXIV, 41r
Valori, Niccolò di Bartolomeo	2,128	XXIII, 25r
Vanni, Vanni di Niccolò di ser, & Co.	9,952	XXIII, 156r, 21r; XXIV, 45r; XXV, 105r; XXVIII, 3r

APPENDIX F

THE *UFFICIALI DEL BANCO,* 1427–1433

I. From November 27, 1427, to December 31, 1428. Reference: *PCUB,* XXIII, f. 1r.

    Antonio di Jacopo Canigiani
    Donato d'Ugolino de'Bonsi
    Bernardo di Lamberto Lamberteschi
    Jacopo di Piero Baroncelli
    Palla di Nofri Strozzi
    Francesco di Pierozzo della Luna
    Domenico di Tano, *coltricciaio*
    Cosimo de'Medici
    Niccolò di Bartolomeo Valori
    Lionardo di Salvestro, *brigliaio*

II. From December 5, 1430, to September 1431. Reference: *PCUB,* XXIV, f. 1r.

    Tommaso di Bartolomeo Corbinelli
    Gianozzo di Bernardo Manetti
    Bartolomeo di Giovanni di Michelozzo
    Giovanni di messer Forese Salviati
    Antonio di Salvestro Serristori
    Filippo di Giovanni Carducci
    Francesco di messer Simone Tornabuoni
    Piero di Francesco di ser Gino
    Andrea di Guglielmino de'Pazzi
    Lorenzo di Bertino di Guccio

III. From September 22, 1431, to January 1431/32. Reference: *PCUB,* XXVII, f. 1r.

    Giovanni di Tommaso Corbinelli
    Giovanni di Matteo dello Scelto
    Schiatta d'Uberto Ridolfi
    Lutozzo di Jacopo Lutozzo

Piero di Lorenzo d'Agniolino
Antonio di Salvestro di ser Ristoro [Serristori]
Giovanni di messer Forese Salviati
Masino di Piero dell'Antella
Giovanni di Pagolo Morelli
Jacopo di Jacopo del Zacheria
Filippo di Giovanni Carducci
Giovanni di Simone Altoviti
Francesco di Francesco della Luna
Giovanni d'Andrea Minerbetti
Baldassare d'Arrigo di Simone
Cosimo di Lorenzo de'Medici
Giuliano di Francesco di ser Gino
Filippo di messer Biagio Guasconi
Andrea di Guglielmino de'Pazzi
Puccio d'Antonio di Puccio

IV. From January 25, 1431/32, to June 1432. Reference: *PCUB*, XXVIII, f. 1r.

Andrea di Lipaccio de'Bardi
Luti di Michele di Luti
Gianozzo di Bernardo Manetti
Bernardo di Lamberto Lamberteschi
Vanni di Niccolò di ser Vanni [Castellani]
Bianco d'Agostino Spinelli
Francesco di Jacopo Ventura
Cosimo di Giovanni de'Medici
Andrea di Guglielmino de'Pazzi
Jacopo di Giovanni Villani
Banco di Sandro, *coltricciaio*
Puccio d'Antonio di Puccio

"Di poi a dì xviii d'Aprile 1432 si fece al nome di Dio una agiunta a'decti dodici d'altrettanti."

Bernardo d'Antonio da Uzzano
Mariotto di Dinozzo Lippi
Antonio di Salvestro di ser Ristoro [Serristori]

Francesco d'Altobianco degli Alberti
Cante di Giovanni Compagni
Domenico di Lionardo Buoninsegni
Adoardo Giachinotti
Pierozzo di Francesco della Luna
Taddeo di Zanobi Gaddi
Bartolomeo di Luca di Piero Rinieri
Stefano di Nello Nelli
Jacopo di Giovanni Bischeri

V. From June 1432 to August 17, 1432. Reference: *PCUB,*
XXIX, f. 1r.

Lorenzo di Giovanni Grasso
Duccio di Taddeo Mancini
Giuliano di Francesco di ser Gino
Lodovico di ser Viviano di Neri
Cristofano d'Antonio, *coreggiaio*

VI. From August 18, 1432, until November 1432. Reference:
PCUB, XXX, f. 1r.

Jacopo di Bernaba Filippeschi
Giovanni d'Amerigo Benci
Baldassare di Bernardo Bonsi
Giovanni di Mico Capponi
Giovanni di Giovanni del Bellaccio
Francesco di Cino Rinuccini
Francesco di Piero Dini
Filippo di Giovanni di ser Rucco(?)
Jacopo di Jacopo del Zacheria
Agnolo di Bartolomeo Carducci
Giovanni di Domenico Bartoli
Filippo d'Antonio del Buono
Pagolo di Niccolò Cuti(?)
Stagio di Matteo Bonaguisi
Bartolomeo d'Antonio di ser Bartolomeo
Parente di Michele di ser Parente
Lorenzo di Bartolomeo di ser Fanti

Neri di Domenico Bartolini
Bernardo d'Antonio de'Medici
Simone di Michele, *feraiuolo*

VII. From November 24, 1432. Date of dismissal unknown. Reference: *PCUB,* XXXI, f. 1r.

Messer Giuliano di Nicolaio Davanzati
Filippo di messer Biagio Guasconi
Pagolo di Vani Rucellai
Francesco di Francesco della Luna
Giovanni d'Andrea Minerbetti
Averardo di Francesco de'Medici
Niccolò di Bartolomeo Valori
Andrea di Guglielmino de'Pazzi
Banco di Sandro, *coltricciaio*
Domenico di Tano, *coltricciaio*

INDEX

HARVARD HISTORICAL MONOGRAPHS

33. Concordia Mundi: The Career and Thought of Guillaume Postel (1510-1581). By W. J. Bouwsma. 1957.

34. Bureaucracy, Aristocracy, and Autocracy: The Prussian Experience, 1660-1815. By Hans Rosenberg. 1958.

35. Exeter, 1540-1640: The Growth of an English County Town. By Wallace T. MacCaffrey. 1958.*

36. Historical Pessimism in the French Enlightenment. By Henry Vyverberg. 1958.

37. The Renaissance Idea of Wisdom. By Eugene F. Rice, Jr. 1958.*

38. The First Professional Revolutionist: Filippo Michele Buonarroti (1761-1837). By Elizabeth L. Eisenstein. 1959.

39. The Formation of the Baltic States: A Study of the Effects of Great Power Politics upon the Emergence of Lithuania, Latvia, and Estonia. By Stanley W. Page. 1959.*

40. Conservation and the Gospel of Efficiency: The Progressive Conservation Movement, 1890-1920. By Samuel P. Hays. 1959.

41. The Urban Frontier: The Rise of Western Cities, 1790-1830. By Richard C. Wade. 1959.

42. New Zealand, 1769-1840: Early Years of Western Contact. By Harrison M. Wright. 1959.

43. Ottoman Imperialism and German Protestantism, 1521-1555. By Stephen A. Fischer-Galati. 1959.*

44. Foch versus Clemenceau: France and German Dismemberment, 1918-1919. By Jere Clemens King. 1960.

45. Steelworkers in America: The Nonunion Era. By David Brody. 1960.*

46. Carroll Wright and Labor Reform: The Origin of Labor Statistics. By James Leiby. 1960.

47. Chōshū in the Meiji Restoration. By Albert M. Craig. 1961.

48. John Fiske: The Evolution of a Popularizer. By Milton Berman. 1961.

49. John Jewel and the Problem of Doctrinal Authority. By W. M. Southgate. 1962.

50. Germany and the Diplomacy of the Financial Crisis, 1931. By Edward W. Bennett. 1962.

51. Public Opinion, Propaganda, and Politics in Eighteenth-Century England: A Study of the Jew Bill of 1753. By Thomas W. Perry. 1962.